Contradictory Subjects

Contradictory Subjects

*Quevedo, Cervantes, and
Seventeenth-Century Spanish Culture*

George Mariscal

Cornell University Press

Ithaca and London

Cornell University Press is grateful for a subvention
from the University of California, San Diego,
that aided in bringing this book to publication.

First published 1991 by Cornell University Press.

International Standard Book Number 0-8014-2604-9
Library of Congress Catalog Card Number 91-13369
Printed in the United States of America
*Librarians: Library of Congress cataloging information
appears on the last page of the book.*

 ∞ The paper in this book meets the minimum requirements
of the American National Standard for Information Sciences—
Permanence of Paper for Printed Library Materials, ANSI Z39.48-1984.

In memory of
Marguerite Molina and Martha Isabel Villa—
my godmother, Tiny, who wrote us stories,
and my Uncle B.

Contents

Preface   ix

1. The Subject of Hispanism   1

2. Tracking the Subject in Early Modern Spain   31

3. Francisco de Quevedo: Individuation and Exclusion   99

4. Miguel de Cervantes: Deindividuating Don Quixote   153

   Afterword: The Exigencies of Agency   200

   Bibliography   213

   Index   225

Preface

Long before my interest in the issue of subjectivity led me to the idea of this book, the reality of being a member of an ethnic minority in the United States had positioned me in ways I was still unequipped to analyze. The myth of a universal and transhistorical individualism exerted a particularly powerful fascination for me since to be an "individual" was what U.S. culture has consistently set forth as the ultimate achievement. At that time, some twenty years ago, the construction of subjectivity was not yet widely discussed in intellectual circles, much less in "Mexican-American" middle- and working-class homes. But what I could not know then, as a nineteen-year-old Chicano drafted into the army in 1968, now seems self-evident—that the privileges of self-determining individualism were unavailable to me and in fact were unavailable to entire groups of people.

As I look back across two decades, it is therefore clear that the "choices" made by some of us during the Vietnam era were the results of our limited access—as members of minority and working-class communities—to discourses of resistance and ultimately to alternative forms of subjectivity. To put it another way, many of us who went ahead and served were unaware that the situation in which we found ourselves was historical in the strong sense, that is, not an incontrovertible "given" but a situation fraught with contradictions and therefore open to debate and contestation.

My autobiographical overture is in no sense designed to reduce history to an individual case study, but rather to give an account of how I came to recognize the importance of reconceiving the subject as a product of culture and society. The complex process by which a dominant ideology manages ethnic and class differences and sanctions only certain forms of agency for certain groups is no less pressing an issue for young Asian Americans, Latinos, and African Americans today. Within the rarefied atmosphere of the academy, however, the consequences of that process remain utterly foreign to a majority of traditional literary scholars. Even the concept of a different kind of subject, constituted across a wide range of contradictory discourses, perpetually in process, and neither completely free nor always co-opted by the so-called dominant continues to be unthinkable. And yet I would argue that every form of subjectivity is constructed precisely in this way. These are complex matters that have been foregrounded by the infusion of critical theory into literary studies; in this regard my book is the product of recent changes in the profession of literary criticism, specifically the materialist approaches of the last decade. My more specific purpose here is to rethink a particular moment of Spanish culture in light of these changes.

Because I have written it from the outer edges of what was once the Spanish empire, *Contradictory Subjects* enjoys an uneasy relationship to its subject matter. Despite the seminal work of Américo Castro, the idea of an aestheticized and homogeneous "Golden Age Spain" continues to be central to the thinking of the vast majority of scholars in Spain. It is not surprising that it does, inasmuch as Spain has been a relatively monoracial society for at least the past three hundred years. Spanish friends have already complained that my representation of early modern Spain as a culture premised on issues of blood purity is "very British," that is, it perpetuates the Black Legend initiated by Spain's enemies in the sixteenth century. I am not suggesting that Spanish social practices were any more or less rigid than those of other early modern European nations, but I do want to question the idea of a utopian Golden Age in which contemporary literary critics working around the world are still so heavily invested. Perhaps it is only fitting that I attempt to reproblematize this complex moment of Spanish culture from the multiethnic context of California in the 1990s.

To some, perhaps nonspecialist English-speaking readers, this period of Spanish history will seem an esoteric object for investigation not only because it is chronologically distant but also because Spain has functioned as a kind of "other" to Anglo-American culture at least since the sixteenth century. It was my sense of the importance of the late sixteenth and early seventeenth centuries—when the alterity of Spanish culture was initially constructed throughout the rest of Europe at precisely the same moment that the otherness of America was being written through Spain's colonial project—that brought me to trace the outlines of early modern Castilian cultural practices and the forms of subjectivity they produced. Only after I had become immersed in the historical and literary material did I realize that Spain in this period is an especially rich field of inquiry for the issues confronting the human sciences as we approach the turn of the twenty-first century.

As I write these pages, the revolution in literary theory is a quarter century old, and not unlike the revolution in Mexico, it has been institutionalized. "Theory" is now a salable commodity in literature departments across the country. Within the field of Hispanism, however, the struggle between the old and new ways of reading is far from over. At professional meetings one hears complaints about the new language, about abstractions and the abandonment of the text. Not long ago a well-established colleague in Golden Age studies asked me: Why do you want to cozy up to the poststructuralists? The opposition implied by this remark between their body and our body indicates how some kinds of theory continue to be cast in the role of other, an other that must be excluded and kept far from the imagined community of Spanish studies. Recently, an influential Hispanist warned against the "extreme nihilism of the deconstructive school of criticism." In a similar gesture made over a century ago, George Ticknor, the founder of modern Hispanism, condemned Emerson and the wild young metaphysicians of his time and warned: "The professional scholar must keep himself consecrated to letters and safe from the enthrallment and degradation of politics and the passions."

The fact is that those who would hold off the barbarians have arrived too late. The discipline of literary studies is now fully engaged in an ongoing realignment, and already a variety of strategies for dealing with the new conjuncture have emerged. One strategy has been to resist theory for being destructive and hostile to literature, which is thought to be a privileged form of writing. Others have found a way to keep the profession safe and have their theory too—thus the easy passage in Spanish departments from one formalism to the next, from stylistics to structuralism to narratology. Still others have attempted to domesticate theory's radical potential and only then allow it entry into the city of scholarship. It is because of this maneuver that we hear much talk about feminine writing but little about feminism, a great deal about the *pharmakon* but not much about the politics of culture, still more about Garcilaso's psyche but nothing about the exclusionary tactics of liberal humanism or the need to rethink the notion of the individual itself. In this scenario, new idealisms replace the old, careers are made and unmade, and the institutional work we do as intellectuals remains unexamined.

Many of us involved in the writing of a "new" Spanish Golden Age want to intervene where Ticknor would not tread. We want to show how literary history and criticism are always unavoidably linked to broader social and political issues, that the theoretical languages we adopt bring with them ideological baggage that is not easily gotten rid of, that any poststructuralism inattentive to historical problems will ultimately transform earlier cultures into false images of our own. It is my hope that this book will shed some light on what Hispanism has been in the past and, more important, what it might be in the future.

Portions of Chapters 1 and 4 appeared in earlier versions as "History and the Subject of the Spanish Golden Age," *The*

Seventeenth Century 4 (Spring, 1989), and "The Other Quixote" in *The Violence of Representation: Literature and the History of Violence,* ed. Nancy Armstrong and Leonard Tennenhouse (London: Routledge, 1989). I thank the editors for permission to use this material in expanded form here.

Translations of Petrarch reprinted by permission of the publishers from *Petrarch's Lyric Poems* by Robert M. Durling, Harvard University Press, Cambridge, Massachusetts, Copyright © 1976 by Robert M. Durling. Translations of Garcilaso's sonnet 11 and Quevedo's poem 131 from Elias L. Rivers, *Renaissance and Baroque Poetry of Spain,* pp. 36, 267, Copyright © 1966, reissued 1988 by Waveland Press, Inc., Prospect Heights, Illinois, reprinted with permission of the publishers.

Grants from the University of California, San Diego, enabled me to do research in Madrid in the summer of 1987 and facilitated the publication of this book. I am obliged to Judith Bailey for her excellent suggestions during the editorial process. For their support and encouragement I am grateful to members of the Department of Literature and my colleagues in the Spanish Section. In particular, *Contradictory Subjects* has profited greatly from conversations with Carlos Blanco Aguinaga, Page duBois, Don E. Wayne, and especially Lisa Lowe. My thanks to all of them. What I have learned from Leonard Tennenhouse and Nancy Armstrong cannot be briefly summarized. They have helped me to rethink productively most of what I had been taught about literature and culture. More important, they showed me how a rigorous criticism of colleagues' work-in-progress could be done in a spirit of friendship and collectivity.

Above all I thank Elizabeth, who means more to me than I could ever put into words.

GEORGE MARISCAL

Cardiff by the Sea, California

Contradictory Subjects

CHAPTER I

The Subject of Hispanism

It's a very long and difficult job, how to carry through this
very powerful task, which is to see how, in the very detail of
composition, a certain social structure, a certain history, dis-
closes itself. This is not doing any kind of violence to that
composition. It's precisely finding ways in which forms and
formations, in very complex ways, interact and interrelate.

—Raymond Williams, interview (1986)

I

The radical renewal of literary studies in the United
States, precipitated by the revolution in theory, is now in its
third decade. The varied and often contradictory forms of poststructuralist thought, which initially gave rise to a comprehen-
sive project of rereading the major texts of the Western tradition,
have consistently interrogated the literary profession's most fundamental principles—the author, the canon, the category of
literature itself. Even as faculties both here and in Europe felt
compelled to integrate theory into their curricula and scholarly
publications because of its ever-increasing value within the aca-
demic marketplace, there was an unspoken anxiety that these
discourses would eventually do away with the discipline of literature as it had been constituted for the past two hundred years.
But as we enter the 1990s, it is clear that "literature" and even
the traditional institutional structures of the literary profession
have not only survived but flourished in the last twenty years.
The example of Shakespearean studies is especially instructive.
Rather than delegitimate what for decades had been the most
sacred of specialties in the Western academy, the infusion of new

theoretical approaches, even those claiming to demystify, deconstruct, and decanonize, have had the effect of generating still more writing about Shakespeare and thus have safeguarded his position as the most desirable of all literary objects.

For those of us who work within the field of Hispanism, especially "Golden Age" studies, the developments of the last few years present an intriguing set of problems. Because our discipline has been slow to accept those methodologies and languages produced by the theoretical debates, traditional categories persist in the critical literature about our period. The canon of classic Spanish texts remains in place, and certainly few among us are willing to problematize, let alone to abandon, the conventional notions of the author. Clearly, the process of rewriting literary history can be successfully accomplished only with a great deal of sensitivity to historical difference and an awareness of the danger of transforming earlier cultures into images of our own, but every day it becomes more obvious that the productive and invigorating force of theory is gaining increased access to all forms of writing produced in early modern Spain. The question now, therefore, is whether all methods have equal capacity to shed light on that culture as well as on our own.

This book, although it takes off from the premise that any poststructuralist reading must be informed by an interest in history, could not have been written were it not for the central debates initiated by poststructuralist thought, especially the debate about subjectivity. The term *subjectivity* denotes a complex and unresolved problematic that has alerted us to the limitations of traditional concepts of the "individual" or "self" even as it reminds us that any attempt to revise the idea of the "subject" will produce a number of contradictory meanings according to the disciplinary frame being used; in some significant contemporary discourses its very existence has been denied.[1] A project

---

[1] A vast amount has been written about subjectivity in the last twenty years. Almost all theoretical schools have addressed the issue: discourse theory, various types of feminism, sociology, psychoanalysis, Marxism, film theory, deconstruction. Two useful summaries of the major arguments from distinctive points of view are Alex Callinicos, *Making History: Agency, Structure, and Change*

such as mine, which seeks to map out an entire historical and cultural field with the aid of so-called nonliterary texts and contemporary theory, must begin by interrogating the category of the subject.

Subjectivity is a category of central importance here for at least two reasons: first, the historical material itself, early modern Spanish writing, is the site of an intense competition between rival discourses and ideologies and thus figures forth a variety of subject forms and, second, recent attempts to introduce poststructuralist theory into the field of "Golden Age" literary studies have often lacked an appreciation of the different ways subjectivity is produced in different contexts. The individual, for example, in which most literary scholars continue to invest a great deal, is by no means a historical constant; its classic form as the unified and self-determining "I" is in fact a relatively recent invention, a consequence of the hegemony won by the European middle class in the last century.

Thus my primary thesis is a simple one. Those literary and historical studies that would have us believe seventeenth-century Spaniards shared our contemporary view of "man" have misled us. I want to show that the idea of the subject in Spain in the 1600s, as it was constructed through a variety of discourses including literature, was in no way fixed and was something quite different from those forms that dominate literary criticism and the humanities in the West today. Although a basic principle of this book is that some of the writing produced in early modern Spain worked to elaborate an emergent variant of the subject as individual, I would quickly add that the inability of traditional literary studies to recognize any other kind of subject produces several undesirable consequences: first, the notion of history as fixed, stable, and homogeneous; second, the idea of an unchanging human nature that remains the same regardless of social and historical context; and third, the exclusion of women and ethnic minorities from our definition of "man." These three unsatisfac-

---

in Social Theory (Cambridge: Polity Press, 1978); and Paul Smith, *Discerning the Subject* (Minneapolis: University of Minnesota Press, 1988).

tory principles are in fact different aspects of the same problem, to which liberal ideologies have contributed a great deal. In particular, the idealist notion that "man" is unchanging has driven some of our most perceptive critics to mistake seventeenth-century poets for existentialists and fictional hidalgos for Freudian case studies.

As I have suggested, a serious problematizing of the subject has only recently begun to affect Hispanic criticism. In anglophone Golden Age studies in particular, the individual of liberal humanism continues to thrive, relatively unendangered even when constituted by the languages of deconstruction and psychoanalysis. The long reign of bourgeois man is the result of a powerful cultural inheritance, articulated most strongly in assertions such as the one with which Ramón Menéndez Pidal opened *España y su historia* (1957): "The facts of history do not repeat themselves, but man the maker of History is always the same."[2] For U.S. Hispanism in particular, underwritten by the native ideology of "rough and ready" individualism, the individual attained an almost unassailable position, nowhere more apparently than in the work of a relatively marginal yet powerful defender of Man, Progress, and Art: Otis Green. Green's writings, including the monumental four-volume study *Spain and the Western Tradition* (1963–1966), were rooted in the belief that the idea of the rugged individualist informed all literary characters and should be the model not only for the humanist scholar but even for the nation-state. The Golden Age ended, Green once claimed, because Spain "failed to meet life's challenges."[3] I mention Otis Green because his work, in its profound commitment to the bourgeois subject, is symptomatic of virtually all canonical studies of early modern Spanish literature written in English. Compared to the postmodern notion of the subject as an over-

---

[2] Ramón Menéndez Pidal, *España y su historia*, vol. 1 (Madrid: Minotauro, 1957), p. 13. All the translations in this book are my own unless otherwise noted.

[3] Otis Green, *Spain and the Western Tradition: The Castilian Mind in Literature from "El Cid" to Calderón*, vol. 3 (Madison: University of Wisconsin Press, 1968), p. 466.

determined effect of ideology, the universal individual stands as a comforting and unassailable beacon for a traditional criticism.[4] But so long as we assume that the bourgeois individual has always been the dominant player on the stage of history, we will be unable to understand the ways in which literature and writing in general work to shape alternative forms of subjectivity. The problem of the subject, then, is my primary focus in the following pages. Here, I am not interested in epistemological or metaphysical concepts of the subject. Rather, I posit the subject as a content-free form that is "filled in" differently according to specific social and historical conditions. My argument, therefore, dissolves the notion of a unified individual, even of a role-playing individual, just as it erases the absolute *cogito* of Cartesian thought as well as ideas about "pure consciousness" or the desiring ego, the products of phenomenology and psychology respectively, which, in their more generalized form as "self," continue to exert tremendous influence over a traditional literary scholarship. These initial moves must be made in order to show that the subject is in fact constituted by multiple and often contradictory subject positions and thus is always only a provisionally fixed entity located at various sites (positionalities) within the general relations of production, systems of signification, and relations of power. I propose that early modern culture produced subjects through a wide range of discourses and practices (class, blood, the family, and so on) and that to view any of these as autonomous and originary is to efface the ways in which the construct of the individual was emerging from competition between discourses and was being constituted within writing itself.

By denying the bourgeois individual an exclusive status and insisting that it is but one form of subjectivity among many, I am not claiming with some proponents of poststructuralist thought

[4]With regard to traditional methods, Foucault reminds us, "Making historical analysis the discourse of the continuous and making human consciousness the original subject of all historical development and all action are the two sides of the same system of thought." *The Archaeology of Knowledge*, trans. A. M. Sheridan Smith (New York: Harper and Row, 1972), p. 12.

that the literary or social text is a process without any subject whatsoever. To say that the subject is divided or decentered because it is positioned, implicated, or inscribed in a wider context is not to say that it no longer exists, or even that it is hopelessly subjugated. The forms of subjectivity available within Castilian culture under the Habsburgs were admittedly restricted; yet because the subject is always a subject-in-process (permanent unity being merely a desire, at best a transitory condition) and because early modern social relations were the site of pronounced struggle, there was always a potential for agency and for imagining alternative positions.[5] Once we begin to understand the subject as a series of positions lacking any permanent closure, the potential for contradiction and praxis becomes real since there will always be disjunctions among the various positions.[6] Thus in the final section of this book, I refer to the "agent" as a third term that is neither the culturally specific "individual" nor the "subject" per se but, rather, the subject at the moment it is reconstituted according to a new conjuncture. The reshuffled network of discourses and practices may be conducive to further investment in, improvisation on, or calling into question of the subject's previous positions. In any of these cases, the moments of contingent centeredness or unity are the result of specific relational contexts; thus the agent will always be either limited or enhanced by the agency of others. It is my contention that the issue of human agency is central to the texts

[5] Although Foucault focuses his remarks on Protestantism and its concerns, I would argue that the crisis he describes was felt just as strongly in Counter-Reformation Spain: "All those movements which took place in the fifteenth and sixteenth centuries and which had the Reformation as their main expression and result should be analyzed as a great crisis of the Western experience of subjectivity and a revolt against the kind of religious and moral power which gave form, during the Middle Ages, to this subjectivity." "The Subject and Power," *Critical Inquiry* 8 (1982): 782.

[6] Antonio Gramsci sensed the importance of this productive heterogeneity when he attempted to explain "personality" as a construct composed in a "strange way" ("mode bizarre") of disparate traces of history. See *Selections from the Prison Notebooks of Antonio Gramsci*, ed. and trans. Quintin Hoare and G. N. Smith (New York: International, 1978), p. 324.

of Cervantes and Quevedo; both writers are intensely interested in how human beings in society act out, extemporize on, and even subvert the ideological scripts that history assigns them. The cultural texts I will investigate are representations of all these conflictive issues and the dynamic promise they generated in early modern Spain.

Any project that seeks to problematize subjectivity will of necessity challenge some of Hispanism's most durable critical beliefs, especially for those of us in the United States who study Spanish culture and were brought up on the myth of the Spanish individual. Spain was somehow different from the rest of Europe, we were told, because it was the home of great eccentrics both in literature and in real life. Don Quixote and Don Juan were simply the spontaneous reflections of national characteristics acted out through unconventional behavior. This view of the Spanish "character" was elaborated and welcomed in Spain, especially by those political factions that sought to ward off the effects of "Europeanization" from the sixteenth century through the 1960s. It should surprise no one that from the late eighteenth century on, subjectivity itself, which had been a virtual obsession for the writers of the early modern period, was considered so unproblematic that it was rarely discussed and almost never theorized in Spanish letters.

But if we can no longer focus our critical attention on national character or even on individuals according to traditional definitions, then neither can there be coherent portraits of single authors in any simple sense (for example, Quevedo the reactionary). One of the primary oppositions I have chosen to interrogate, therefore, is the one that positions Cervantes, supposed to have somehow transcended his own historical moment and to be, therefore, more "like us," against Quevedo, said to have been hopelessly blinded by his stagnant class biases.[7] Ernst Mérimée

[7]The Quevedo-Cervantes rivalry remains in place even in important materialist readings of the period: "The point is that Quevedo—the other side of the coin—in contrast, let us say, to Cervantes . . . has a strictly medieval view of the ideal society" ("Y es que Quevedo—la otra cara de la moneda—, a diferencia,

argued in his 1886 study of Quevedo that Cervantes possessed the *raison* and *bon sens* needed to create a masterpiece, but Quevedo was too given to his passionate and irrational instincts to accomplish a similar feat. In the last century, Cervantes was the object of a totalizing criticism that attempted to construct a whole body out of multiple and often contradictory texts in the belief that all human activity follows a "natural" evolution. Quevedo, according to the traditional opposition, has been marked as unnatural insofar as his corpus has consistently refused unification. This kind of thinking, which assumes that each author constitutes a unified consciousness to be recuperated and classified by later generations, has worked to contain critical discourse within modern or strictly aesthetic categories (progressive/reactionary, humanism/religion, light/dark, irony/satire), thereby obscuring the hybrid nature of the production of both writers.

The stature of Cervantes outside the Spanish-speaking world need not be outlined here: he is virtually the only Spanish writer who has been allowed entry into the canon of Western literature. Within Hispanic culture, his value as symbolic capital is equaled only by that of Shakespeare in the rest of the industrialized countries. Cervantes is the most beloved author of Spain, the inventor of the modern novel, the creator of transcendent characters who incarnate the "Spanish spirit." Quevedo has enjoyed much less fame on the international scene; his texts continue to be unknown to the vast majority of non-Hispanists. Within the Hispanic world, however, his name assumed an almost legendary status early on, and it has been used in a wide range of cultural functions, from a universal emblem for satire and humor to an icon for revolutionary politics. To cite only one example, the Spanish reformers of 1868, in their plans for a secular pantheon of great men designed to rival Philip II's Escorial, included the name of Quevedo. No mention was made of Cervantes. In the more limited sphere of literary studies, the two writers have

---

digamos, de Cervantes . . . tiene una visión puramente medieval de la sociedad ideal"). Carlos Blanco Aguinaga, Julio Rodríguez Puértolas, and Iris Zavala, *Historia social de la literatura española*, vol. 1 (Madrid: Castalia, 1978), p. 329.

traditionally been represented as cultural antagonists. Cervantes is the most approachable of the classic authors and thus the one who lends himself most easily to a subjective and personalizing criticism; Quevedo, on the other hand, is the great enigma that for nearly four hundred years we have been unable to decipher. It is not my intention to undertake exhaustive studies of both writers or to attack or defend these characterizations, although it is important that we ask what is at stake for our own culture in their perpetuation. I will insist, however, that Quevedo and Cervantes are not two integral pillars of the "Golden Age." Rather, each of these names by itself stands for a complex intersection of competing ideologies and practices. My title, therefore, is meant to suggest not that Quevedo somehow "contradicts" Cervantes but that contradictions are at work *within* the writings of each of them.

It will readily become clear that a large number of cultural and literary investigations inform this study. I cannot possibly enumerate all my debts to my precursors; nonetheless, I sincerely hope that my respect for the scholarly tradition that stretches from Marx to the sociological poetics of the Bakhtin circle to Raymond Williams and Michel Foucault will be apparent to the reader. Because this book assumes a certain familiarity with the historical intertext that underlies its argument, I do not rehearse the details of the so-called decline of Spain or the global crisis of European society in the seventeenth century.[8] In a very real way, however, what I say about literary representations of the subject cannot be understood apart from these matters.

As a synecdochic prologue to the exigencies of this complex historical moment, the dismantling of traditional structures, the emergence of new forms of subjectivity, and the problematizing of conventional ones, I want to cite a text from a somewhat earlier period, which captures an attitude destined to become

---

[8] For Spain, the standard accounts continue to be Antonio Domínguez Ortiz, *El antiguo régimen: Los reyes católicos y los Austrias* (Madrid: Alianza, 1973); and J. H. Elliott, *Imperial Spain, 1469–1716* (New York: New American Library, 1963).

even more widespread in the following decades, although more difficult to articulate. In a fictional dialogue between a king and a laborer thought to be from the era of Fernando and Isabel (late fifteenth century), the king makes this unusual admission: "Today's world is such that no one is content with his life. Given all you have said, when you look at our courts you think that the reality of our lives is what it appears to be. I say that you are mistaken; I believe that we desire the life that you have just as often as you desire ours" ("El mundo que hoy tenemos es de tal suerte, que á ninguno haze contento la vida que passa. Tú piensas cuando miras las nuestras córtes con todo quanto dexistes, que tal sea el ser de lo que sentimos como la aparençia dél. Digo que yerras; porque non menos vezes creo desseamos la vida que teneys, que vosotros la nuestra").[9] This is by no means the conventional "world-upside-down" motif. As we will see in subsequent passages, the entire document is symptomatic of an ambivalence concerning subject position, an intense desire for the class-other, and thus a profound questioning of social relations in general. Its powerful invocation of a consciousness of class, its analysis of economic matters, its fiercely critical tone—all are suggestive of the imminent breakup of traditional society which would characterize the entire early modern period beginning in the late fifteenth century. Fernando de Rojas's dramatic representation of the struggle between competing interests in *La Celestina* (1499) is only the most striking literary example of similar writings that together constituted an emergent discourse on class.

By the middle decades of the sixteenth century, class distinctions were being openly articulated in those texts indebted to Erasmian humanism. The anonymous and influential *Crótalon* (1553?), for example, without which *Lazarillo de Tormes* (1554) and certain sections of *Don Quixote* might not have been written, contains a stunning attack against the arrogance of aristocrats: "Their presumption is so great that they think that all there is in the world is for them and their children only, and that all other

---

[9]José Amador de los Ríos, "Sobre el libro llamado de los pensamientos variables," in *Historia crítica de la literatura española*, vol. 7, app. 4 (Madrid: Joaquin Muñoz, 1865), p. 586.

men who live in the world are refuse. . . . In conclusion, their haughtiness and ambition is such that they think it obvious that all other men should pay *them* for the right to be their servants" ("Es tanta su presunción, que les parece que para solos ellos y para sus hijos y descendientes es poco todo lo que en el mundo hay, y que todos los otros hombres que en el mundo viven son estiércol. . . . Es, en conclusión, tanta la soberbia y ambición déstos, que tienen por muy averiguado que todo hombre les debe a ellos salario por quererse dellos servir").[10] In its critique of traditional hierarchies, *El Crótalon* sets the stage for future conflicts between the ideology of virtue and dominant ideas about inherited nobility.

By the seventeenth century, the reconfiguration of social discourses and practices and thus the realignment of positions for the subject, the desire to be "something else," together with (and in opposition to) the intensified efforts to sustain essentialist concepts of subjectivity based on both blood and status, were being represented in a wide range of cultural products. That some of these were literary texts later to be fixed as monuments in a dehistoricized canon does not obscure the fact that *Don Quixote*, for example, and Quevedo's poetry are signs of historically specific conflicts, not unmediated reflections of a socioeconomic background but forms of writing that, together with the other transformations, generated a variety of new positions for the subject. In the light of a cultural materialist methodology, Américo Castro's description of this moment in Spanish history as an "age of conflict" ("edad conflictiva") has never seemed more fitting.

II

The idea of the Golden Age has been used to describe the period in Spanish history from approximately 1517 to 1680, that is, from the ascendency of Charles V to the death of Calderón.

---

[10]Cristóforo Gnósofo [pseud.], *El Crótalon*, ed. Augusto Cortina (Buenos Aires: Espasa-Calpe, 1942), p. 269.

As a theoretical construct it has had a powerful and often positive influence on representations of an otherwise heterogeneous series of historical moments. By mapping out a wide range of writers and texts deemed worthy of examination, the concept of the Golden Age produced a delimited and systematic discipline that has attempted to fix the diachronic movement of history so that it might be reconstructed and analyzed by later generations of scholars. In a real way, the model itself was a synthesis of the fascination of early modern culture with the idea of utopia and the nineteenth-century nostalgia for the perceived unity of the Habsburg empire.[11] For literary studies in particular, an important consequence of this desire was the production of the critical trope of Golden Age Spain. The eventual aestheticizing of the entire cultural record would have been inconceivable without the projection of an essentially modern longing for wholeness back onto the sixteenth and seventeenth centuries and the representation of a series of complex historical conjunctures and their contradictions as a single monolithic "age."

Despite Hispanism's silence on the subject and the many studies that unselfconsciously reproduce the inherited idealism of the literary profession, this enterprise can no longer hold together. The use of a synchronic model always carries with it serious drawbacks for all but the most formalist critical methods, and the continued use of the term *Golden Age* more often than not blocks our ability to be precise about what the function of literature was in 1554, for example, and what it may have been fifty or seventy-five years later. My point is that once the changing

---

[11] Although it conveyed a decidedly more limited range of meanings, the term *golden age* had already been used in seventeenth-century courtly rhetoric: "Great happiness attends the government of this fortunate monarchy: the reign of the king, our lord, Philip IV is a golden age for Spain" ("Gloriosa corre la felicidad en el Gobierno desta dichosa Monarquía: siglo de oro es para España el reinado del Rey, nuestro señor, Felipe IV"). *Cartas de Andrés de Almansa y Mendoza: Novedades de esta corte y avisos recibidos de otras partes, 1621–1626* (Madrid: M. Ginesta, 1886), p. 53. Four hundred years later, in the euphoria surrounding the five hundredth anniversary of the "discovery" of America, we sense the durability of this myth: "The year 1492 ushered in Spain's Golden Age. The year 1992 may well mark another." *Town & Country* (April 1990).

contexts of early modern Spanish life were collapsed into one another, it was a relatively simple critical move to appropriate them to a global project founded on the notion of an autonomous aesthetic realm that mysteriously progressed from "Renaissance" to "Baroque." It then became much more difficult, if not altogether impossible, to recognize the heterogeneity of the various periods. The work of those critics with a strong sense of history has indicated how writers working in the 1620s produced very different texts for very different reasons from those of their predecessors in the 1520s. One could even cite examples of texts produced in the same moment which share few if any ideological or stylistic affinities (for example, those of Avellaneda and Cervantes). Nevertheless, the aestheticizing and universalizing impulse of much contemporary critical thought requires that we continue to problematize the concept of the Golden Age, that we repeatedly expose the notion to the light of historical discontinuity.[12]

Fernand Braudel's monumental *La Méditerranée et le monde méditerranéen à l'époque de Philippe II* (1949) has been received by Hispanists with a certain awe for years, but its fundamental insights have yet to be developed for literary and cultural studies. Braudel's demand that history no longer be viewed as objective, unified, or predicated on the actions of a transcendental subject potentially calls into question much that has been said about sixteenth- and seventeenth-century Spanish literature for at least the past two hundred years. Sensing the threat not only to his own project but to Hispanism in general, Américo Castro

---

[12] A few years before his death, José Antonio Maravall gave the most cogent articulation of the problem I am describing: "I begin with the thought that one must banish the term 'Golden Age,' not in order to diminish the value of Spanish culture in that imprecise period, but because it is a hopelessly rhetorical term that distorts any historical reading" ("Empiezo por creer que hay que desterrar la expresión 'Siglo de Oro,' no para reducir el valor de las letras españolas en ese impreciso período, sino porque es una expresión insoportablemente retórica que perturba toda lectura histórica"). See "Sobre el pensamiento social y político de Quevedo (una revisión)," in *Homenaje a Quevedo* (*II Academia literaria renacentista*), ed. Victor García de la Concha (Salamanca: Universidad de Salamanca, 1982), p. 100.

felt compelled to warn his readers: "The purpose of the new historiography is to eliminate the individual and all forms of differentiated particularism" ("El propósito de la nueva historiografía es eliminar al individuo y a toda forma de particularismo diferenciado").[13] This spirited defense of the individual was to be expected given Castro's own ideological bias, which will figure prominently in my account. But it was not that Braudel and the practitioners of a synthesizing approach to all the human sciences (the *Annales* school) wanted to do away with human beings as such. Rather, Braudel's call for the "decomposition of man"[14] signaled the end of the myth of a unified self (the bourgeois individual) and prepared the way for a rethinking of the subject as a series of shifting positions within the social field.

Braudel's attempt to reconstitute subjectivity from a historian's point of view was a crucial test case because it resisted the temptation merely to replace traditional Platonic concepts of "self" with newer and no less transcendent ones. The rivalry between Castro and Braudel was regrettable since the strategies Castro dismissed as "dehumanized history" ("la historia deshumanizada") and "the new socioeconomic gospel" ("el nuevo evangelio económico-social") actually might have achieved what Castro himself openly desired, that is, a coming to terms with the contradictions of early modern Spanish society and an understanding of "the currents of life" ("las fluencias de vida") which constitute history itself. By refusing to problematize the subject of liberal humanism and by claiming that the future of Spanish historiography and cultural studies was jeopardized by two irrational schools of thought (those defending a mystified

[13] Américo Castro, *De la edad conflictiva: Crisis de la cultura española en el siglo XVII*, 4th ed. (Madrid: Taurus, 1976), p. xvii.

[14] The first English translation of this passage obscured Braudel's profound questioning of the subject of history by converting "la décomposition de l'homme en un cortège de personnages" into the essentially phenomenological phrase "to divide man into a multitude of selves." See *The Mediterranean and the Mediterranean World in the Age of Philip II*, vol. 1, trans. Sian Reynolds (New York: Harper Colophon, 1972), p. 21. A slightly preferable reading is that of Sarah Matthews: "the breaking-down of man into a succession of characters" in Fernand Braudel, *On History* (Chicago: University of Chicago Press, 1980), p. 4.

castizo Spain versus those who in his opinion practiced vulgar economism), Castro lost the opportunity to engage in a productive dialogue with Braudel.[15]

Despite the long-lasting hegemony of liberal criticism and its unwavering belief in a transcendental self, genius, and the heroic individual within the language of Hispanic studies, alternative positions occasionally took shape in the work of writers who sought to rethink the category of the subject. This is an important point because it reminds us that theorizing subjectivity is not merely a foreign importation but forms part of a rich, though little-known tradition in Spain itself. Even among those writers who today are most closely associated with "Spanish individualism," one finds occasional signs of doubt as to the historical accuracy and methodological usefulness of such a concept. The texts of a thinker as central to twentieth-century Spanish culture as Miguel de Unamuno, for example, often seem to cry out for a reevaluation of what has usually been read as Unamuno's romantic obsession with individuality, his "yoísmo." More specifically, Unamuno's distinction between "individualism" and "personality" has not been sufficiently emphasized. In a 1902 essay whose title translates as "Spanish Individualism," Unamuno wrote: "My idea is that the Spaniard has, as a general rule, more individuality than personality; that the intensity with which he asserts himself in opposition to everyone else, and the energy with which he creates dogmas and circumscribes himself within their limits, is not due to any richness of his intimate spiritual life, for it is rare indeed for him to show any degree of complexity" ("Mi idea es que el español tiene, por regla general, más individualidad que personalidad; que la fuerza con que se afirma frente a los demás, y la energía con que se crea dogmas y se encierra en ellos, no corresponde a la riqueza de su contenido espiritual íntimo, que rara vez peca de complejo").[16]

---

[15]Castro claimed: "Because we are moving from the myth of Numantia to that of the dogmas of historical materialism" ("Porque estamos pasando del mito de Numancia al de los dogmas del materialismo histórico"). *De la edad*, p. xvi.

[16]Miguel de Unamuno, "El individualismo español," *Ensayos*, vol. 1, ed. Bernardo G. de Candamo (Madrid: Aguilar, 1970), p. 445. I owe my under-

Unamuno's differentiation, which anticipates later theoretical moves of Habermas and others, is essentially between public and private spheres: "individuality" is the result of pressures that originate outside the subject and the limitations that constitute the social itself; "personality" is the product of an interior consciousness conceived against the social. Clearly, Unamuno's distinction continues the process by which the subject was converted into "the individual," an idea tentatively elaborated in Renaissance humanist discourse and central to nineteenth-century thought. But elsewhere in his work, Unamuno is decidedly hostile to the traditional opposition between individual and society:

> The error originates in the superficial opposition usually established between individual and society, without stating that the individual is as much a condensation of society as society is an expansion of the individual. To imagine that the subject and its surroundings are things that come together from different worlds, or the like, is the height of foolishness. The subject makes its surroundings and the surroundings make the subject.

> (El error arranca de la superficial oposición que suele establecerse entre el individuo y la sociedad, sin advertir que es tanto el individuo condensación de la sociedad como ésta expansión de aquél. Imaginarse que el sujeto y su ambiente son cosas que vienen a unirse partiendo de distintos mundos, o poco menos, es el disparate de los disparates. El sujeto hace el ambiente y el ambiente hace el sujeto).[17]

It is one thing to reject the specious self/society dichotomy as Unamuno, following Marx, has done so powerfully in this state-

---

standing of Unamuno's complex exploration of subjectivity to the work of Carlos Blanco Aguinaga. See Blanco's "Unamuno's 'yoísmo' and Its Relation to Traditional Spanish 'Individualism,'" in *Unamuno Centennial Studies*, ed. Ramón Martínez López (Austin: Department of Romance Languages, University of Texas, 1966).

[17] Miguel de Unamuno, "El individuo, producto social" (1897), in *Obras completas*, vol. 9: *Discursos y artículos* (Madrid: Escelcier, 1971), p. 699.

ment. It is quite another to attempt to reconcile the desire for an autonomous, self-determining individual, which was consistently and energetically produced by a number of important Renaissance writers, from Petrarch to Montaigne, Cervantes to Quevedo, with our own late twentieth-century understanding of the origins of that desire.

From the historical perspective of almost one hundred years of critical writing, it is clear that Unamuno's concept of the subject was problematized to an even greater extent than that of Américo Castro, despite the fundamental role Castro's theory of castes played in demythologizing the concept of *castizo* Spain. By rereading the history of Spain as the interaction of Jewish, Muslim, and Christian identities, Castro rejected the notion of racial purity, which had been used as a tool of reaction from at least the fifteenth century until well into the Franco years, and reconstructed Spanish individualism on the scene of *convivencia*, the living together of the three religions. But despite this important political gesture and the centrality of all Castro's work on early modern Spain, the phenomenological underpinnings of his project produced a variation on the figure of an autonomous and unified agent of history, which, even in its disguised form as the collective "Spain," built its personal empire relatively unimpeded by external constraints. The primary category of Castro's historicism was that of the "living space" ("morada") within which the historical subject resides. Castro insisted that his was not an essentialist term, "not a finished and static reality, analogous to the classic substance; it is a dynamic reality . . . a certain horizon of living possibilities (preferences) and impossibilities (denials)" "no es una realidad estática y acabada, análoga a la sustancia clásica; es una realidad dinámica . . . un cierto horizonte de posibilidades [preferencias] e imposibilidades [rechazos] vitales"). Nevertheless, Castro's concept retained both the image of a fixed space ("mansion") and the sense of a solitary monad safely removed from history itself: "But when calm is restored and the inhabitant returns to his living space, he will prefer to inhabit some rooms rather than others" ("Pero cuando se restablece la calma, y el morador se reintegra al dentro de su morada, aquél preferirá habitar en unas estancias más bien que en otras").[18]

It should be noted that elsewhere in Castro's work are statements suggestive of a more complex sense of how the subject is constituted,[19] and that Castro and his students such as Stephen Gilman have played an extremely important part in enabling us to view imperial Spain as a heterogeneous and conflictive society rather than an Iberian *Gemeinschaft*. For a more radical rethinking of the subject within the field of Hispanic studies, however, we must look outside the accepted canon of critical works. Here I am thinking particularly of the writings of Enrique Tierno Galván, a university professor and Renaissance scholar whose literary studies never achieved canonical status; Tierno practiced a rigorous Marxist criticism and was active on the Spanish Left, founding the Partido Socialista Popular and later becoming the Socialist mayor of Madrid after the death of Franco.

In a long essay relatively ignored by North American Hispanists, Tierno asserted that the so-called Baroque "presents itself as a culture of the convention—repetitive, tedious, and irreplaceable . . . creating a communal mentality that necessitates rebellion. . . . This nonconformity is at the root of that which has commonly been interpreted as personality or Spanish individualism. In reality, it is the opposite. . . . Lived rebellion becomes a

[18]Américo Castro, "En el umbral de la historia," *Nueva revista de filología hispánica* 7 (1953): 242–45. The way in which Castro's "saving" of the bourgeois subject coincided with the discourse of Hispanism as practiced in the United States should not be overlooked. John Beverley has remarked on the underlying elitism of Castro's approach, a result of liberal humanism's exclusionary strategies. See Beverley's "Class or Caste: A Critique of the Castro Thesis," in *Papers of the Américo Castro Centennial Symposium* (Syracuse, N.Y.: Syracuse University Press, 1988).

[19]Castro writes, for example: "The unity of the person does not consist of *being* an *I* (for us a *he*) substantial and fixed, but rather of the will to be what one desires to be. In this way, the person splits into a current of varied representations" ("La unidad del personaje no consiste en *ser* un *yo* (para nosotros un *él*) fijo y sustancial, sino en la voluntad de ser lo que se quiere ser. El personaje se escinde así en un fluir de representaciones variables"). See Prólogo to *El ingenioso hidalgo Don Quijote de la Mancha*, 19th ed., ed. Castro (Mexico City: Editorial Porrua, 1979), p. xlvi.

solution to the lack of dialectic and the repetition of contrast" ("se presenta como cultura del lugar común, reiterado, tedioso e insustituíble . . . constituyendo una mentalidad comunitaria, que obliga a la rebeldía. . . . Esta disconformidad está a la base de lo que comúnmente se ha interpretado como personalidad e individualismo español. En el fondo es lo contrario. . . . La rebeldía vital se ofrece como una solución a la falta de dialéctica y la repetición del contraste").[20] Tierno thus powerfully introduces the issue of "rebellion," or what in another context might be called "resistance" or "agency." The issue of agency is at the center of current writings about subject formation, and I will have something to say about it in my concluding remarks. For now, I want simply to point out a preliminary difficulty with Tierno's formulation: the kind of communal mentality to which he refers, instead of making resistance inevitable, more often than not produces a utopian sense of well-being and ideological "comfort" which precludes the articulation of any effective oppositional practice. Given this view, if Spanish culture was the site of endlessly repeated oppositions upon which the dialectic could not work, we must ask how any contestation of traditional discourses and thus any reshaping of the hegemonic order could have occurred.

Within the field of early modern studies, Tierno's contention that the "Spanish individual" was the product of an unusually constraining social environment was developed by José Antonio Maravall, especially in his studies of the forms of early modern theater (*comedia*) and what he referred to as the culture of the Baroque. Focusing on specific writers, Tierno had convincingly argued that Quevedo, for example, was "the first Spanish victim of an attempted intimacy that, if it had not been for the baroque context, would have developed into one of the most complex examples in all of Europe" ("la primera víctima española de una intimidad en conato, que de no haber sido por la circunstancia barroca habría madurado hasta ser una de las más matizadas de

[20]Enrique Tierno Galván, "Notas sobre el Barroco," in *Desde el espectáculo a la trivialización* (Madrid: Taurus, 1961), p. 183.

Europa").[21] Within a frame more properly functionalist than Marxian, Maravall went on to show in general terms that all those characters of Spanish literature who have traditionally been taken for "great individuals" are in fact little more than exaggerated figures molded by the limitations of a rigidly aristocratic and exclusionary society. In his important study of the phrase "I am who I am" ("soy quien soy"), Maravall wrote:

> To our way of seeing, from all the data we have gathered, it is clear that "I am who I am" is not a principle that obliges one to be faithful to oneself in the sense of realizing through one's actions that internal nucleus of personality in each person which defines it as a unique being. On the contrary, it is a principle that is always spoken in relation to social behavior, as an obligation to function in a certain way that is proper according to qualities of estate.

> (A nuestro modo de ver, de todos los datos que hemos reunido resulta claro que "soy quien soy" no es un principio que obligue a ser fiel a sí mismo, en el sentido de realizar en sus actos aquel núcleo interno de la propia personalidad que la define, en cada uno, como un ser sí mismo. Es, por el contrario, un principio que se enuncia siempre en relación al comportamiento social, como una obligación de obrar de cierta manera—que es la propia, en atención a su calidad estamental.)[22]

In Maravall's account, individual behavior is predetermined by social position and subjected to continual manipulation by a dominant social order that allots even the emotions according to rank. Elsewhere, Maravall had laid the groundwork for such a position by rejecting any idealist bias: "Individualism is not—on this we must insist—an invention of philosophers but a social phenomenon" ("El individualismo no es—insistimos en ello—una ocurrencia de filósofos, sino un fenómeno social").[23] Given the hegemonic status of the bourgeois self within the discourse of

---

[21]Ibid., p. 189.

[22]José Antonio Maravall, *Teatro y literatura en la sociedad barroca* (Madrid: Seminarios y Ediciones, 1972), p. 100.

[23]Maravall, *Estado moderno y mentalidad social (siglos XV a XVII)*, vol. 1 (Madrid: Revista de Occidente, 1972), p. 408.

Spanish historiography and literary criticism, this kind of statement was crucial if the subject was to be reconceived as a social construct and not a transhistorical constant. I have already stated my reservations about a theoretical model that reduces the subject to an embodiment of ideological effects. Subjectivity may be socially constructed, but this is not to say that human beings are incapable of resisting or investing in any given set of positions. A concept of the dominant which is as totalizing as it comes to be in Maravall's *Cultura del Barroco*, for example, leads to problems reminiscent of those surrounding Louis Althusser's *Träger* (subjects as systemic supports), not the least of which has to do with the potential for oppositional movements and social change. The thesis that the *comedia* was little more than a well-oiled propaganda machine designed to reproduce and disseminate the ideology of the ruling elites ignores the complicated functioning of the public *corral* and seriously understates the potential for multiple and even contestatory responses within the performance text itself (for example, carnivalesque inversions such as *bailes* and *mojigangas*). Elsewhere, it should be noted, Maravall sensed the impossibility of any "total system" and reminded us that in seventeenth-century Spain, "we are faced with a society energized in its traditional elements, but in new circumstances. . . . Now, the restored tradition is more or less debated, or at least it is not exempt from questioning" ("Estamos ante una sociedad que se ve vigorizada en sus elementos tradicionales, pero también en circunstancias nuevas. . . . Ahora, incluso, la tradición restaurada se encuentra en mayor o menor medida discutida, o, por lo menos, no deja de ser puesta en cuestión").[24] It is this suggestive thesis that continues to make Maravall's work central to any deaestheticizing approach to early modern Spanish culture. In the end, Maravall's most significant contribution may have been his dramatic reopening of the entire

[24]Maravall, *La cultura del Barroco: Análisis de una estructura histórica* (Barcelona: Ariel, 1975), p. 201. An English translation is available: *The Culture of the Baroque*, trans. Terry Cochran (Minneapolis: University of Minnesota Press, 1986). An important supplement to the otherwise totalizing study of baroque culture is the earlier *La oposición política bajo los Austrias* (Barcelona: Ariel, 1972) in which Maravall outlines contestatory practices in early modern Spain.

issue of the social construction of the subject in the "classic"
period of Spanish literature.

III

The problematizing of the unified and autonomous subject in
the work of Braudel, Tierno, and Maravall may be seen as part of
a tradition originating with Marx himself. While it is safe to say
that the founders of Marxism did not formulate a full-scale
theory of the subject as did classical philosophy—culminating in
the thought of Hegel, Feuerbach, and others—it is nonetheless
true that a profound rethinking of subjectivity is implicit in the
Marxist project. In the 1845 critique of Feuerbach, we are told:
"But the human essence is no abstraction inherent in each single
individual. In its reality it is the ensemble of the social relations"
(thesis 6). And in the 1857 introduction to the *Grundrisse*—"The
human being is in the most literal sense a political animal, not
merely a gregarious animal, but an animal which can individuate
itself only in the midst of society"—we see that Marx was one of
the first modern thinkers to recognize the complex relationships
between subjectivity and social life.[25]
   In his well-known essay "Reification and the Consciousness of
the Proletariat" Georg Lukács would go on to elaborate another
of Marx's insights, this from the *Critique of Hegel's Philosophy of
Right*: "The essence of man does not possess any true reality."[26]
In Lukács's hands, this fundamental challenge to traditional
literary, historical, and philosophical studies becomes a call for
the disintegration of any humanism founded upon an absolute
concept of Man. At this juncture we encounter a way to understand the difficult issue of the decentered subject, for by turning

[25] Karl Marx, *Theses on Feurbach* in *The Marx-Engels Reader*, 2d ed., ed. Robert
C. Tucker (New York: W. W. Norton, 1978), p. 145; Karl Marx, *Grundrisse:
Foundations of the Critique of Political Economy*, trans. Martin Nicolaus (New York:
Vintage, 1973), p. 84.
   [26] Karl Marx, *Contribution to the Critique of Hegel's Philosophy of Right* in *Early
Writings*, ed. and trans. Tom Bottomore (New York: McGraw-Hill, 1964), p. 43.

the dialectical method on the human being we are able to see subjectivity not as a thing but as a process. Again, Tierno is one our most insightful commentators:

> The concept of the dialectic applied with rigor, as an intellectual procedure of being in praxis, destroys the humanist concept of independent subjectivism, even if it is situated and interested in the world. By pushing to the limit the potential of the concept of the dialectic, we find reciprocal negation, an idea that in itself implies the negation of substantiality as it is understood by humanist subjectivism.

> (La noción de dialéctica aplicada con rigor, como un procedimiento intelectual de estar en la praxis, destruye la noción humanista del subjetivismo independiente, aunque metido e interesado en el mundo. Apurando al límite las posibilidades de la noción dialéctica, encontramos la negación recíproca, idea que a su vez implica la negación de la sustancialidad, tal y como el subjetivismo humanista la entiende.)[27]

The notion of the subject as substance, that which is "in itself and conceived through itself" (according to Spinoza's characterization of the Cartesian formulation), is necessarily undone by the movement of historical contradictions and the discontinuities that exist between subject positions. Dialectical materialism, Tierno suggests, breaks definitively with any and all metaphysical concepts of subjectivity, a break theorized long before more recent attacks on the "Western tradition" initiated from within a more properly philosophical discourse (for example, by Derrida and his followers).

To follow Tierno's attack on traditional humanism and my

---

[27]Enrique Tierno Galván, "Humanismo y sociedad" (1964), in *La novela picaresca y otros escritos* (Madrid: Tecnos, 1974), p. 285. In one of his last interviews (Jan. 20, 1984), Foucault made a similar assertion. The subject, he said, "is not a substance; it is a form and this form is not above all or always identical to itself." See "The Ethic of Care for the Self as a Practice of Freedom," in *The Final Foucault*, ed. James Bernauer and David Rasmussen (Cambridge: MIT Press, 1988), p. 10.

own insistence on problematizing subjectivity with a gesture toward the work of Jean-Paul Sartre would seem contradictory at best. No other major writer of this century has been more closely associated with questions of freedom and the "full" individual or more the target of the attacks of emergent poststructural thought. But in later texts such as the *Critique of Dialectical Reason* (1960), Sartre abandoned an earlier existential model of individualism and theorized the forces (for the most part, the products of human activity) that work to constitute the subject. Attributing any simple concept of the subject to Sartre is misleading, therefore, for in fact Sartre is the only major thinker who has attempted to develop a complex Marxist theory of subjectivity. While I do not intend to give an extended account of the Sartrean project, we need to understand how the relationship between praxis and objective conditions (what Sartre calls "the material") is rethought in the *Critique*.

The passage I have selected is of particular interest because it returns us to Spain in the early modern period. Taking Braudel's study of the Mediterranean as his point of departure, Sartre proposes to discuss Spanish hegemony and the economic structures that arose in Europe on the heels of the colonization of America. Spain, he argues, was the sealed container into which New World metals had to be delivered in order for them to become "human quantities." Sartre than poses the following question and answer:

> Should this crucible, this unbreakable vessel (unbreakable in theory at least) be called material, on the grounds that the very nature of the Spanish frontiers (the sea, the Pyrenees) constitutes in itself a natural barrier, and that institutions, social structures and the system of government are crystallised practices? Or should it be called *praxis*, on the grounds that governments pursuing a precise policy and supported by the ruling classes appointed quite definite people—administrators, policemen, customs officials, etc.—to keep watch over the outflow of gold and silver?
>
> In reality, it is completely impossible to separate the first interpretation from the second: at this point we reach concrete and fundamental reality. Matter as the receptacle of passivised prac-

tices is indissolubly linked to lived *praxis*, which simultaneously
adapts to material conditions and inert significations, and renews
their meaning, reconstituting them by transcending them, if only
to transform them.[28]

This passage foregrounds the dialectical movement between
wholeness and multiplicity which is crucial for understanding
the relationship between subjectivity and agency. The determining macrotext appears to be a "closed" totality, but its wholeness
is provisional at best because "society" is a process of continual
change produced by the living out of discourses and ideologies.
From our vantage point at the conjuncture of consumer capitalism and postmodernism, we might add that subjects themselves,
whether they are members of the ruling class or their "subjects,"
are constituted not through single but through multiple discursive positions, and therefore they must negotiate at any given
moment the various contradictions and interests that intersect
them. This last methodological move is a necessary correction of
the tendency in Sartre's thought toward privileging the notion of
the "actor" as a unified and noncontradictory subject. It is useful,
I think, to show that the decenteredness of subjectivity enhances
the potential for disruption and transformation of objective conditions; the subject as agent functions within limited options, yet
nevertheless is capable of being reinscribed and of rearranging
"prescribed" reality as he or she is reconstituted by new discursive configurations. These are complex questions that will not be
resolved here, but I want to ask them in relation to a specific
period in Spanish cultural history and to trace their effects across
a series of literary and nonliterary texts.

It will strike the attentive reader that the one traditional genre
I have chosen not to investigate is that with the most obvious
political and social implications for the seventeenth century: the
theater. Because early modern dramatic spectacle comprised
many complex economic and cultural practices and because the

[28]Jean-Paul Sartre, *Critique of Dialectical Reason*, trans. Alan Sheridan-Smith
(London: Verso, 1982), p. 168.

representation of subjectivity on stage relied heavily on spectator response, physical conditions in the theater, and other factors not directly associated with reading and writing, I have decided to focus on the textual and cultural processes that produce the subject forms of poetry and the novel.[29] Despite the modern critic's desire to convert certain characters into bourgeois heroes according to the nineteenth-century model, the collective nature of theatrical practice virtually precluded the textual construction of the subject as individual which we will see at work in Cervantes and Quevedo.

In a real sense, traditional *comedia* criticism has been especially guilty of seeing the individual where it is not since, by founding itself upon an ahistorical concept of "human nature," it erased the contradictions that make up the subject. Even as brilliant and influential a critic as A. A. Parker, in an essay that sought to expose those ways of reading which privileged modern and realistic genres such as the novel and to offer a new theoretical model for a generation, fell prey to such idealist tendencies: "It does not matter in the least if the plot of a play is untrue to life in the sense of being untrue to normal experience, provided that its theme is true to human nature."[30] What that nature might have been for Quevedo or Cervantes or Lope is no easy riddle to solve, but clearly it bore a scant resemblance to our own twentieth-century versions. And if we accept for the moment the argument I advance in my next chapter—that Spanish culture was the site of various contradictory definitions of "man"—then human nature would have signified different things to different writers even though they inhabited the same cultural and historical space.

If this book does not seek to explicate texts from all genres, neither does it directly address the issue of gender. After reviewing the historical material, I am convinced that the category of gender as it is understood in contemporary middle-class culture is premised to a great degree on the effacement of kinship relations by a strictly economic division of labor. Thus modern gender is a discourse that situates women in ways quite unrelated to those produced by seventeenth-century Spanish social practices. This is not to say that the complex sex/gender system of early modern culture did not produce and reproduce sexual difference within a misogynist context. It most certainly did, and in ways no less oppressive than those of earlier or later historical moments. But the aristocratic subject that is the focus of this book is undeniably a masculinist construct; virtually all forms of subjectivity in this period depended on different degrees and kinds of "maleness," rather than on the historically more recent male/female binomial. Thus, although I will discuss certain aspects of early modern sexuality, the category of gender itself must be understood in relation to other symbolic orders (blood, status, class) that were more often determinant in the final instance. As for the subject of religious discourse, it figures only occasionally in this book and then only as a means to foreground the nature of secular texts. Nevertheless, the issue of religion is closely linked in the period to that of blood and is an important topic for future study. In a real sense, my proposition that subjectivity be rethought as the intersection of contradictory discursive positions is anticipated by the Spanish ruling-class practice of inventing neologisms (for example, *alborayque*) to describe the "species-less" *converso* (Jewish convert to Christianity). This and other cultural mechanisms, such as the intricate process that gave rise to the subject of mystic literature and its attendant forms of Christian "individualism," could be adequately addressed only in a separate study.[31]

Thus I will delineate only some of the categories and contradictions at work within the dominant ideologies of seventeenth-

---

[31] For a historical study employing the category of gender, see Mary Elizabeth Perry, *Gender and Disorder in Early Modern Seville* (Princeton: Princeton University Press, 1990). On the subject of mysticism, see the writings of Michel de Certeau, for example, "Mystic Speech," in *Heterologies: Discourse on the Other*, trans. Brian Massumi (Minneapolis: University of Minnesota Press, 1986).

century Spanish culture as well as those discourses and practices against which the dominant struggled to maintain itself. Chapter 2 attempts to reconstruct the cultural field through which various forms of subjectivity took shape. In employing the vocabulary of early modern Spanish culture, I am not interested in composing a totalized narrative of the period; instead, I want to map the different oppositions, negations, and syntheses that worked to produce subjects. My claim is not that we will thereby come to understand fully how early modern men and women viewed themselves. On the contrary, rejecting and breaking up the traditional concept of the Golden Age and its "individuals" will permit us to see what the past can tell us about our own assumptions and biases.

By way of concluding, I want to insist that Chapter 2 is not the "outside" to the "inside" of the chapters on specific literary writers, the context to their text. The various discourses (medical, legal, economic) to which I refer cannot be considered prior to or separate from the discourse of literature itself. All these material practices worked together to give shape to the emergent and traditional forms of subjectivity that struggled for dominance in seventeenth-century Spain. In my final two chapters, then, I sketch the outlines of this struggle as it is represented in the texts of Cervantes and Quevedo, again not in order to privilege literature or to produce a totalized vision of each author but rather to trace the kinds of subjects figured forth by two specific modes of early modern writing, lyric poetry and the extended narrative. In Chapter 3 I speak only in passing of Quevedo's nonpoetic output. His two extended narratives, *Historia de la vida del buscón llamado don Pablos* (1604?) and the *Sueños* (1607–1622), were undertaken early in his career; that he rarely returned to the narrative form hints at the ways in which the pressures of courtly power dynamics determined literary production. At the same time, the so-called serious and burlesque poems offer us a more explicit positioning of the reading and writing subject as it was both constrained and liberated by the various poetic forms themselves. The noncanonical picaresque poems are of particular interest, for they may well constitute the most powerful figuration of Quevedo's near obsession with the emergent idea of the individual. For his part, Cervantes, as innumerable critics have taught us, exploded the potential of the sustained narrative and in the process "invented" the modern novel (and if we accept the nineteenth century's verdict, helped to invent the modern individual as well). Chapter 4 traces a number of issues surrounding the formation of subjectivity in the Cervantine text, in particular the attempts to deindividuate the radical subject of the 1605 novel, and outlines the ways in which the second *Don Quixote* seeks a settlement with the traditional discourses of seventeenth-century culture.

In Chapters 3 and 4, I argue that both authors struggle with an emergent form of the subject which since the nineteenth century we have come to take for granted as the "eternal" nature of man.[32] I want to make clear, however, that by purposely placing my discussion of Quevedo before that of Cervantes I hope to move away from the idea of "progress" in the historical constructions of the subject. I think we must reject the notion of an inevitable evolution toward "higher stages," culminating in twentieth-century forms. Rather, each specific context produces conditions in which existing elements are rearticulated and, in some cases, win hegemony. Thus, the subject as individual has passed through a variety of incarnations, from the twelfth-century burgher to the early modern *Homo faber*, from Rousseauean man to the *Homo economicus* of the last century.

A final word about the relationship between subjectivity and the social field: although my book has a stake in the issue of agency, it is in no way calling for a return to voluntarism or for the reinstitution of the myth of a radically autonomous individual,

---

[32] In the first of several interesting studies on Cervantes, John Weiger reproduced the developmental notion of "self" which continues to inform the discourse of Hispanism: "From Cervantes' point of view, then, it is essential to know one's strengths and weaknesses, in order to be an individual in the sense in which I have been employing this term, namely to realize one's full potential as a person." This position is incompatible with the basic premise of my own work. See Weiger, *The Individuated Self: Cervantes and the Emergence of the Individual* (Athens: Ohio University Press, 1979), p. 7.

an entity that works to sustain the oppositions I am seeking to problematize. The authors I study here were determined by their specific contexts. It will therefore be necessary to draw on some biographical and a great deal of cultural material, not as earlier positivist or reflection theories might have done but rather in order to understand the limitations and pressures that affected the production of the text. This is not to say, however, that the ways in which each writing subject wrote and was "written" by his culture were irrevocably predestined. Determination in the sense I am using it means only that a network of boundaries and interests is always in place before and during the production of any cultural artifact. This "formation" is constituted not only by the pressures of the social macrotext but also by the constraints of the literary mode employed. In some cases, these pressures and constraints lead to a reaffirmation of established norms, in others to their disruption and rearticulation. My point is that no matter how closed the society, the potential for action and change always exists within the cultural field, even though it may be circumscribed and seemingly unavailable to many. Those of us who make culture, both past and present, the object of our analysis can only continue the work of identifying the sites of that potential and, whenever possible, realizing it through praxis.

CHAPTER 2

Tracking the Subject
in Early Modern Spain

Man is not an abstract being squatting outside the world.
—Marx, *Critique of Hegel's Philosophy of Right*

No, you had rather stay always the same, neither more nor
less, like a figure in a tapestry.

(¡No, sino estaos siempre en un ser, sin crecer ni menguar,
como figura de paramento!)
—Sancho Panza to his wife, *Don Quixote*

I

Any contemporary discussion of subjectivity is governed by certain terms. Within the general movement toward
more elaborate forms of individuation which characterized nineteenth-century discursive practices, Marx claimed that human
activity could not be understood apart from the society that both
produced and was produced by it. Men and women do not
inhabit some ontological space outside social life; rather, they
appear as individuals only because of their interconnected relationships shaped by general relations of production. Thus Marx
began to problematize the notion of a homogeneous and unified
man which stands at the center of bourgeois thought.

One logical elaboration of Marx's model is the figure of "man"
caught somewhere in the world. Not unlike a figure made up of
the intersection of numerous threads of a tapestry, the subject,
according to this view, occupies an a priori and immutable posi-

tion within society. The possibility of change is slight, since a necessary precondition is the unraveling of the entire social fabric. The static image of the tapestry, therefore, is misleading insofar as it denies both the dynamic nature of subject formation and the often contradictory process of positioning within the social field. It reveals the undesirability of an essentialized self-hood that forecloses the ongoing movement within limitations through which subjects are constructed.

My reading of this issue is based on the assumption that the opposition of individual and society which structures traditional discussions of subjectivity and most literary criticism is a basic misunderstanding of how subjects are constituted. The division between inside and outside has obscured the fact that all forms of subjectivity in any specific historical moment are the consequence of practices that make up the culture at large. It is an equally important point that these multiple practices may be negotiated in a number of ways, and in fact seventeenth-century European writing used many rhetorical gestures to figure forth an "individual" who exists independent of social relations and is therefore able to enter into contractual arrangements with society. In its later variants, this figure would become the protagonist of the social contract and of liberal humanism. Despite competition from other ideological positions, it continues to dominate contemporary mainstream literary studies.

In this chapter we will begin to glimpse two very different figures, the aristocratic subject of seventeenth-century Spain and the still-tentative form of its singular or individuated rival. Given what I have said so far, the term *aristocratic subjectivity* itself may be misleading insofar as it suggests a unified essence no less substantial than the false dichotomy between "self" and society or the notion of the bourgeois individual. I want to move away from structural-functional models, then, to argue that the aristocratic subject itself was the intersection of a variety of contradictory positions and that in concrete practice any single subject was simultaneously situated in a multiplicity of ways. According to this view, the "aristocratic subject" per se is an irretrievable object from the cultural past. Even for the seventeenth century, it was a nonessential construct and thus never really existed in practice, at least not as a unified and clearly delimited entity. The subject of Castilian legal discourse, for example, which invoked blood as the source of its authority, was distinctly opposed to the subject figured by religious writing, which cited virtue. The interplay of subject positions, moreover, was continually transformed and rearticulated as the material conditions and discursive formations of the early modern period shifted. This last point is important because it reminds us that the contradictory subject, which I outlined in the previous chapter, is not a universal formed in the same way across the ages; it changes its composition according to particular social and historical conjunctures. The tropes I will examine in the following pages, therefore, serve to fill in the content of the category "subject" as it was constituted by Castilian writing during the first half of the seventeenth century. Not all of them played an equally decisive role in literary discourse either in earlier or later periods, but the texts of Cervantes and Quevedo cannot be understood historically unless they are juxtaposed to other forms of writing that were no less important for the elaboration of early modern subjectivity.

The interplay of subject positions is strikingly represented in the following anecdote in which San Juan de Dios, walking through Granada one day, accidentally brushes against an aristocrat, whose cape (a sign of his status) falls into the street. The nobleman exclaims:

"Hey, dimwit, picaro! Don't you watch where you're going? With much patience, he [San Juan] said: "Excuse me, brother, I did not notice what I did." With these words and because he had used the familiar form of address [*vos*] and called him brother (as he always did with everyone), the nobleman became even more angry and turned and slapped him in the face. Juan de Dios said: "I am the one who erred so I deserve it. Hit me again!" The noble, since he was still being spoken to in the familiar form, said to his servants: "Take care of this ill-bred peasant!" At this point, as people gathered, a local resident and important gentleman named Juan de la Torre approached: "What is all this, brother Juan de Dios?" As soon as the offended noble heard the name, he threw himself on the ground saying that he would not get up until he had kissed the saint's feet: "Is this the Juan de Dios who is known throughout the world?" Juan de Dios lifted him from the ground and each, with much weeping, begged forgiveness from the other. The nobleman wanted to take the saint to dine with him, but he excused himself, and later the noble sent him fifty gold escudos for the poor.

("¡Ah, bellaco, pícaro! ¿No mirais cómo vais?" Y él, con mucha paciencia, díxole: "Perdóname, hermano, que no miré lo que hice." Y él, con estas palabras, como le dixo de vos y hermano (como acostumbrava decir a todos) mucho más airado volvió a él y dióle una bofetada en el rostro; y Joan de Dios, dixo: "Yo soy el que erré, que bien la merezco: ¡dadme otra!" Y él, como todavía le decía de vos, dixo a sus criados: "¡Dadle a ese villano mal criado!" Y estando en esto, como se juntó gente, salió un vecino de allí, hombre principal, llamado Juan de la Torre; "¿Qué es esto, hermano Joan de Dios?" Y como el que le había injuriado le oyó nombrar, echóse a sus pies diciendo que no se levantaría de allí hasta que se los besase, diciendo: "¿Es este Joan de Dios tan nombrado en el mundo?" Y Joan de Dios le levantó del suelo abrazándole, y pidiéndose perdón el uno al otro con muchas lágrimas. Le quería el caballero llevar consigo a comer y él se excusó de ir, y después le envió cincuenta escudos de oro para los pobres.)[1]

This account reminds us that within religious discourse the holy man enjoyed a certain superiority so that, once his true identity was revealed, the aristocrat was obliged to surrender his own privileged status, itself the product of coetaneous, yet contradic-

[1] Francisco de Castro, *Historia de la vida y santas obras de Joan de Dios* (1585), quoted in Luis Rosales, *Cervantes y la libertad*, vol. 2 (Madrid: Sociedad de Estudios y Publicaciones, 1960), p. 31. The conflict between inherited nobility and "holiness" could lead to dramatic results. Baltasar Porreño reports that Philip II "greatly respected the dignity of the priesthood and therefore ordered the beheading of a gentleman who had fired a harquebus at the canon of Toledo and had the same done to another who struck a priest" ("honró mucho la dignidad sacerdotal, y así, a un caballero que disparó un arcabuzete contra un canónigo de Toledo, lo hizo degollar y lo mismo hizo con otro que dió a un Sacerdote una bofetada"). *Dichos y hechos del rey D. Felipe II* (1628), ed. Angel González Palencia (Madrid: Saeta, 1942), p. 168.

tory discourses that I will elaborate in this chapter. The varying sites upon which each subject was positioned could shift rapidly: San Juan insists on his own inferiority and demands that violence be employed to signify it even while such passive humility enhances his stature according to spiritual values. The noble attempts to mitigate his untenable situation at the end through the conventional use of charity as a means to exculpate the conscience of the ruling class.

The anecdote is useful as a paradigmatic model for the cultural dynamics of the period. It illustrates how the dominant ideology was not limited to a single institution or group, how within the flux of lived social relations it could be pragmatically rearticulated by rival and no less powerful discourses. The relativistic shifting of position can be understood only when we stop viewing the subject as an isolated monad and begin to place it in combinatory relationships with other subjects. This of course is the great lesson of the 1615 *Don Quixote*, but it is equally central to an understanding of Quevedo's lyric speakers if not of all literary characters in general. Here, Antonio Domínguez Ortiz's remark about Spanish legal traditions in the seventeenth century is crucial: "The social body was not an inorganic aggregate of individuals, of atoms, but of complex molecules: guilds, colleges, brotherhoods, municipalities, associations. . . . Privileges were granted not to the individual as such, but only to the member of one of these organisms" ("El cuerpo social no era un agregado inorgánico de individuos, de átomos, sino de moléculas complejas: gremios, colegios, cofradías, ayuntamientos, corporaciones. . . . Los privilegios no recaían sobre el individuo en cuanto tal, sino en cuanto miembro de uno estos organismos").[2]

Each of the ensembles described by Domínguez Ortiz functioned as a site upon which subjects were constituted, and in a real sense the concept of subjectivity as the intersection of multiple subject positions is impossible to understand without first understanding "society" as a configuration of different group

[2] Antonio Domínguez Ortiz, *Las clases privilegiadas en el antiguo régimen*, 3d ed. (Madrid: Istmo, 1985), p. 12.

interests and investments. To take a well-known example: Don Quixote's abandonment of his place within the body of the *hidalguía* propels him into the anachronistic and potentially subversive "group" (within its new context) of knights-errant. His return to the larger collective of the church at the end of the second novel merely underscores that his brief experiment in subjectivism and individual autonomy is bounded on all sides by the pressures of group affiliations. In a similar fashion, Quevedo's poetic speakers, although they point haltingly toward the modern figure of the autonomous and fully interiorized individual, are implicated in a variety of ensembles ranging from the *gremio* of courtly poets to the power of the literary tradition itself and have relatively little to do with the private psychology of the man who gave them written form.

Contemporary social theory may help to clarify the issues surrounding the question of subjectivity. What objectivize human beings and constitute them as subjects are what Foucault has called "systems of exclusion," that is, sets of prohibitions and controls which map out and regulate divisions on the field of material life.[3] In different social configurations and in different textual practices certain discourses take priority over others: economic class may be a determining factor in some situations; in others, questions of blood purity will be the final basis for inclusion or rejection. In reality, all these categories indicate the continual struggle being waged on the field of subjectivity even as institutions work to privilege certain forms necessary to the maintenance and reproduction of their hegemony. Early modern Spain provides an especially rich example because the qualities associated with aristocratic forms of subjectivity permeated the entire social fabric. The ideology of the ruling elites was inordinately successful in representing itself as the only medium through which one could become a subject, so that questions of blood and lineage were no less important to the Castilian peasant than they were to the king himself.

Raymond Williams has argued that while any historical mo-

[3] All Foucault's work is concerned with different aspects of this problem. For a brief summary statement, see "The Subject and Power."

ment may be viewed as a synchronic system governed by hege-monic groups or institutions, it is also important to delineate the movement of elements within a given conjuncture. The practices and ideologies of seventeenth-century Spain may be differenti-ated according to what Williams identifies as dominant, emer-gent, and residual elements in a cultural field, all of which work to construct the subject, although often in contradictory ways.[4] By the sixteenth century, for example, the ideology of blood was already a residual element in Spanish culture; it continued to produce forms of subjectivity having more to do with past than with present social formations and continually ran up against alternative forms articulated by both economic and religious discourse. Religion itself had a double function. Even though much of its ideological baggage was essentially residual (tradi-tional morality, hierarchy), certain teachings (universal brother-hood, "cada uno es hijo de sus obras") worked against the domi-nant idea of inherited privilege. More radical forms of a "new" subjectivity were the consequence of emergent practices asso-ciated with the rise of new economic structures. Throughout the period, however, these products of capitalist activity were to remain significantly mediated by other cultural factors; for this reason, they do not come to dominate Spanish literary discourse until well into the nineteenth century. In all seventeenth-century representations of the subject, even in those in which the dis-course of class is clearly the principal factor, we will find the insistence of blood or religion as complementary determinants that mediate economic considerations. This is also the case with the family, itself a site of profound transformation in the early modern period.

This complex process, then, was played out in a variety of

---

[4]See Raymond Williams, *Marxism and Literature* (Oxford: Oxford University Press, 1977), pp. 121–27. Braudel posits a similar concept of the social: "It would be misleading to think that confronted with the mounting strength of the economy . . . the other sectors and society as a whole did not continue to play their part. . . . Every·society is shot through with currents, bristling with obstacles, with obstinate relics of the past that block the way." *Civilization and Capitalism, 15th–18th Century*, vol. 2: *The Wheels of Commerce*, trans. Sian Rey-nolds (London: W. Collins, 1982), p. 461.

cultural arenas, not the least important of which was literary writing, where the representation of the subject was a partial figuration of struggles taking place in society at large. What interests me here is not so much the real-life existence of certain social types as the ways in which literary texts, through rhetorical strategies and slippages, constituted diverse forms of the subject. Quevedo's poetic speakers, for example, work to map out the aristocratic subject through exclusionary gestures. In so doing, they simultaneously invoke figures of otherness (women, heretics, picaros) without which the dominant itself could not take shape. In a more general sense, the combination and repetition of specific textual figures in the writings of both Quevedo and Cervantes worked to produce a form of the subject which in the coming centuries would become the dominant figure on the stage of Western culture—the individual.

At best, the idea of an autonomous individual was limited in the seventeenth century in Spain to a humanist anthropology that had been significantly co-opted and transformed by residual discourses and by the mechanisms of the absolutist state. Thus we must view this particular appearance of the individual not as the triumphant and crowning moment of the history of mankind but as a temporary and unstable prominence within the limited sphere of European writing. The "discovery of man," which Jakob Burckhardt marked as the identifying gesture of Renaissance thought and whose origins Giovanni Gentile located within a detached philosophical discourse, was in fact the consequence of a lengthy process through which a historically specific subject took shape in a variety of high-cultural forms. The conjuncture of contradictory and competing discourses which figured the early modern "individual" was no less the product of material conditions than were those moments that produced its earlier and subsequent variants.

Having said this, I would insist that the structure of the present chapter, divided into separate discussions of specific categories, must be understood only as a heuristic device; in reality, each interactional medium continually intersected every other. The various discourses form no series or hierarchy; they function together to make up the general social formation. In the anecdote involving San Juan de Dios we have already seen examples of the conflicts produced by such exchanges and competitions. The trope of the "body," for example, cannot be understood apart from that of "blood" since both participated in a physiological discourse that ultimately tended to mask the origins of the dominant social order. Nor can the trope of "blood" be separated from that of "class," as is well illustrated by the blood-purity (*limpieza de sangre*) statutes, which to a great degree were designed to contain an emergent middle class of wealthy conversos. An understanding of these dialectical relationships is crucial to a reading of Quevedo's poetry and *Don Quixote* because it helps us to rethink literary representations of subjectivity as constructs that depend upon multiple and often contradictory practices and affiliations. The cultural critic can reduce the concepts of "author" and "character" to single points of consciousness only by extreme oversimplification.

Throughout each section I have referred to contemporary methods of tracking the subject in order to bring to the foreground the differences between the early modern understanding of subjectivity and our own. This approach, too, must be viewed as a product of local circumstances. Indeed, every methodology is implicated in the social and political context in which it is practiced and, because of its position within the discipline of literature and institutions of higher education, also contributes to the reproduction of that context.

II

The aristocratic subject of seventeenth-century Spain was marked off from its European counterparts in large measure by the ideology of blood.[5] The constitution of both the subject and

[5] Domínguez Ortiz has written of the hierarchy of blood: "This was a medieval inheritance which the other European states did not have, or if they did it was to such a small degree that its influence was quickly absorbed. . . . This was

the social body was premised on a substantialist notion of blood which set the limits of a rigid hierarchical system based on imaginary wholeness and ethnic homogeneity. We cannot underestimate the effect of this complex issue on social relations in general; by representing subject position as the consequence of "natural" forces, the ideologues of blood attempted to control the distribution of power in Spanish society and ensured the marginalization of certain groups considered to be inferior.

As was the case with virtually all discourses that worked to construct the subject, there were contradictions within the category of blood itself. It is well known that the Spanish peasant could claim greater blood purity than his aristocratic counterpart: hence the claims made by Sancho Panza throughout *Don Quixote*. At the level of social relations, such claims had little effect since the issues of status or class were always more powerful in the last instance. The "purebred" peasant was still a peasant. The aristocrat, although in many cases tainted by converso ancestry, was nonetheless secure in his superior position in the hierarchical order. As we shall see in Quevedo's burlesque poetry, the picaresque speaker who tells us: "If the king has pure blood, so must his louse" ("Si tiene buena sangre el rey, tendrá tan buena su piojo") is appealing to a theoretical equality based on biology which in practice was effaced by a strict ordering according to genealogy, status, and economic position.

Even on the level of official discourse, the belief that inferior blood necessarily signified a lesser form of subjectivity was openly questioned by those who sought to replace it with a more tolerant, though by no means egalitarian, social policy. The Spanish church was in the awkward situation of having drawn many members of its ruling elite from those with converso ori-

---

what distinguished Spain in terms of social issues, and if it is not the key that explains everything, it is a crucial factor for an understanding of our national essence in those centuries" ("Esta era una herencia medieval que los demás estados europeos no tuvieron, o en tan pequeña medida que sus huellas fueron pronto absorbidas. . . . Tal fue el hecho diferencial hispánico en material social, y si no es la clave que lo explica todo, sí es un factor imprescindible para la comprensión du nuestra esencia nacional en aquellos siglos"). *Las clases privilegiadas*, p. 14. On the issue of blood, the work of Américo Castro is seminal.

gins. It is not surprising, therefore, that minority factions within the church (and occasionally the Inquisition itself) pushed for reforms of the purity statutes from the late 1500s onward. Although rarely calling for the total elimination of such statutes, texts such as Fray Agustín Salucio's *Discurso sobre los estatutos de limpieza* (1599) argued against the division of society on the basis of blood and led to heated debates in the highest circles of state and ecclesiastical authority. At an even earlier moment of Habsburg hegemony, the Valencian thinker Fadrique Furió Ceriol had claimed: "All good people, whether they be Jews, Moors, Gentiles, Christians or from some other religion, are from the same land, from the same house and blood, and likewise for all bad people" ("Todos los buenos, agora sean judío, moros, gentiles cristianos o de otra secta, son de una mesma tierra, de una mesma casa y sangre, y todos los malos de la misma manera").[6] It is in this kind of text that we see most clearly the increasing competition between the discourse of virtue and that of inherited nobility.

It would be a mistake, however, to conclude from the debate about blood that early modern Spanish society was tolerant and free of racism. Such claims, most often founded on a naïve empiricism that admits only that which is verifiable in archival material and thus is incapable of mapping the complex distribution of social power, may lead to the unconvincing conclusion that the purity statutes were nothing more than "a major inconvenience."[7] What is important about the problematic status of the category of blood is that it reveals the dynamic composition

[6] Fadrique Furió Ceriol, *Concejo y consejero del Príncipe* (1559), quoted in Biblioteca de autores españoles, 36 (Madrid: Atlas, 1950), p. xx.

[7] This argument has recently been put forward by Henry Kamen, who suggests that the debates over the purity statutes (in which conversos participated on both sides) proves that the Inquisition was not racist: "Even the Inquisition, especially between 1580 and 1640, adopted an open position against the practice of racism" ("Incluso la Inquisición, principalmente entre 1580 y 1640, adoptó una postura abierta contra la práctica del racismo"). "Una crisis de conciencia en la Edad de Oro en España: Inquisición contra 'limpieza de sangre,'" *Bulletin Hispanique* 88 (1986):321. Kamen only vaguely hints that such debates were possible because the issue of blood was increasingly challenged by the emergent issue of class privilege.

of the dominant ideologies themselves. Far from being a mono-lithic fortress, the category of blood was the site of diverse interests not unlike those that competed on the field of subjec-tivity. In the end, it matters little that the purity statutes, for example, were never incorporated into the Spanish legal code—an omission given undue weight by modern apologists for the Inquisition. Although the statutes were indeed binding only in military and religious orders, colleges, and the other private organizations that adopted them, the more important point is that juridical discourse itself was always already determined by questions of racial difference. As a contribution to the formation of the cultural discourse of the period, the debate about blood was symptomatic not of a tolerant society but rather of one in which race was at the center of all discussions about social relations and subjectivity.

The centrality of race and blood is especially evident in the physiological discourse of the period. The attempt by ruling interests to formulate a social order premised on the symbolic body of the aristocracy and thus separate from that of other groups on the basis of biology depended in large part on the hierarchical theory of humors in which a limited quantity of blood required protection from external pollutants. Once the social whole had been totalized as an organism analogous to the human body, the practice of purgation (that is, bleeding) became a logical strategy for the elimination of excesses or contamina-tion, perhaps nowhere more strikingly than in the symbolic use of menstruation. Throughout the medieval and early modern periods, menstruation was employed to signify inferiority. Bibli-cal authority as well as popular folklore reworked by authors ranging from Pliny to Agrippa was consistently invoked to "ex-plain" female weakness and to justify what were traditionally considered appropriate subject positions for women, that is, what women were supposed to be as women. In Spain this com-plicated argument by which the female body was constructed as naturally subservient to its male counterpart was transferred to other groups considered defective, especially Jews and Moors. A memorial from the year 1632 directed to Fray Antonio de Soto-mayor, confessor to Philip IV, claims:

This treacherous rabble of the Jews, a rebellious nation, unbeliev ing, tyrannical, cruel, base, bothersome, ferocious, perjured, arrogant, obstinate, stubborn, despicable, without honor in anything even though they everywhere desire it, separated from the Kingdom and the Priesthood, exiled, wandering, captive, placed in perpetual servitude, and hated by all, as Galatino says, among other bodily and spiritual curses which they suffer, inside and outside of the body, for having persecuted the true Messiah, Christ our redeemer, to the point of placing him on a Cross, is that *every month many of them suffer a flowing of blood from their posterior, as a perpetual sign of infamy and shame.* . . . Many authors say therefore that when Pilate said, according to Saint Matthew, that he was innocent of the Just One's blood, all those Jews who shouted and said let his blood be on them and their children they and all their descendants remained with this blemish, plague, and perpetual sign so that *every month they suffer a flow of blood like women.*

(Esta perfida canalla de los Judios, rebelde nación incredula, tirana, cruel, infame, molesta, feroz, perjura, sorberbia, obstinada, pertinaz, abatida, sin honra en todas partes, si bien apetecedora siempre della, privada del Reyno y Sacerdocio, desterrada, vaga, cautiva, puesta en perpetua servidumbre, y aborrecida de todos, como dice Galatino, entre otras maldiciones que padece corporeal y espiritualmente, dentro y fuera de su cuerpo, por aber perseguido el verdadero Mesias Christo nuestro redentor, hasta ponerlo en una Cruz, que todos los meses muchos dellos padecen flujo de sangre por las partes posteriores, en señal perpetua de ignominia y oprobio. . . . Dicen pues muchos autores que todos aquellos judios que cuando Pilatos dijo, como refiere San Mateo, que estaba inocente de la sangre del Justo, clamaron y dijeron que la sangre dél fuese sobre ellos y sobre sus hijos, quedaron con esta macula, plaga, y señal perpetua y todos sus descendientes afectos a ella que cada mes padeciessen flujo de sangre como las mujeres.[8]

---

[8]Juan de Quiñones, *Memorial de Juan de Quiñones dirigido a F. Antonio de Sotomayor, inquisidor general, sobre el caso de Francisco de Andrada, sospechoso de pertenecer a la raza judía, discutiendo sobre los medios de conocer y perseguir a ella* (Biblioteca Nacional, Madrid, VE, Box no. 16), my emphasis. The attribution to Jewish males of menstruation was commonplace in such documents. See also *Discurso contra los judíos traducido de lengua portuguesa en Castellano por el Padre Fray Diego Gavilán Vela* (1630): "Others say that on Good Friday all Jewish men and women experience a flow of blood, and for that reason they are almost all pale"

This passage clearly represents the process by which the body of the other (be it female or Jewish) was constituted against the male aristocratic body, constituted as inferior and subversive. The author, Juan de Quiñones, an official in the royal court, links what he considers to be physical and spiritual suffering, locating their common origin in the act of a rebellious people ("rebelde nación") against their natural lord. The sign of menstruation, then, participates in a semiotics of the body designed to exclude and purge sectors of society judged to be undesirable and potentially threatening. "The sign," writes Quiñones, "is for no other reason except to mark the difference between others so that they are not confused . . . and when recognition is difficult from the look of the face, one should resort to the hidden signs of the body. . . . it is my opinion that this will serve to indict and bring them to trial, as is done with those who are found to be circumcised" ("La señal no es otra cosa que poner algo para que aya diferencia entre las otras, que no se confunda con ellas . . . y quando el reconocimiento es difícil por el aspecto del rostro, se ha de recurrir a ver las señales ocultas que ay en el cuerpo. . . . me parece que bastará para inquirir y formar proceso contra ellos, como contra los que se hallasen circuncidados").⁹ The Jew is doubly marked, by both circumcision and menstruation, and it is through his body that the seemingly separate codes of race and sexuality collapse into each other. In a parallel move, the presumably Old Christian inquisitor functions as reader of the accused's body and interpreter of his alterity.

While such documents formed part of a body of folklore with deep roots in the ideology of the ruling elites, the issue of blood played a no less important role in the more properly "scientific" discourse of the period. Medical treatises were inclined to reproduce the symbolic values assigned to various bodily func-

---

("Otros dizen que el Biernes sancto todos los Iudios, y Iudias, tienen aquel día fluxo de sangre, y que por este respecto son casi todos de color pálido"). Quoted in Josette Riandière La Roche, "Du discours d'exclusion des Juifs: Antijudaïsme ou antisémitisme?" in *Les problèmes de l'exclusion en Espagne (XVIe–XVIIe siècles)*, ed. Augustín Redondo (Paris: Publications de la Sorbonne, 1983), p. 65 n. 37.
    ⁹Quiñones, *Memorial de Juan de Quiñones*.

tions, and the theory of bodily humors complemented the strict divisions that structured the social body. The shift from a hierarchical to a systemic concept of the body, however, which began in the seventeenth century, would profoundly affect social relations, representations of the body, and the ways in which subjects could be constructed. The Spanish reception of William Harvey's claims about the circulation of the blood, first made public in England in 1616, was mixed at best, and throughout the century its proponents and detractors carried on a spirited polemic. As late as 1677, the anatomist Matías García noted that Harvey's theory was doing "immense damage" ("immenso daño") to medical studies in Spain; ten years later, although still the cause of much debate, it was finally introduced into the curriculum at the University of Zaragoza by Juan Bautista Juanini.[10]

Had the circulation of blood been accepted as biological fact, it would have problematized identity in ways that threatened the deepest structures of Spanish society; indeed, it had this effect in other cultures where it was introduced earlier. Once the hierarchical theory of humors was replaced by a systemic model in which function mattered more than substance, both the physical and the social body had to be reconceived. In the first place, the veneration of the body as an essential whole was immediately challenged by the alternative theory of the body as an instrument never wholly identical to its blood. Thus, Harvey's isolation of a closed circulatory system called into question the notion that the condition of the blood alone ensured the health of the body or, to state the homologous structure on the social level, the status of the aristocracy determined the well-being of society. Given its potential for cultural disruption, it is no surprise that throughout the early seventeenth century the idea of circulating blood was repressed in Spain, considered at best a suspicious hypothesis. For most of the century, the idea of static blood continued to form the basis upon which subjectivity could be conceived.

In short, traditional thought held aristocratic blood to be the

---

[10] See Luis S. Granjel, *La medicina española del siglo XVII* (Salamanca: Universidad de Salamanca, 1978), pp. 143–45.

very substance of the social body, requiring the summary purgation of pollutants and contamination. The notion of an individualized subject premised on an autonomous consciousness was virtually unthinkable. As we have seen, however, throughout the early modern period a struggle *within* the ideology of blood opposed a biological aristocracy (*lo godo*) to a more properly genealogical one. At the same time, additional terms such as *virtue, service*, and *wealth*, each a divided and contradictory sign in itself, entered into competition with blood as important determinants of the subject. As early as the fifteenth century we find the claim that the productive classes, not the noble elites, were the new life-force of society. In the dialogue between a king and a laborer cited in the last chapter the laborer draws the analogy of the social and human bodies, suggesting that if the king is the heart, the laboring class,[11] not the aristocracy, is the blood that makes it function: "Fortunate king, in my opinion the function of the blood in the human body is a great example for those who govern this miserable world. The blood always rushes and attends to that part of the body where there is weakness or debility. . . . And I, illustrious prince, am moved to say what I say not because I want to exhalt those like me but because it seems to me that help is needed most there; I come there first like blood" ("Bienauenturado rrey, á mi pareçer el ofiçio que la sangre en los humanos cuerpos tiene gran exenplo para los gouernadores deste mísero mundo, la qual sienpre socorre é aconpaña aquella parte del cuerpo do más flaqueza ó mengua conoçe. . . . E yo, ilustríssimo príncipe, non porque á los tales como yo quiera primero aupar, me mueuo á lo que digo; mas porque me pareçe ser allí más neçessario el socorro, vengo allí primero como la sangre").[12] The attempted displacement of the aristocracy from its essential function which is implicit in this passage is little more than an

---

[11] As I will argue in a later section of this chapter, the term "class" is problematic for any study of early modern society. My references to "productive classes" and "laboring class," therefore, should not be misunderstood as having the same signification as they would in the nineteenth or twentieth centuries (i.e., "workers"). The principal Spanish terms are *villanos, jornaleros*, and *labradores*.

[12] Amador de los Ríos, "Sobre el libro llamado," p. 588.

inversion of the traditional hierarchy. Nevertheless, it already suggests the problematic status of blood as a determining factor in the production of subjects.

The category of blood was to be increasingly contested by certain segments of society, but not out of some abstract sense of justice or equality; rather, the rival discourses of class and virtue had begun to force the category of blood out into the margins of Spanish culture. When Teresa de Avila, for example, voiced her support of the concept of virtue as the ultimate determinant of the subject, she did so because of her own converso ancestry but also because of her affiliation with important members of the merchant class on whose financial backing her institutional projects depended. The account of the founding of a monastery in Toledo in 1568 is revealing: "During the time I worked with Alonso Alvarez on the foundation, there were many people who disapproved, and they told me so, because they [the merchants] were not illustrious men and gentlemen" ("En los días que había tratado de la fundación con Alonso Alvarez, eran muchas personas a las que parecía mal, y me lo decían, por parecerles que no eran ilustres y caballeros"). The future saint was well aware that without the support of the merchants (most of whom shared her converso lineage and thus were considered "inferior" by her aristocratic patrons) her projects could not continue. Thus she rejected the advice of the blooded nobility and counseled: "If I had followed the vain opinions of the world, to that which we are able to understand, it would have been impossible to have such comfort [in the monastery], and an injustice would have been done to someone who with such good will had shown us charity" ("Si hubiera mirado a las opiniones vanas del mundo, a lo que podemos entender, era imposible tener tan buena comodidad, y hacíase agravio a quien con tanta voluntad nos hizo esta caridad").[13]

For a variety of reasons, then, the ideology of virtue, opposed to that of blood, was a counterdiscourse through which alterna-

[13] Teresa de Avila, *Libro de las fundaciones* (written 1573; pub. 1610), in Biblioteca de autores españoles, 53 (Madrid: Atlas, 1952), p. 205.

tive forms of subjectivity were constructed. Within the category of virtue, too, however, is a competition between contradictory positions similar to the one we have seen at work in the trope of blood. This is evident in a passage from the *Examen de ingenios* (1575) in which Juan Huarte de San Juan attempts to rewrite the term *hidalgo* and to account for its multiple significations:

> The Spaniard who invented this noun, *hijodalgo*, understood well the doctrine we are discussing. Because according to his opinion men have two types of birth: one is natural, in which all men are equal; and the other is spiritual. When a man does some heroic deed or some unusual exploit or accomplishment, then he is born again and gains better parents and loses the being that he formerly had. Yesterday he was called the son of Pedro or the grandson of Sancho; now he is the child of his deeds, from which originates the Castilian proverb: each man is the child of his deeds. And because Scripture calls good and virtuous deeds "something" (Acts 5) and vices and sins "nothing" (Job 1), this noun *hijodalgo* was coined and now means: the descendant of he who performed some unusual deed for which he and all his descendants deserved to be rewarded by the king or the republic for ever and ever.
>
> The law of the Partida says that *hijodalgo* means child of wealth. And if by this is meant temporal wealth the law is mistaken because there are many poor *hijosdalgo* and many rich men who are not *hidalgos*. But if by wealth is meant virtues, then it has the same meaning of which we spoke.

> (El español que inventó este nombre, hijodalgo, dió bien a entender la doctrina que hemos traído. Porque según su opinión tienen los hombres dos géneros de nascimiento: el uno es natural, en el cual todos son iguales; y el otro espiritual. Cuando el hombre hace algún hecho heroico o alguna extraña virtud y hazaña, entonces nasce de nuevo y cobra otros mejores padres, y pierde el ser que antes tenía. Ayer se llamaba hijo de Pedro y nieto de Sancho; ahora se llama hijo de sus obras, de donde tuvo origen el refrán castellano que dice: cada uno es hijo de sus obras. Y porque las buenas y virtuosas llama la divina Escritura "algo" (Act. 5), y a los vicios y pecados "nada" (Io. 1), compuso este nombre hijodalgo, que querrá decir ahora: descendiente del que hizo alguna extraña

virtud, por donde maresció ser premiado de rey o de la república, él y todos sus descendientes para siempre jamás. La ley de la Partida dice que hijodalgo quiere decir hijo de bienes. Y si entiende de bienes temporales no tiene razón, porque hay infinitos hijosdalgo pobres, e infinitos ricos que no son hidalgos. Pero si quiere decir hijo de bienes que llamamos virtudes, tiene la mesma significación que dijimos.)[14]

In this passage, Huarte attempts to place the emphasis on virtue and deeds in contrast to earlier definitions, which insisted that the suffix -*algo* referred only to inherited nobility. Covarrubias, for example, in a long entry for *fidalgo* records several of the more tortured versions of the blood-based reading, such as: "Others are of the opinion that this word is a corruption of *sons of Goths*, *filgod*, and transposing the consonants l, d, and adding the vowels a, a, one would say *fidalgo*." ("Otros son de opinión que este vocablo está corrompido de fijo de godo, filgod, y transmudadas las consonantes l, d, y añadiéndoles sus vocales a, a, dirá fidalgo").[15] The appeal to Gothic Spain as a prelapsarian moment before the tainting of the blood by Semitic invaders would continue to be made throughout the period. The debate over the meaning of *hidalgo* was a real ideological struggle, not easily resolved. Its consequences reached far beyond the texts of historians and etymologists into the deepest recesses of Spanish social life.

The idea that those lacking inherited nobility could inaugurate their own noble lineage, repeated by Covarrubias and insisted upon by Huarte, is well known as a principle central to the construction of subjectivity in *Don Quixote*. What is less familiar to modern readers is the belief that the execution of some heroic deeds leads to a rebirth of the subject through which it abandons its former identity ("then he is born again and gains better

[14] Juan Huarte de San Juan, *Examen de ingenios* (1575), in Biblioteca de autores españoles, 65 (Madrid: Atlas, 1953), p. 480.
[15] Sebastián de Covarrubias, *Tesoro de la lengua castellana o espanola* (1611) (Madrid: Turner, 1977).

parents and loses the being that he formerly had"). This process is also a basic component in the early stages of Don Quixote's project, and it is contained in Sancho Panza's disapproval of those who would passively accept a prescribed position. For Sancho, even a peasant may be inserted into a new conjuncture of discourses and thereby rearrange the composition of the entire social fabric. This potential for change is clearest in *Persiles y Sigismunda* (1617), Cervantes's final extended narrative, where all the major characters are continually transformed on their way to spiritual and social well-being according to seventeenth-century Catholic ideology.

In more than a few cases the ideology of blood continues to contribute to the formation of the subject in the Cervantine text. For example, "The Little Gipsy Girl," "The Power of Blood," and others of the *Exemplary Stories* (1613) insist on the idea of lineage as destiny. In the longer prose texts, however, the rival discourse of virtue and deeds wields considerably more power. Throughout Cervantes's opus, unlike the staunch traditionalist position defended in Avellaneda's *Don Quixote*, an ambiguity surrounds the issue of blood. In the extended narratives in particular, with their complex stitching together of multiple discourses, Cervantes represents one of the basic contradictions of Spanish culture in a transitional moment. It is not so much that the two *Don Quixotes* (1605 and 1615) reject the dominant ideas being represented elsewhere in Spanish writing. Rather, the two novels figure forth the conflicts and oppositions at work within the dominant itself. Blood could no longer be viewed as the only determinant in the construction of the aristocratic subject; Huarte, in fact, ranks blood as only third of his six requirements for honor and valueless in itself: "There are those who compare nobility [of ancestry] to the zero of arithmetic. By itself it has no value, but joined to another number it increases the latter's worth" ("Algunos suelen comparar la nobleza al cero de la cuenta guarisma, el cual solo por sí no vale nada, pero junto con otro número le hace subir").[16] By the mid–sixteenth century, the traditional dis-

---

[16] Huarte de San Juan, *Examen*, p. 481. That blood must be supplemented by virtue is a recurring idea throughout the period. In Antonio de Eslava's *Noches de*

course of blood was incapable of producing subjects until it had been joined to other, increasingly powerful categories.

Some have argued that the hegemonic social groups of Habsburg Spain never considered the symbolic value of virtue equal to that of blood.[17] This view is corroborated in later writings such as Juan de Zabaleta's *Día de fiesta por la mañana* (1654): "Those who have seen the truth say nobility is not acquired through birth but by deeds. If by this they mean the generous application of virtue, they are correct; but the world does not equate virtue with nobility, and it is not that the world is so blind that it does not see that virtue is a greater attribute than nobility of blood, but this attribute has a different name. Only the purity of one's forefathers is given the name nobility." ("Los desengañados dicen que la nobleza no se adquiere naciendo, sino obrando. Si ellos entienden por nobleza las aplicaciones generosas de la virtud, dicen muy bien; pero el mundo no tiene a la virtud por nobleza, y no es tan ciego el mundo que no vea que la virtud es atributo mejor que la nobleza de sangre, pero este atributo tiene diferente nombre. La claridad de los abuelos solamente tiene por nombre nobleza").[18] Despite the powerful status of the ideology of blood, an ambivalence about its relationship to virtue, which we have separated out heuristically as oppositions between different kinds of texts in Cervantes's project, was openly figured in many other writings. Antonio de Eslava, for example, makes the appeal to virtue but immediately undercuts

---

invierno (1609) (Madrid: Saeta, 1942), Fabricio claims: "And thus I remember having seen in Rome, next to the Appian gate, a place on which was built a sumptuous temple to Honor, a temple built in such a way that no one could enter it without first passing through another nearby temple dedicated to virtue" (Y así me acuerdo haber visto en Roma, junto a la puerta Apia, un lugar donde estaba edificado un sumptuoso templo dedicado a la Honra, con tal artificio que no podía ninguno entrar en el templo, sino que entrasen primero por otro cercano templo de la virtud") (p. 379).

[17] Domínguez Ortiz, for example, declares: "No one took seriously the idea of nobility of virtue or of letters despite what one reads in the texts" ("Nadie tomó en serio la nobleza de la virtud o de las letras, a pesar del apoyo que encontraba en los textos"). *Las clases privilegiadas*, p. 186.

[18] Zabaleta, *Día de fiesta por la mañana* (1654) in *Costumbristas españoles*, vol. 1, ed. Evaristo Correa Calderón (Madrid: Aguilar, 1964), p. 223.

it by suggesting that those who lack aristocratic blood, despite their virtuous deeds, remain inferior: "Even though a man is not noble by blood, if he is by virtue he should be more esteemed because virtue is the soap with which one cleanses the stain of the lower caste" ("Aunque un hombre no sea noble por generación, si lo es por virtud, ha de ser más tenido, porque ella es el jabón con que se quita la mancha de la baxa casta").[19]

While it is true that the kind of definitive shift apparent in Huarte's *Examen* from a biological to a genealogical theory based on virtue or deeds may have been a minority position and may never have had practical consequences, the change nonetheless marked a significant gesture in the direction of the "individual." The heroic stature of those men who had "performed some unusual deed" set them apart from the community, and whereas autonomy and complete self-determination were still relatively unthinkable, a space *was* being cleared for what in a different context (where the subject would be constructed through discursive formations in which the category of blood no longer figured) would become the bourgeois subject. The competition between physical and spiritual "deeds" was also being waged simultaneously in the period, as we have seen in the anecdote involving San Juan de Dios and his aristocratic antagonist. This competition also sets the terms for the movement from the 1605 to the 1615 *Don Quixote*. It is little wonder that modern criticism has consistently privileged the first *Don Quixote* over its sequel, for the 1605 text, by figuring a form of autonomous subjectivity based on heroic exploits rather than spiritual worth, corresponds more closely to the modern notion of individualism. The second novel shifts its emphasis toward more traditional categories and thus distances itself from secularized variants of the subject as individual.

Blood, virtue, and deeds, therefore, all functioned as homologous but fundamentally rival discourses within the economy of

[19] Eslava, *Noches de invierno*, p. 380. For a discussion of how the category of virtue shifted in the seventeenth century to that of service (to the monarchy), see Ignacio Atienza Hernández, *Aristocracia, poder y riqueza en la España moderna: La casa de Osuna, siglos XV–XIX* (Mexico City: Siglo XXI, 1987), pp. 55–60.

power. In the end, the debate over whether blood or virtue was the basis for subject formation was merely an argument between two easily reconciled metaphysics. By abstracting and idealizing the normative grounds upon which subjectivity would be founded, these two discourses drove subject formation away from material reality and into an imaginary realm of purity and wholeness. The emergent category of deeds, however, eventually produced a more concrete space for a tentative concept of an individual subject constituted by physical and intellectual accomplishments. Yet it was not long before that new space was itself split into the opposition of arms versus letters, an opposition fundamentally designed to consolidate the absolutist state by privileging military and bureaucratic practices. Despite this kind of ongoing competition within the ideological field, the residual discourse of blood (as we will see in the remaining sections of this chapter) remained powerful and persisted well into the final decades of the seventeenth century and beyond.

III

The representation of the human body is always a figure of the social order. Contemporary anthropology has taught us that a central element in any cultural practice and its attendant constructions of subjectivity is the issue of how human biology is imagined and interpreted. Many passages from Cabrera de Córdoba's chronicle of activities in the court reveal the conflation in the early modern period of aristocratic culture with the royal body, whose health was central to the maintenance of society at large. Cabrera's text is structured upon the complementary concerns of the well-being of the socioeconomic body (the arrival of American metals, royal incomes) and the status of the aristocratic body (illnesses, marriages, births). No item of news touching upon these two matters is considered too trivial for inclusion; thus the report that the Prince of Savoy had contracted malaria is juxtaposed to word of a delay in the arrival of a shipment of New World silver.

The Prince of Savoy is ill with malaria, and for this reason his two younger brothers have not gone out with the King and Queen today; nor did they travel with them Wednesday morning to the wedding of the Marquis of Fuentes which was held in the palace; nor to the plaza where the bulls were run. . . . On the 25th of last month, the fleet arrived at San Lucar, from which one ship had been lost in Santo Domingo, and the silver has not arrived.

(Está malo de tercianas el príncipe de Saboya, y por esta causa no han ido los otros dos hermanos menores con los Reyes esta jornada; ni el miércoles de mañana salieron con sus Magestades a la boda de los marqueses de Fuentes que se hizo en Palacio; ni tampoco a la tarde a la Plaza donde se corrieron los toros. . . . A los 25 del pasado llegó a San Lúcar la flota de la Nueva-España, de la cual se perdió un navío en Santo Domingo y no trae la plata.

Elsewhere, we read that Philip III and members of his family suffered from a painful eczema, which the doctors treated without success, at the same time that we are presented with a catalog of the net worth of important ecclesiastical and royal offices.[20]

Together, the aristocratic body and its political analogue, the state, constituted a space that encompassed all those discursive practices available for the construction of subjects. Each practice was confined within a rigid hierarchical organization that structured the entire cultural field, and although the categories of blood and rank were extremely powerful, they were nonetheless affected by rival discourses of psychology, physiology, and biology. These earliest manifestations of these disciplines should not be confused with later nineteenth- and twentieth-century variants. If the figure of the social body in seventeenth-century Spain, that is, the nation-state, was slowly beginning to resemble those forms more closely associated with the modern age, the figure of the material human body still shared little with later representations produced by modern science. In this regard, the early modern discourse of sexuality is especially interesting, for

[20]Luis Cabrera de Córdoba, *Relaciones de la cosas sucedidas en la corte de España desde 1599 hasta 1614* (Madrid: J. Martín Alegría), Oct. 4, 1603, Apr. 8, 1600.

it was markedly distant from our own constructions and stood in a very different relation to the relatively modern category of gender.

The construction of women in the dominant culture of seventeenth-century Spain, for example, was grounded in discursive practices inherited from the medieval tradition of misogyny and so thoroughly masculinist that it is difficult for modern readers to imagine the extent of its consequences in the social realm. In general terms, we can say that modern thought has consistently argued that biology determines essence; the theorists of the early modern period, however, believed that an already sexed essence preceded the constitution of the material body. Put another way, anatomical differences were thought to be not a cause but an effect of a basic difference in the substance of being. Obviously, in its essentializing of the sexes this extreme biologism surpasses even the most traditional attitudes in our own century. In earlier periods, the category "female" functioned less as the oppositional binomial it would be in later centuries than as a homologous and inferior position within the hierarchical order.[21] Even the relatively enlightened Huarte de San Juan uncritically reproduces the ancient belief that "femaleness" is inherently inferior, and in his influential *Examen de ingenios* (1575) he devotes an entire chapter (Chapter 18) to strategies designed to prevent the birth of female children. In a culture preoccupied with questions of blood and lineage, the future itself was thought to be in jeopardy if the male line were to be corrupted or, worse still, come to an end.

The rigidity of the hierarchical chain inherited from the classi-

---

[21] In chap. 1 of *La perfecta casada* (1583), Luis de León equates the "perfect wife" with "manliness": "What we refer to here as *woman of value* we might also call a *manly woman*, as Socrates, following Xenophon, calls the perfect wife" ("Lo que aquí decimos *mujer de valor*, y pudiéramos decir *mujer varonil*, como Sócrates, cerca de Jenofón, llama a las perfectas casadas") (Madrid: J. Pérez del Hoyo, 1972), p. 30. In the beatification and canonization proceedings of Teresa de Avila, she was consistently praised for being a "virile woman." See Alison Weber, *Teresa of Avila and the Rhetoric of Femininity* (Princeton: Princeton University Press, 1990).

cal and medieval traditions, in which aristocratic masculinity signified perfection, meant that early modern Spanish subjectivity would be constructed in part from exclusions based on sexuality. In its diverse manifestations, the dominant sex/gender system was structured on correspondences that produced a repertoire of tropes that varied only slightly according to their textual elaboration. In Juan de Pineda's *Agricultura cristiana* (1589), for example, the word *woman* is linked to the flesh and to sin, whereas *male* signifies the bones and virtue, and this correspondence is invoked to explain why the parents' joy should be greater at the birth of a male child.[22] A generation earlier, the readers of the 1542 Castilian translation of Francesc Eiximenis's *Lo libre de les dones* (Catalán ed. 1495) had been invited to speculate about whether or not a woman who ascended to heaven would change her shape for a man's. Because the "body in glory" was thought to be perfect, the female form would necessarily "be restored to the greatest dignity and nobility of the human species, which is the male form" ("sean restituydas a la mayor dignidad y nobleza de la especie humana que es la de varón").[23] It is on the basis of such textual evidence that we must wonder about the very possibility of imagining modern forms of female subjectivity within early modern culture. This is not to deny that specific women were positioned within equally powerful rival discourses, and thereby exercised an effective kind of agency. Teresa de Avila is perhaps the best-known example of those women who successfully participated in dominant practices, but most women constructed an altogether alternative figure of the body as a dispersed site for the workings of nature and divine intervention.[24]

---

[22] Juan de Pineda, *Diálogos familiares de la agricultura cristiana* (1589), in Biblioteca de autores españoles, 163 (Madrid: Atlas, 1963), pp. 11–12.

[23] Francesc Eiximenis, *Carro de las donas* (1542), quoted in Carmen Bravo Villasante, *La mujer vestida de hombre en el teatro español* (Madrid: Mayo de oro, 1988), p. 66 n. 26.

[24] Research on the writings of Spanish religious women has increased dramatically in recent years. See, for example, Electa Arenal and Stacey Schlau, *Untold Sisters: Hispanic Nuns in Their Own Works* (Albuquerque: University of New Mexico Press, 1989). See also the special issue of *Journal of Hispanic Philology* 13 (1989) edited by Alison Weber.

It is within dominant medical discourse, however, that masculinist assumptions assume their strongest form. Medical traditions posited the coexistence of two sexed types of "seed" (*simiente*), either capable of fulfilling the function of procreation (*el agente*) or of nourishment (*alimento*). This functional interdependence would seem to suggest a certain equality of the sexes, and in fact sexual difference was most often discussed in terms of homologous rather than oppositional structures. The female seed was occasionally even thought to be the source of procreation, the male seed being relegated to the role of nourishment. But despite the greater potential of the female seed for "agency" in some cases, the product of the female seed was necessarily judged to be inferior. Thus Huarte (following Galen) writes: "The man born of the woman's seed is incapable of being ingenious or talented because of the coolness and dampness of this sex. Therefore it is clear that the birth of a discreet and prudent male child is an infallible indication of its having been born of the father's seed. If he is awkward and slow, it shows that he was formed from the mother's seed" ("Y el hombre que se hace de simiente de mujer no puede ser ingenioso ni tener habilidad, por la mucha frialdad y humedad de este sexo. Por donde es cierto que en saliendo el hijo discreto y avisado, es indicio infalible de haberse hecho de la simiente de su padre. Y si es torpe y necio, se colige haberse formado de la simiente de su madre").[25] The responsibility for the production of inferior male children, then, is displaced onto the woman and the intrinsically flawed materials she brings to the reproductive process. The origin of the more desirable form of sexuality (male) is even located in a particular physical space within the female body: "The final condition was to ensure that both seeds, that of the husband and that of the wife, fall on the right side of the uterus; because Hippocrates says that it is in that place that male children are made; and females are made on the left" ("La última condición fue procurar que ambas simientes, la del marido y la de la mujer, caigan en el lado derecho del útero; porque en aquel lugar dice

---

[25] Huarte de San Juan, *Examen de ingenios*, p. 515.

Hipócrates que se hacen los varones, y en el izquierdo las hembras").[26] The right side is consistently privileged over the left to such a degree that reproductive discourse is rigidly constructed upon the signifying couplet masculinity-right. In such a physiological schema, the "place of the female," whether it be the inferior seed, the left side of the uterus, or the left breast, is in reality a nonplace from which nothing good can arise. It is no surprise that for traditional culture the left side marked the site of both the feminine and the diabolical (*siniestro*).

How this biological hierarchy was reread back into the social world from which it had originated can be gathered from another section of Huarte's influential text. Once again using the authority of Hippocrates as a screen, Huarte suggests not only that there is a real biological basis for sex-differentiated behavior but that the feminization of males threatens the very existence of the species: "Thus Hippocrates records that the principal men of Scythia were very effeminate, womanish, ladylike, inclined to do woman's work such as sweeping, washing, and baking, and therefore their seed was unable to engender. And if a male child was born to them it was either a eunuch or a hermaphrodite" ("Y así cuenta Hipócrates que los hombres principales de Scitia eran muy afeminados, mujeriles, mariosos, inclinados a hacer obras de mujeres, como son, barrer, fregar y amasar, y con esto, eran impotentes para engendrar. Y si algun hijo varon les nacía, o salia eunuco o hermafrodita").[27] The grammatical logic of the passage is striking: men doing female labor are deprived of their masculine reproductive powers. Within the intertext of classical literature, the Scythians were emblematic of outsiders and invaders. Thus all heterogeneous groups with origins perceived to be outside of the peninsula, especially Muslims and Jews, were necessarily represented as both nonmale and non-Spanish. Huarte's point here is that the Scythians cannot function as men precisely because they do not "act" like Castilian men. The connective "therefore" ("y con esto") signifies the immense authority of common sense to which such an assertion appealed. What this

[26] Ibid., p. 500.
[27] Huarte de San Juan, *Examen*, p. 498.

attitude meant for the positioning of women and other feminized groups within the discursive and institutional field should be fairly obvious. The subversive potential of behavior considered improper according to prescribed categories of sexuality and race threatened not only traditional forms of subjectivity but the entire social order as well.

The link between impure blood and feminization ran deep in the ideological assumptions of all the groups that made up seventeenth-century Castilian society. The popular collections of folktales and humorous stories such as Juan de Timoneda's *Sobremesa y alivio de caminantes* (1563) helped perpetuate the belief that any claim to subjectivity not founded on Christian and male categories was to be denied access to power and in fact to be considered "outside" culture. Two excerpts from Timoneda's text, although identical in their ideological message, permit us to see the various ways in which aristocratic activities (in these two cases, hunting and chess) supplied a language suitable for the representation of the important issues of sexuality and blood.

> A castrated soprano passed in front of a ragman who was a notorious Jew, old and withered [circumcised], who in order to mock the musician said:
> —Sir, how is your hunting falcon without bells?
> The castrato replied:
> —The same as yours that has no hood.

> (Paseábase un músico tiple y capado, por delante de un ropavejero, famosísimo judío, viejo y retajado, el cual, por burlarse del músico, le dijo:
> —Señor, ¿cómo le va a su gavilán sin cascabeles?
> Respondió el capado:
> —Como al de vuesa merced sin capirote.)

> A soldier who returned from Italy very prosperous was invited to dinner by an old friend. Sitting at the table, there was a famous wit who was known to be a Jew, who, implying that the soldier was a sodomite, took the chicken's rump with the point of his knife and put it in front of the soldier, saying:
> —Check.

Then the soldier, quickly, took a slab of bacon and put it in front
of the wit, saying:
—Checkmate.

(Viniendo un soldado de Italia muy próspero, fue convidado por
un grande amigo suyo. Estando en la mesa, había un extraño
decidor que tenía fama de judío, el cual, por tratar al soldado de
puto, tomó con la punta del cuchillo el obispillo de la gallina, y
púsoselo delante, diciendo:
—Jaque.
Entonces el soldado, de presto, tomó asimesmo una lonja de
tocino, y púsosela delante, diciendo:
—Mate.)[28]

These cultural materials regarding blood, the body, and sexuality reveal that many categories functioned not so much to
distinguish between men and women as to determine the distribution of power among men. The debate within aristocratic
discourse between pure blood and earned virtue was possible
because it was always framed by masculinist assumptions; those
forms of subjectivity thought to be tainted by a lack of male-
related qualities and the suspicion of "impure" blood, however,
were necessarily excluded from participation in the culture at
large or at least were castigated and ultimately forced into the
margins. But by at least the mid–sixteenth century, it was clear
that new space would have to be cleared for those groups that
had formerly been excluded from the definition of "Spanishness." The attempt to reinscribe the bodies of others (Amerindians, Jews, and so on) was particularly dramatic in Spain,
where institutions such as the Inquisition refined and supplemented traditional disciplinary techniques of public torture and
shame long before the so-called Great Confinement of the later
seventeenth century.

The shifting discursive formations of the period would allow
for alternative subject positions, but the hegemony of masculine

---

[28]Collected in Maxime Chevalier, *Cuentecillos tradicionales en la España del Siglo
de Oro* (Madrid: Gredos, 1975), pp. 183–84.

discourse would remain unchallenged for centuries. Where contestation did occur, the interests of blood and status precluded the formulation of effective feminism in any of its modern forms. Here I am thinking of the texts of María de Zayas, in which the aristocratic woman contests her exclusion from such processes of cultural production as writing but reconfirms the dominant ideology by insisting on the centrality of blood and relegating members of non-noble classes to the status of animals. In Zayas's "Noche décima," for example, Lisis, the narrative voice traditionally associated with Zayas herself, claims: "Male and female servants are household animals and necessary enemies to whom we give away and [on whom we] waste our patience and our money" ("los criados y criadas son animales caseros y enemigos no excusados que los estamos regalando y gastando con ellos nuestra paciencia y hacienda").[29] The lack of solidarity among women represented in this passage is a sign that racial and class affiliations, rather than gender, usually provided the sites of subject formation for preindustrial women. More generally, the alterity of all nonaristocratic groups worked to define the borders of the aristocratic body, even as categories of maleness determined the extent to which all groups, including aristocratic females, would gain or be denied access to subjectivity itself.

IV

Much of our contemporary understanding of subjectivity is the product of psychoanalysis, itself a construction of a specific

[29]María de Zayas, "Noche décima," in *Desengaños amorosos—parte segunda del Sarao y entretenimiento honesto* (1647) (Madrid: Aldus, 1950), p. 458. The modern reader is often surprised to hear relatively "progressive" attitudes spoken by Spanish noblemen. Don Alonso de Avalos, for example, reportedly argued: "God gave me, and I took, my wife as a companion and not as a slave; her parents turned her over to me as a sister, not as a prisoner" (Dióme Dios, y tomé yo, mi mujer por compañera y no por mi esclava; entregáronmela sus padres por hermana, y no por cautiva"). See Tomé Pinheiro de Veiga, *Fastiginia o fastos geniales* (1605) (Valladolid: Colegio de Santiago, 1916), p. 85.

historical moment, the nineteenth century, in which private life was increasingly seen as a refuge from social life. We must keep in mind that middle-class notions of the family were relatively unknown in the early modern period if we are to avoid the kind of distortion of history which results from the universalizing of nineteenth- or twentieth-century (historically and culturally specific) models. It would serve us better to begin with the assumption that early modern ideas about the family were distinct from and independent of the majority of structures today associated with the family and thus with the constitution of individuals. Although my own work obviously draws on contemporary theory, I want to suggest that models such as Freud's oedipal narrative or Lacan's dual spheres of the imaginary and symbolic can be useful to us only if we are attentive to the differences between the contexts in which they were produced and those of earlier cultures. I will have more to say on this subject later in this section.

Although its economy of relations differed fundamentally from that of its middle-class variant, the aristocratic family was nevertheless a site for the production of subjectivity, and we must look there in our search for both traditional and developing forms of the subject. As Philippe Ariès's important study of childhood taught us, the seventeenth century was a transitional moment in which the modern idea of the family first began to take shape.[30] That is, the preoccupation with bloodline and family name (the "house" in the ancestral sense) was slowly joined to and in some cases replaced by the notion of the family as the locus of moral and spiritual values where the individual, the interiorized subject, might be constituted. Marx once astutely noted that the hegemony of the bourgeoisie marked the triumph of "the family over the family name." In Spain the completion of this crucial transformation would be deferred until well into the nineteenth century. In previous periods, the function of the family unit was thought to be not at all autono-

[30] Philippe Ariès, *Centuries of Childhood: A Social History of Family Life*, trans. Robert Baldrick (New York: Random House, 1962).

mous or inseparable from broader social and economic relations. In his entry for *familia*, Covarrubias traces the significations of the word from its classical origins, when it designated only a group of servants, to its more inclusive early modern usage: "And by this word *family* is understood the lord and his wife, and all others subject to their command, such as children, servants, slaves" ("Y debaxo desta palabra familia se entiende el señor y su muger, y los demás que tiene de su mando, como hijos, criados, esclavos").[31] In the seventeenth century, the nuclear family as we understand it today was little more than a barely imaginable entity; all dependents were grouped together, and no group was particularly favored.

Within the extended body of the early modern family, children were positioned as merely one group within a continually shifting coalition dependent on economic exigencies. Thus, rather than receiving their identity solely from their parents, children from an early age participated in a wide range of practices that put them in contact not only with distant relatives but with complete strangers or so-called *amigos*.[32] We should remember, for example, that Don Quixote's household includes a member of his own extended family, a niece, as well as an anonymous "lad for the field and market" ("mozo de campo y plaza"). In my opinion, the oedipal triangle, which Freud made the basis for our modern understanding of the subject, must be carefully rethought before it can be relevant to the study of seventeenth-century aristocratic culture. The early modern practice of "farming out" children, either to the care of wet nurses and servants or as apprentices, significantly mediated the role of the parents in subject formation. A "psychology" of literary characters premised on middle-class structures and anxieties will be of limited value unless such differences are taken into account.

Given the overall dispersion of the family's power to produce

[31] Covarrubias, *Tesoro de la lengua.*
[32] See James Casey and Bernard Vincent, "Casa y familia en la Granada del antiguo régimen," in *La familia en la España mediterránea, siglos XV–XIX*, ed. Casey (Barcelona: Crítica, 1987), pp. 172–211.

subjects, aristocratic children knew little of the mechanisms of intimacy through which some modern children bond with their parents; even the nursing of infants was considered unworthy of highborn women as was child care in general: "Today it is taken as a point of honor for mothers not to raise the children to which they give birth, but rather to give them to other women to raise" ("Ya se tiene por punto de honra no criar las madres a los hijos que paren, sino darlos a otras que los críen").[33] Philip II's son Fernando, for example, had eight different wet nurses, and the future Philip III was handed over to the wife of a high-ranking bureaucrat on the day of his birth. Seventeenth-century medical practice was already attempting to modify this attitude in manuals such as J. Gutiérrez de Godoy's 1629 *Tres discursos para probar que están obligadas a criar a sus hijos a sus pechos todas las madres* (Three discourses to prove that all mothers are obligated to nurse their children). But for the most part such appeals had little to do with a sentimental desire for increased contact between mother and child. Gutiérrez, for example, is more interested in the abuses of nonaristocratic wet nurses (*nodrizas*) and their possible effects on aristocratic blood: "Some turn up pregnant and they are so unscrupulous that, sensing that they are burdened with this impediment, they do not hesitate to kill the son of some great lord with their bad milk" ("Unas amanecen preñadas y son tan poco escrupulosas que, sintiéndose con este impedimiento, no reparan en matar con su mala leche un hijo de un gran señor").[34] For Gutiérrez and other ideologues of blood, the removal of the aristocratic child from the immediate control of the natural parents and its contact with representatives of inferior social classes was a threat to group purity. More important, the child's exposure to nonaristocratic practices made the potential for alternative subject formation all too real. The influential preacher Alonso de Cabrera warned his listeners: "How many times has it

---

[33] F. Juan de las Ruelas, *Hermosura corporal de la Madre de Dios* (1621), quoted in Ricardo del Arco, "La vida privada en la obra de Cervantes," *Revista de archivos, bibliotecas y museos* 56 (1950): 602.

[34] Quoted in J. L. Morales, *El niño en la cultura española*, vol. 1 (Madrid: n.p., 1960), p. 142.

happened that your young daughter or some other young girl in your home loses her purity by being influenced by a vile duenna or a dishonest maid?" ("¿Qué de veces tu hija doncella y la otra mozuela que tienes en casa pierde su limpieza persuadida de la dueña ruin y del ama deshonesta?").[35] This attitude would be represented in a variety of writings and cultural spectacles, especially in the public theater.

Within the relatively diffused structure of aristocratic families, then, the gap between adulthood and childhood was bridged much more quickly than it would be in later cultural and class contexts. The child was implicated in a variety of institutions at an early age, and major career decisions were often made by the father when the child was between six and eight. In some cases, even the taking of holy orders was accomplished before the age of nine; the receiving of *hábitos* in the military order of Santiago could be completed as early as age seven. This accelerated socialization was typical of a system in which aristocratic children were considered "miniature men" and occupied multiple subject positions in early life.[36] Unlike their modern counterparts, they were not limited to the function of family member, nor were they necessarily protected from the harsh realities of early modern existence. In 1572, for example, Antonio de Léon Pinelo reported that a religious confraternity had responded to the need to aid the "many children who appeared on doorsteps, some dead, and others in the wells and fountains of the Prado" ("muchos niños que amanecían por las puertas, algunos muertos y otros en

---

[35] Alonso de Cabrera, *Sermones*, vol. 1, *Nueva biblioteca de autores españoles*, 3 (Madrid: Bailly, 1930), p. 21.

[36] The term is Stephen Gilman's. See *The Spain of Fernando de Rojas: The Intellectual and Social Landscape of "La Celestina"* (Princeton: Princeton University Press, 1972), p. 218. With regard to the changing concept of childhood in Spain, no study is comparable to that of Ariès, but see the opening chapter of Richard L. Kagan, *Students and Society in Early Modern Spain* (Baltimore: Johns Hopkins University Press, 1974), as well as Casey, ed., *La familia de la España mediterránea*; Augustín Redondo, ed., *Autour des parentes en Espagne aux XVIe et XVIIe siecles: Histoire, Mythe, et Litterature* (Paris: Sorbonne, 1987); Luis Cortés Echánove, *Nacimiento y crianza de personas reales en la corte de España, 1566–1886* (Madrid: CSIC, 1958).

los pozos y estanques del Prado").[37] Given these conditions, we can be fairly sure that the sentimental privileging of the child as a "special" creature was far less prevalent than it is today in middle-class culture; in fact, tenderness toward children was associated with nonaristocratic classes: "It is the custom of laborers and widows to love their children tenderly" ("Es costumbre de labradores y de viudas, que aman tiernamente a sus hijos").[38]

Certainly, aristocratic parents had little interest in equal treatment of their children. The institution of primogeniture, known in Spain as the *mayorazgo*, sanctioned by biblical sources, persisted throughout the early modern period in both Catholic and Protestant countries. Even in England, where Puritan ideology was already constructing all children as special members of the domestic space and thus deserving of equal treatment, it was held that the eldest son alone should inherit the family estate.[39] In Castile, partible inheritance was more widespread and was extended even to female descendants, but this practice did not reveal an economic and cultural movement toward equal distribution of property to all members of a nuclear family. Instead, it was designed to protect the purity of the bloodline by blocking transference of wealth to collateral males. In a curious way, the Spanish insistence on blood as constitutive of both individual and group subjectivity enhanced women's access to economic

[37] Antonio de León Pinelo, *Anales de Madrid (desde el año 447 al de 1658)*, ed. Pedro Fernández Martín (Madrid: Instituto de estudios madrileños, 1971), p. 109. In most cases, aristocratic attitudes toward both children and members of the subordinate classes were collapsed; servants were considered simple, childlike charges. See Leah S. Marcus, *Childhood and Cultural Despair: A Theme and Variations in Seventeenth-Century Literature* (Pittsburgh: University of Pittsburgh Press, 1978).

[38] Martín Pérez de Ayala, *Discurso de la vida* (1566) (Buenos Aires: Espasa-Calpe, 1947), p. 16.

[39] Joan Thirsk, "The European Debate on Customs of Inheritance, 1500–1700," in *Family and Inheritance: Rural Society in Western Europe, 1200–1800*, ed. Jack Goody, Thirsk, and E. P. Thompson (Cambridge: Cambridge University Press, 1976), pp. 177–91. See also David E. Vassberg, *Land and Society in Golden Age Castile* (Cambridge: Cambridge University Press, 1984); Bartolomé Clavero, *Mayorazgo: Propiedad feudal en Castilla, 1639–1836* (Madrid: Siglo XXI, 1974).

power. Under the system of primogeniture, however, the consequences for younger children could be dramatic. Younger males, effectively excluded from the structures of blood and wealth, were necessarily constituted as subjects through alternative and often disruptive discourses. On the seventeenth-century stage, this process is clearly visible in figures such as Tirso de Molina's Don Juan (*El burlador de Sevilla*, ca. 1620) and Juan Ruiz de Alarcón's Don García (*La verdad sospechosa*, 1619–1620), both of whom are displaced from their natural position in the family hierarchy and subsequently become a threat to its survival.

Thus the idea of the family as an isolated group of nurturing individuals set in opposition to society, which seems to us both natural and historically constant, was in fact relatively alien to early modern culture. It is not surprising, therefore, that the experience of privacy was a recent phenomenon in the seventeenth century. The interiorization of the subject, the formulation of the idea of the "individual" as we understand it, was only just beginning to take place through the changing material conditions of everyday life. The private room, the practice of solitary and silent reading, the intensified emphasis on individual piety in both Protestant and Catholic discourse—all these developments gradually transformed what in an earlier period had been a virtual lack of distinction between the public and private.[40] Azorín was among the first to identify the lack of realist description in *Don Quixote* as symptomatic of an emerging culture marked by neostoical values, which, unlike earlier aristocratic and future bourgeois traditions, placed relatively little value on domestic trappings.[41] Cervantes does not describe the house of Diego de Miranda, for example, in any detail, and he represents it not as a place of warmth and nourishment but of mystery and silence. Within his own historiographical model, Maravall convincingly argued that the development of the bourgeois house-

---

[40] For a discussion of these issues in early modern France, see *Histoire de la vie privée*, vol. 3: *De la Renaissance aux Lumières*, ed. Roger Chartier (Paris: Seuil, 1986).

[41] See José Martínez Ruiz [Azorín], "La casa de Miranda," in *Con permiso de los cervantistas* (Madrid: Biblioteca nueva, 1948), pp. 187–88.

hold can be directly related to many of the innovations in the function of literature: the desire for privacy and relative autonomy intensified in direct proportion to the incursion of printed texts into the domestic space.[42] Certainly, in the case of Don Quixote an extreme form of subjectivism was intensified to a large degree in proportion to the number of books that entered the confines of his house: "He sold many acres of cornland to buy these books of chivalry to read, and in this way brought home every one he could get" ("Que vendío muchas hanegas de tierra de sembradura para comprar libros de caballerías en que leer, y así, llevó a su casa todos cuantos pudo haber dellos").[43] Even in larger aristocratic households throughout the seventeenth century, there was a progressive movement of the book from communal halls to the intimacy of bedrooms and private chambers.[44]

The importance of the shift from reading aloud in groups to reading silently alone should not be underestimated. It was a crucial step in the construction of the individual as an entity separate from the community. The lingering practice of communal reading is of course everywhere in *Don Quixote*; yet the originary moment of the text presumably transpired during those times when Don Quixote sat alone with his chivalric novels. Thus we are faced with still another transitional moment, this time on the level of modes of communication. The gradual transition from oral to manuscript to print culture, which abstracted the human body (formerly involved through voice, gesture, and so on) from the act of reading, would profoundly affect forms of subjectivity and intersubjectivity, that is, the ways in which individual and collective mentalities were constructed.[45]

---

[42] José Antonio Maravall, "Interés personal por la casa propia en el Renacimento," *Revue de littérature comparée* 52 (1978): 255–66.

[43] Miguel de Cervantes, *Don Quijote de la Mancha*, ed. Martín de Riquer (Barcelona: Juventud, 1971), pt. 1, chap. 1, hereafter cited in the text by part and chapter. English translations throughout this book are from *The Adventures of Don Quixote*, trans. J. M. Cohen (London: Penguin, 1982).

[44] See Roger Chartier, "Les pratiques de l'écrit," in *Histoire de la vie privée* 3:141.

[45] The important concept of mode of communication is being theorized in the

For most early modern Spaniards, the direct aesthetic experience of corporality would survive, especially in the public readings of the *venta* and in the *corral*; for a small minority of intellectuals, however, the idea of solitary reflection had already begun to replace communal experience, producing a heightened awareness of the potential for individual autonomy. Quevedo's poem 131 suggests that solitude was beginning to be understood as a desirable state in the seventeenth century not only for ascetic reasons but for reasons of personal and intellectual pleasure as well:

> Retirado en la paz de estos desiertos,
> con pocos, pero doctos libros juntos,
> vivo en conversación con los difuntos
> y escucho con mis ojos a los muertos.
>
> Si no siempre entendidos, siempre abiertos,
> o enmiendan, o fecundan mis asuntos;
> y en músicos callados contrapuntos
> al sueño de la vida hablan despiertos.
>
> Las grandes almas que la muerte ausenta,
> de injurias de los años, vengadora,
> libra, ¡oh gran don Iosef!, docta la emprenta.
>
> En fuga irrevocable huye la hora;
> pero aquélla el mejor cálculo cuenta
> que en la lección y estudios nos mejora.

(Withdrawn into the peace of this desert, having gathered together some books, few but learned, I live in conversation with the deceased and I listen with my eyes to the dead. If not always understood, yet always open, they [the books] either correct or fertilize my actions; and in silent musical counterpoint they, awake, speak to the dream [sleep] of life. The great souls which death takes away are freed from the damage of the years, oh great Sir Joseph, by an avenger, the learned printing press. In irrevocable flight the hour

---

work of H. U. Gumbrecht. See, for example, "The Body versus the Printing Press: Media in the Early Modern Period, Mentalities in the Reign of Castile, and Another History of Literary Forms," *Poetics* 14 (1985): 209–27.

flees; but that hour scores the highest which improves us by reading and study.)[46]

This poem is a composite of emergent and residual discourses; its final tercet figures the humanist belief in learning and education over against the second quartet's restatement of the ascetic ideology of "life is a dream." At the same time, the allusion to the modern technology of the printing press produces the synesthetic image of "listening with ones eyes" to deceased authors. The first stanza itself is nothing less than an ode to the joys of reading in seclusion.

By the middle decades of the century, the diplomat Bernardino de Rebolledo was describing the privacy of reading: "All these exercises are done without leaving a single room . . . from whose isolation I rarely depart so that no one can disturb such enjoyable solitude" ("Todos estos ejercicios se hacen sin salir de un aposento . . . cuya clausura rompo pocas veces por que no me embarace tan entretenida soledad nadie").[47] The transformation of the private sphere, then, was the necessary precondition to the elaboration of a myth of the individual subject, constructed in opposition to society or to the public domain. This slow and difficult metamorphosis was only just beginning in early modern Europe, and the resistance of the traditional structures of Castilian culture would problematize its development to an even greater degree than in other national contexts.

Clearly, those of us who would study early modern Spanish culture with the aid of psychoanalysis must reformulate many of the recurring tropes that determine the narrative of modern

[46]Throughout this book I use José Manuel Blecua's edition of Quevedo's poetry, *Obra poética*, 4 vols. (Madrid: Castalia, 1969–81), citing it in the text by poem number. The English translation of poem 131 is by Elias Rivers and appears in his *Renaissance and Baroque Poetry of Spain* (Prospect Heights, Ill.: Waveland Press, 1988), p. 267. All other translations are mine unless otherwise indicated.

[47]Bernardino de Rebolledo, *Ocios* (1660) quoted in María Concepción Casado Lobato, "Autores franceses en la biblioteca de un escritor del siglo XVII: Bernardino de Rebolledo (1597–1676)," in *Livre et lecture en Espagne et en France sous l'ancien régime: Colloque de la Casa de Velásquez* (Paris: AOPF, 1981), p. 127.

criticism. I have already pointed out that the oedipal story, dependent on the bourgeois family as its site of operation, can be a critical handicap if we try to force it on familial units that were configured differently. Psychological practice in general (especially as it has developed in the United States) continues to be premised on the notion of "individuals" who must struggle against one another within a family situation in order to be whole. The individual is a form of the subject which I have already tried to situate historically and about whose universal claims I have voiced reservations. With the dual concepts of the bourgeois individual and the bourgeois family at the center of most psychoanalytical readings of early modern literature, we are often unable to recognize other forms of subjectivity and social behavior, the products of cultural formations only marginally related to our own.

The passage from traditional Freudian readings of seventeenth-century Spanish literature to readings based on the work of Jacques Lacan has been relatively easy and in some sense logical insofar as the "French Freud" is a language-based project that has been made to coincide with the formalist interests of many English-speaking Hispanists. What has been given less attention, of course, is Lacan's radical decentering of the subject and its consequences for literary and cultural studies in general. For Lacan, individuals as such are absent from the oedipal scene since it is language itself (the symbolic) that determines subject positions and in fact is a prerequisite for any subjectivity at all. On this view, signifiers replace human agents at the moment the entry into language is accomplished. It is not my intention to repeat the entirety of the Lacanian program. I want only to suggest that the problems we have seen with more conventional uses of psychoanalysis in literary studies are replaced here by the no less serious problem that Lacan's symbolic is presented as a universal and transhistorical dimension that functions identically regardless of specific sociocultural contexts, ultimately sustaining the strict separation of feminine and masculine and blocking the potential for agency and resistance. That the so-called symbolic (like Freud's family) is a concept wholly contingent on history and that it could not have been constructed in the early modern period precisely as it was in the nineteenth century or as it is today is an idea those of us who write about literature have yet to address adequately.

My remarks on contemporary theory are less a digression than an attempt to resituate critical discourse within a more properly seventeenth-century context. The subjection of literary characters from earlier cultures to the rigors of modern psychological reading strategies reduces those cultures to reflections of ourselves. But reread through the lens of a method premised on the social construction of the subject, the literary and historical material reveals the failings of all such dehistoricizing operations. Cervantes's understanding that subjectivity could not be conceived apart from the social, for example, renders inoperative the widely influential and relatively recent opposition between individual and society. The family as a mediating agent between two opposed spheres of action, which to a great extent defines the great novels of the nineteenth century, is virtually absent in early modern Spanish literature. When it does appear, as in the case of Don Diego de Miranda in the 1615 *Don Quixote*, the specific details of family life are left unstated. We read only of the son's interest in poetry and learn nothing at all about his mother, Doña Christina. This is not to suggest that new forms of the family were not already being constructed in Spain. Just as the subject as individual was beginning to take shape in discourse, so too was the bourgeois family, and it is not an insignificant detail that in the 1615 *Don Quixote* one of the minor voices that joins in the criticism of Don Quixote's earlier subjectivism is a Castilian bourgeois. As the knight rides through the streets of Barcelona, his critic exclaims: "How have you got here alive after all the beatings you've received? You're a madman. If you had been mad in private and behind closed doors you would have done less harm. . . . Go back home, idiot, and look after your estate and your wife and children, and quit this nonsense that worm-eats your brain and skims the cream off your intellect" ("¡Cómo que hasta aquí has llegado, sin haberte muerto los infinitos palos que tienes a cuestas? Tú eres loco, y si lo fueras a solas y dentro de las puertas de tu locura, fuera menos mal. . . . Vuélvete, mentecato, a tu casa, y mira por tu hacienda, por tu mujer y tus hijos, y déjate destas vaciedades que te carcomen el seso y te desnatan el entendimiento") (2:62). This unusual intervention by a proponent of familial responsibility in a proto-middle-class sense ("look after your estate and your wife and children") alerts us to the changing concept of the family at this historical moment. In sharp contrast to the image invoked by the Castilian's advice, we know that elsewhere in Cervantes's text family groupings are consistently represented in conflict and under duress as members are confronted by alternative discourses that reconstitute their subjectivity over and against the family (for example, Catholicism in the case of Zoraida in the 1615 *Don Quixote*).[48] The domestic unit attributed a civilizing function in the later bourgeois novel is in Cervantes more often than not a space that is itself in need of civilizing.

In the early seventeenth century, because the subject could not be conceived of as separate from social relations, the idea of the family continued to be more generally understood in the form of broader collectives such as the clan, the monarchy, or the church. The few decrees issued from the Councils of Trent dealing directly with family matters attest to the church's lack of understanding of the emergent idea of the nuclear family, which continued to be associated with the heretical sects of the North. Some historians have even argued that it was the Counter-Reformation church's hostility to the development of the modern family which blocked the construction of the subject as individual in Mediterranean culture.[49] On this view, Don Quixote's return "home" at the end of the 1615 novel has less to do with the nucleus composed of his housekeeper and his niece than with his reintegration into the religious community: "Don Quixote's end came, after he had received all the sacraments"

[48]Luis Murillo has suggested that the entire Cervantine text is constructed upon a "structure of separation" through which characters are displaced from their natural environment, reconstituted as subjects, and then return as potentially disruptive elements. See "Narrative Structures in the *Novelas Ejemplares*: An Outline," *Cervantes* 8 (1988): 234–35.

[49]See John Bossy, "The Counter-Reformation and the People of Catholic Europe," *Past and Present* 47 (1970): 51–70.

("llegó el último de don Quijote, después de recibidos todos los sacramentos"). The positioning of the subject within religious practice, therefore, was considered far more important than the more private sphere of the family, a sphere only just beginning to take on the features of spiritual intimacy and child-centeredness with which we associate it today and which was being consolidated elsewhere in Europe through the ideology of Protestantism.

v

In our own time, class continues to be the dominant category through which subjects are constructed in the industrialized West, but in the seventeenth century, social differentiation on the basis of economic factors was still inextricably bound to other determinants with long-standing cultural histories, what Lukács once referred to as the "inter-worlds," which escape analysis based exclusively on class. Blood, status, and kinship relations precluded the operation of any "pure" or "rational" Weberian economic model; thus subjectivity was constituted through a wide range of complex networks rather than through any single practice. It would be difficult to argue convincingly that all early modern conflicts were class based and that therefore what seems to be the effect of other discursive practices is merely a mask for the relations of production. Although it is clear that economic structures identifiable as market relations already existed in the period, it is no less evident that they did not yet make up the autonomous and hegemonic force observable at later stages of capitalist development. Thus we would do well to remember Maurice Merleau-Ponty's admonition that a strictly "economic analysis would miss criteria essential to the distribution of privileges" in precapitalist or transitional societies, and George Lukács's warning that "Much greater caution is required when applying historical materialism to earlier societies than to changes in society in the nineteenth century."[50]

[50]Maurice Merleau-Ponty, *Adventures of the Dialectic*, trans. Joseph Bien

It is one thing to caution against privileging the economic at the expense of other practices, as Marxist theory itself has consistently done, demonstrating special reluctance toward moving the terms of analysis too quickly to an economic base in precapitalist or early capitalist societies. It is something quite different to deny altogether the usefulness of economic strategies for literary scholarship. In traditional Spanish studies, the use of the terms *class* and *class conflict* has met with opposition for a number of reasons. Aside from the conventional prohibition against inserting what is thought to be political language into any discussion of aesthetic issues (as if culture were not always also political), it is said to be anachronistic to project terms based on nineteenth-century social formations back onto an earlier historical moment. In view of the caveats I have cited, this criticism cannot be dismissed out of hand. Nevertheless, in this section I want to show that its basic proposition, that class consciousness and class relations were not functioning categories in preindustrial Europe, is contradicted by the cultural material.

Despite the appearance of ideological homogeneity produced by particular groupings of canonical literary texts, it would be difficult to deny that antagonistic social groups on the Peninsula understood their economic interests differently according to their local situation. Already in Fernando de Rojas's novel-dialogue *La Celestina*, especially in the expanded text of 1502, we hear the consequences of the violent competition for limited resources. Whereas this intensified splitting-up of the social fabric did not bring about the degree of class consciousness we associate with later historical moments, Rojas's servants clearly set themselves apart from the interests of their masters. In the first act, Celestina herself explains the changing situation to the naïve Pármeno: "Masters these days love themselves more than the servants in their house. And they're right! Their servants should do the same. . . . All these masters use their servants basely and meanly for their own ends; and their servants, even

---

(Evanston, Ill.: Northwestern University Press, 1973), p. 35; Georg Lukács, *History and Class Consciousness: Studies in Marxist Dialectics*, 3d ed., trans. Rodney Livingstone (Cambridge: MIT Press, 1973), p. 238.

those in the lower ranks, should do no less and live by their own law" ("Estos señores de este tiempo más aman a sí, que a los suyos. Y no yerran. Los suyos igualmente lo deben hacer. . . . Cada uno de éstos cautiva y mezquinamente procura su interés con los suyos. Pues aquéllos no deben menos hacer, como sean en facultades menores, sino vivir a su ley").[51] Similar arguments are spoken by servants and other marginal types in later dramatic texts, including Cervantes's *Comedia entretenida* (1611?). But such expressions of class antagonism do not necessarily indicate the presence of a fully developed counterideology.

As Marx wrote in his analysis of France in 1848: "In so far as millions of families live under economic conditions of existence that divide their mode of life, their interests and their culture from those of the other classes, and put them in hostile contrast to the latter, they form a class. In so far as there is merely a local interconnection among these small peasants, and the identity of their interests begets no unity, no national union and no political organisation, they do not form a class."[52] Given this model, we can say that on the level of the mode of economic production, the subordinate groups in Habsburg Spain constituted a class. On the level of social formation, however, they did not develop an ideological apparatus separate from that of the aristocracy and therefore were not a class in the strong sense of the term. This is the point at which the traditionalists' argument against a class analysis of early modern Spain seems to gain credence. But one can reject class considerations only if one refuses to acknowledge that any society in which a proportion of production is kept back and accumulated by a privileged group is necessarily a society

[51] Fernando de Rojas, *La Celestina* (Madrid: Alianza, 1988), p. 69. Translation from *The Celestina*, trans. Lesley Byrd Simpson (Berkeley: University of California Press, 1966), p. 26. For a discussion of the relationship in Rojas's text among the new economic structures of the fifteenth century, class, and the "individual," see José Antonio Maravall, *El mundo social de "La Celestina"* (Madrid: Gredos, 1964), especially the chapter "Individualismo y sentimiento de libertad."

[52] Karl Marx, *Eighteenth Brumaire of Louis Bonaparte* (1852). In *The Marx-Engels Reader*, 2d ed., ed. Robert C. Tucker (New York: W. W. Norton, 1978), p. 608.

with class structures. Despite their investment in aristocratic ideologies and practices (blood, lineage, the so-called honor code), the nonaristocratic groups did constitute a separate and distinct *social force* insofar as their alterity, their radical economic otherness, made possible the construction and reproduction of different and often opposed forms of subjectivity. In effect, despite the absence of political organizations designed to foreground class differences, there was nonetheless a community of interests drawn from among members of the subordinate groups.

It is important to remember that as early as the period of Fernando and Isabel there existed a body of writings (many now presumably lost) that constituted nothing less than an emergent discourse on class. In their weakest form, these texts were part of the medieval inheritance that disguised social difference as nature or fate. There was the popular story originally told by Boccaccio, for example, of a servant who for many years has served his king loyally but without reward. When he complains, he is told to choose between two chests, one filled with jewels, the other with sand. The servant selects the latter and so the king explains that the lack of compensation has nothing to do with decisions made by the king and everything to do with the servant's character and personal failings. In its first Spanish reworking, included in Antonio de Torquemada's *Coloquios satíricos* (1553), the king responds: "Do you think I am to blame? Your fortune is to blame, not your luck or lack of luck, because in reality these are empty words; I say fortune, your negligence and poor judgment, bad timing and missed opportunities." ("¿Piensas que tengo yo toda la culpa? La mayor parte tiene tu ventura, no quiero decir dicho o desdicha, porque de verdad estos son nombres vanos, mas digo ventura, tu negligencia y mal acertamiento, fuera de sazón y oportunidad").[53]

We can be sure that such representations of the attempt by cer-

---

[53]Quoted in M. Herrero García, ed., *Cuentos de los siglos XVI y XVII*, Biblioteca literaria del estudiante, 23 (Madrid: Instituto-Escuela, 1926), pp. 10–12. This story was also included in Timoneda's popular *Sobremesa y alivio de caminantes* (1563).

tain members of the aristocracy to efface class antagonisms were
not beyond the analytical faculties of the subordinate classes,
and in fact the unmasking is already present in a fifteenth-
century document (dated by Amador de los Ríos) in which a
laborer engages in dialogue with a king. Within the literary
frame of the dream-vision, the text is startling for the modernity
of its assertions:

> The men of this miserable world from which we all come were
> equal lords of what God, before their formation, had created for
> them, and thus, if one can speak honestly, those like me should be
> mortal enemies of highborn men since, by having forcibly usurped
> the dominion of the world, they have made us servants. And since
> your majesty claims that that ancient and great custom is now part
> of nature, you should know that we want to reverse things by
> means of those laws through which all this began, because every-
> thing done by force must be undone by force.

> (Los onbres en este mísero mundo venidos todos fueron ygual-
> mente señores de lo que Dios, antes de su formación, para ellos
> auia criado, é desta manera si onestamente dezir se puede, gran
> enemiga deuemos auer é tener los tales como yo con los altos
> varones, pues forçosamente auiéndosse usurpado el señorío, nos
> han hecho sieruos. E puesto que tu majestad diga que aquesta larga
> é gran costumbre es ya buelta en naturaleza, sepa que por aquellas
> leyes por donde lo dicho se principió, querriamos el contrario
> rehacer, porque toda cosa que con fuerça se haze, con fuerza
> deshacer se tiene.)[54]

One would be hard pressed to deny the existence in this passage
of a differentiation between competing economic interests as well
as a lucid understanding of how the ruling elites manipulate
ideology for their own interests. The radical assertion that power
alone maintains social relations and that power can just as easily
rearrange those relations suggests that even within the relatively
contained Spanish situation class conflict was already possible.

[54] Amador de los Ríos, "Sobre el libro llamado," pp. 583–84.

The distinction made by Anthony Giddens is useful here because it alerts us to the unique situation of early modern social formations: "I use the term *class-divided society* as distinct from that of *class society*. A class-divided society is a society in which there are classes, a class relation always being inherently a conflict relation in the sense of opposition of interest; but it is not a society in which class analysis provides the key to unlocking all the most significant features of the institutional order."[55] In the seventeenth century, private capital and property were becoming a means of social domination, but as we have seen in the case of the ideology of blood, residual categories with origins in earlier historical conjunctures continued as equal, if not more effective, means for the establishment of subject positions. Social relations were not generated from a single set of structures (the economic) as they were to a greater extent in the societies analyzed by Marx; rather, they were produced by diverse and often contradictory mechanisms that placed significant restraints on emergent practices and thus transformed the ways in which the economic functioned.

Still, the effects of nontraditional discourses are visible throughout all forms of writing in the period. I will cite only one well-known example: Sancho Panza's economic calculations are not grounded in precapitalist, agrarian planning structures that plot out the immediate future by reproducing inherited patterns derived from nature. On the contrary, they project far into the futures of himself and his family (his daughter's potential for changing class affiliation) and are articulated through contractual agreements made with Don Quixote (the colts and the island). Despite Sancho's subordinate class status, his claim to blood purity allows him to participate in relatively complex economic activities. Sancho's commercial interests are especially striking when he fantasizes about becoming king of Micomicon (1:29). What can be done, he wonders, if his new kingdom is populated

[55] Anthony Giddens, *Central Problems in Social Theory: Action, Structure, and Contradiction in Social Analysis* (Berkeley: University of California Press, 1979), p. 162.

by Africans? He quickly decides: "What do I care if my vassals are black? I've only to put them on board ship and bring them to Spain, where I shall be able to sell them, and be paid in cash. Then with the money I can buy a title or a post on which I can live at my ease for all the days of my life" ("¿Qué se me da a mí que mis vasallos sean negros? ¿Habrá más que cargar con ellos y traerlos a España, donde los podré vender, y adonde me los pagarán de contado, de cuyo dinero podré comprar algún título o algún oficio con que vivir descansado todos los días de mi vida?"). At this point, Sancho is in many ways a more modern figure than his master. Don Quixote's extreme subjectivism and appeal to a general principle of autonomy in the 1605 novel may be finally less important as a literary precursor of a fully developed individualism than is the squire's desire to rearticulate his own subjectivity and that of others through emergent practices of colonial exploitation. What is perhaps ironic is that it is Sancho the peasant who speaks for an entire class of early modern European capitalists. But the irony is diminished once we recall that for virtually all social classes in Spain accumulation and economic activity were less ends in themselves than the means to buy noble status and thus gain entry into the ever-widening body of the aristocracy.

I want to return briefly to the idea of the contract because it is central to the founding of new subject positions in this period. The written contract marked the crucial break with traditional ways of imagining subjects, for it is in the textualization of the contract that the subject, regardless of its blood or lineage, is reconstructed as "individual" and thus may "freely" enter into agreements with other subjects as equals. Throughout the early modern period, however, contractual relationships continued to be strongly mediated by the residual elements of blood and status. These are nowhere more apparent than in Don Quixote's frequent mistreatment of Sancho as an intrinsically inferior being: "Do you think, miserable peasant, that you can go on showing me disrespect and expect me to forgive you?" ("¿Pensáis, villano ruin, que ha de haber lugar siempre para ponerme la mano en la horcajadura y que todo ha de ser errar vos y perdonaros yo?") (1:30, my translation). It is also evident in the duke's insistence in the Clavileño episode that it is his right to change the terms of an agreement should he so desire: "So the price I mean to extract for this governorship is that you shall go with your master Don Quixote to complete and crown this memorable adventure" ("El que yo quiero llevar por este gobierno es que vais con vuestro señor don Quijote a dar cima y cabo a esta memorable aventura") (2:41). This stipulation had not been part of the original contract, but the duke's action makes it clear that it is the aristocrat's prerogative to supplement any agreement according to his whim. The contract was an important cultural mechanism for textualizing the individual, therefore, but it too was limited by older, more powerful, social practices.

It is too often suggested that Spain differed from the rest of Europe in the early modern period because of the undeveloped potential of capital. This generalization, which substitutes the economic structures of a region (Castile) for the whole of the Iberian peninsula, obscures the competition between modes of production which gave Spanish social relations their particular dynamism and intensely problematized subjectivity throughout the early modern period. In southern Spain, for example, questions of blood were considered secondary since *nobles de sangre* were relatively few there. By the early seventeenth century regular trade had been established with American markets, some traditional practices were losing influence, others had emerged, and a powerful merchant class was already in place in the cities of Catalonia and in Valencia and Seville. Maravall has referred to certain "new characters" ("nuevos personajes") who suddenly appeared on the sixteenth-century Spanish landscape.[56] Among them were members of an incipient middle class who did not labor themselves but lived off the labor of others ("ommes de villa que no biven de su trabajo") and also the earliest manifestations of a proletariat class at the mines of Almaden as well as

[56]José Antonio Maravall, *Utopia y reformismo en la España de los Austrias* (Madrid: Siglo XXI, 1982), p. 213.

professional financiers involved in sophisticated forms of exchange. In a later text published in Amsterdam and titled *Confusión de confusiones* (1688), for example, we are told that those who play the "game" of speculation do so "in order to be Men" ("porque todos aspiran en él, a ser Hombres").[57] It is not so much that objective conditions in early seventeenth-century Spain precluded forms of subjectivity which were taking shape elsewhere in Europe; rather, the unusually harsh reaction by the aristocratic and absolutist apparatus against such forms and the persistence of traditional discursive practices heightened the degree of contradiction at work within the Spanish context.

While it is true that investment of capital was slow in coming to the Spanish economy, it is also true that individual labor as a salable commodity existed early in the period and was already being theorized at the beginning of the seventeenth century. The constitution of the subject on the basis of his or her labor power had the effect of breaking traditional dependencies among social groups and produced the idea of a secular, private sphere disconnected from public opinion or questions of blood. Some even suggested that the new labor-based subject be granted privileges traditionally reserved for the aristocracy, including the prestigious exemption from taxes.[58] As for the possible attitudes of the subordinate class itself, at least as they were represented by an anonymous author, we need only listen to some further striking remarks of the laborer to the king:

> Here it should be noted that each man must be his own diligent judge. We, burdened with physical labor and care, spend every day without any pleasure: we, burdened by a thousand miseries, are desperate for many reasons: we, burdened by the tremendous labor from which you kings and great lords reap all the profit. . . . And what greater evil could arise, should one occur, than seeing

[57] Joseph de la Vega, *Confusión de confusiones* (1688), rpt. by the Sociedad de Estudios y Publicaciones (n.p.: n.d.), p. 5.
[58] *Memorial del contador Luis de Ortiz a Felipe II* (1558), rpt. in Manuel Fernández Alvarez, *Economía, sociedad, y corona: Ensayos históricos sobre el siglo XVI* (Madrid: Cultura Hispánica, 1963), p. 453.

the pathetic laborer maintain with his work and sweat royal expenses, the pomp of the great lords, the wasteful madness of the courtiers, the tremendous wealth that is found in the royal treasury?

(E aquí se nota quán diligente juez deue ser cada uno de sí mesmo. Nosotros, llenos del afan é del cuydado, passamos los dias sin ningun plazer: nosotros, llenos de mil miserias, somos por muchas maneras despechados: nosotros, llenos del creçido trabajo de que los reyes é grandes señores os lleuays todo el prouecho. . . . ¿E qué mayor mal puede auenir, magüer que si auiene, que ver el triste labrador del trabajo é sudor suyo mantenerse los gastos reales, la ponpa de los grandes señores, la desgastadiza locura de los cortesanos, la creçida riqueza de aquellos, quen la real hazienda entienden?)[59]

There can be little doubt that the composition of such a text, first reproduced by Amador de los Ríos in 1865, would have been extremely dangerous in the late sixteenth and early seventeenth centuries, although a number of writers seem to have been willing to make similar arguments even in this later period (for example, Pedro de Valencia, Caxa de Leruela, and others). In this particular text I want to emphasize the first line, which articulates a form of subjectivity based on the secularized notion of autonomy and self-interest we have seen at work in *La Celestina* and elsewhere, which is rapidly transformed within the movement of the text into strong class identification. This process is most evident in the repetition of "nosotros" and first-person plural verbs, which are situated in marked contrast to the "os" whose referent is the aristocracy. Such an early representation of class consciousness would seem to call into question Marx's assertion that prior to the Renaissance the predominance of use value created a situation in which the mode of production and subjectivity itself were experienced as a unified field. The idea that the peasant enjoyed an unproblematic relation to his or her conditions of labor may be little more than a utopian myth on the

[59] Amador de los Ríos, "Sobre el libro llamado," p. 585.

order of Hegel's Greece. In reality, the recognition of class difference was always a possibility, and there was always the potential for resistance to prescribed structures and subject positions; without such potential sites of contestation the dominant itself would be unable to take shape, and social change would be an unthinkable category.

If in fact the idea of "economic man" (one variant of the individual) was being articulated in areas of Spain at least as much as it was in other parts of Europe, it is nevertheless clear that throughout the early modern period traditional Castilian institutions and interests worked to block its development. By the late sixteenth century, capitalism and its attendant structures as they were rapidly developing in the cities of Italy and the Low Countries, regions under Spanish political domination, were considered harmful to the well-being of the monarchy. In the Castilian cities, the transition from an artisanal system to one based on manufacture accelerated the process of individuation, but always within the restraints imposed by traditional social relations. It has been maintained, perhaps most forcefully by Alfred von Martin in his *Soziologie der Renaissance* (1932), that the increased division of labor in which the tasks of craftsmen and artisans became progressively more specialized worked to break up the earlier totalizing effects of the guilds and other communal organizations. But here again we are faced with the undeniable fact that the process by which manufacture contributed to the construction of "individuals" was limited by the Spanish, especially the Castilian, situation. While some limited sectors of the population may have participated in these transitional practices, the great mass of underemployed had virtually no experience of technological innovations or of their practical or ideological consequences. Even the relatively few laborers who did continued to be inextricably linked to larger collectives ranging from kinship groups to religious confraternities. The persistence of these traditions, together with economic changes such as the rapid decline of the various Castilian industries (silk and wool, for example), which ceased to be competitive by 1625, inhibited both the development of manufacture on the classic model and its resultant effects on forms of subjectivity.

Meanwhile, according to Vicens Vives, the power of the Spanish bourgeoisie, which had intensified immediately after the discovery of America, declined rapidly after 1550 because of foreign trade monopolies, a lack of economic incentives, and the persistence of residual aristocratic practices.[60] Under these circumstances, the development of a merchant class, which in other contexts would embrace new practices and discourses to produce the figure of the autonomous individual, was made more difficult at every turn. Thus we find in a document written to Philip II in 1558 an entire chapter devoted to legal and cultural restrictions on mercantile activity: "In order for this to cease, it shall be commanded that brokers and other merchants and persons who improve their lot with others' money, besides the penalties incurred through laws and decrees, that they and their wives and their sons and daughters and their descendants should be prohibited from wearing silk, riding on horseback, and enjoying all honors and offices, and that they should be subject to all the prohibitions placed upon those condemned by the Holy Inquisition" ("Para que esto cese, se a de mandar que los canbios y otros mercaderes y personas que se alzaren con aziendas ajenas, de más de las penas que yncurren por leyes y premáticas, ellos y sus mugeres y hijos y hijas, y sus deçendientes, queden ynbalitados [sic] de bestir seda y de andar a cauallo y de todas onrras y ofiçios y en todo lo demás queden tan ynábiles como lo son los condenados por la Santa Ynquisiçion").[61]

The historical evidence suggests that such laws were never consistently enforced. The early years of Philip IV's reign were particularly permissive; merchants received royal favors, and the prohibitions imposed on small-scale businessmen were regularly waived for major capitalist entrepreneurs. The fact remains, however, that for a large segment of the ruling elites throughout the early modern period capitalist activities continued to be associated with undesirable social groups, particularly heretics and rebellious subjects. In Spain there would be no celebration in

[60]Jaime Vicens Vives, *An Economic History of Spain*, vol. 1, trans. Frances M. López-Morillas (Princeton: Princeton University Press, 1969), p. 339.
[61]*Memorial del contador Ortiz*, p. 453.

writing of the new figures of the merchant and financier like those
we find in England during the same period.[62] In the sixteenth
century, the Council of Trent had reiterated Thomas Aquinas's
condemnation of interest and other forms of economic transaction; nevertheless, relative tolerance followed in the early seventeenth century, soon to give way to the enforcement of severe
restrictions. One Old Christian, for example, was stripped of his
hábito and imprisoned for not revealing his previous activity as a
broker.[63] By the end of the century there were numerous reports
on the Inquisition's persecution of the new class that attempted
to make money from money: "The Inquisition had driven out
considerable capital by castigating those who owned it" (1694).[64]

It should come as no surprise that in the *Confusión de confusiones*
the character most heavily involved with economic activity is
associated with a literary figure renowned for his irrational behavior—Don Quixote. In the exchange among a philosopher, a
merchant, and a broker which structures this text is a description
of a group of Dutch merchants: "Building some ships, they sent
them in the 1604 voyage to the West Indies to search out adventures like Don Quixote. . . . The ships chose their direction, and
without finding windmills or enchanted giants, their voyage was
so fruitful . . . that they gained a generous profit" ("Fabricando
algunos navios, los embiaron en el de 1604 à buscar como Don
Quixote, a las Indias orientales sus Aventuras. . . . Eligieron los
navios su rumbo, y sin encontrar con molinos de viento, ni con
gigantes encantados; fue tan feliz su viaje . . . [que] lograron un
luzido lucro"). Later in the same text, we are presented with
satirical explanations of the origins of the stock exchange: "The
Quixotes claim that Sancho Panza invented it, either because

[62] See Laura Stevenson, *Praise and Paradox: Merchants and Craftsmen in Elizabethan Popular Literature* (Cambridge: Cambridge University Press, 1984).

[63] See L. P. Wright, "The Military Orders in Sixteenth- and Seventeenth-
Century Spanish Society," *Past and Present* 43 (1969): 67–68.

[64] Henry Kamen reproduces these reports to substantiate his claim that the
Inquisition's impact on economic development was negligible. One could support Kamen's thesis only by limiting oneself to "empirical evidence" and refusing to acknowledge the profoundly anticapitalist ideology figured in a wide
variety of texts. See Kamen's *Inquisition and Society in Spain in the Sixteenth and
Seventeenth Centuries* (Bloomington: Indiana University Press, 1985), p. 260.

many of those in the market with two *ducados* think they govern two islands, or because they, like Sancho, serve a madman who battles windmills" ("Los Quixotes defienden que lo inventó Sancho Panza, o por haber muchos en el que en viendose con dos Ducados, luego creen que goviernan dos Insulas, o porque sirven como Sancho a un loco que combate con molinos de viento").[65] The pun on *ducados* combines references to Sancho's imaginary island, stage-managed by the duke and duchess in the 1615 *Don Quixote*, and to a type of currency in order to make the point that certain kinds of economic activity have no more basis in reality than did Sancho's governorship. In the end, any form of subjectivity constituted through economic categories bore an inherently negative connotation. Here it is not so much that Don Quixote represents an incipient form of the subject, potentially threatening to the ideology of blood and status (as he seems to have done for some readers at an earlier moment of his reception); rather, he signifies the instability and foolhardiness associated with economic practice, in contrast to the aristocratic moderation and good sense of the philosopher.

The emergence of the figure of the bourgeois individual in Spain, therefore, was a complex process accompanied in large part by the stigma of irrationality and the perverse desire to place oneself above the community by living off others' labor. That many people found the negotiation among contradictory subject positions extremely difficult is clear to us from documents of the period. Confessors' manuals such as Martín de Azpilcueta's *Manual de confesores* (1556) delineated the conditions under which financial dealings could be undertaken without fear of spiritual transgression, and many capitalists paid close attention to such instructions. The powerful German banker Jakob Fugger, for example, often consulted theologians in Bologna before completing a transaction, and Lázaro Doria, a Genoese merchant living in Spain, retired from business in 1577 for reasons of conscience.[66] The case of Gonzalo de la Palma (d. 1595), a businessman from Toledo whose biography was written by his son, is of

[65] De la Vega, *Confusión de confusiones*, pp. 19, 56.
[66] Braudel, *Wheels of Commerce*, p. 564.

particular interest because it reveals a man who before agreeing to any new contract felt compelled to discuss its moral and theological implications with "the wisest men of his time" ("teníalos comunicados con los hombres más doctos de su tiempo").[67] For Gonzalo de la Palma, subjectivity was no mere question of economic position but rather a complex struggle among emergent and traditional discourses and affiliations. Implicated in this contradictory situation, de la Palma and his colleagues pointed toward an anticipatory form of the subject that in a later historical moment Defoe's Moll Flanders would call "an amphibious creature that thing of water and earth, which is called an artisan-knight." In all its forms within the early modern Castilian context, capitalism continued to be strongly mediated by the traditional discourses of blood and religion from which it would not be entirely separated until the nineteenth century.

Given this picture of Spain in the seventeenth century, especially the predominance of residual practices and institutions, it should not surprise us to find that five of Gonzalo de la Palma's eight children followed a religious vocation. But de la Palma was a divided subject on still another level. The suspicion of impure blood was to follow him and his sons for decades, and we can be fairly sure that the family did in fact have converso origins. Thus the subjectivity of this Catholic capitalist with Jewish ancestry was precariously constructed across the categories of religion, blood, and class. The records reveal many other conflicts of this type, some of them uncanny in their renegotiation of conventional restrictions in view of the changing economic context. In villages throughout Castile, the records reveal numerous examples of subjects implicated in multiple positions: hidalgos, for example, who functioned as millers, carpenters, or blacksmiths.[68] One such hidalgo, supposedly of untainted ancestry,

---

[67] A summary of Gonzalo de la Palma's biography is in Julio Caro Baroja, *Las formas complejas de la vida religiosa: Religión, sociedad, y carácter en la España de los siglos XVI y XVII* (Madrid: Akal, 1978), pp. 377–79. Similar cases are recorded in Ruth Pike, *Aristocrats and Traders: Sevillian Society in the Sixteenth Century* (Ithaca: Cornell University Press, 1972).

[68] On the issue of shifting class boundaries in the period, see Noël Salomon,

was forced to practice manual labor because of financial difficulties and was informed by the authorities that his noble status, although not forfeited, was temporarily suspended.[69] He would have to cease manual labor before he could be repositioned at a higher level within the hierarchical chain. The existence of such contradictory and shifting interpellations would seem to explode once and for all the traditional understanding of premodern literary characters as unified individuals free to "develop" themselves, to play roles, even to choose their place in society. As we shall see in the chapters on Quevedo and Cervantes, literary representations more often than not reveal the difficulty with which the idea of a self-determining individual struggled to take shape in Spanish writing.

VI

Even as the category of economic class acquired increasing power with regard to the constitution of subjects, other discourses had begun to efface divisions founded upon class differences. Here I am thinking primarily of nationalism. Despite an earlier interpretive model that isolated the state as the autonomous origin of all change in the early modern period (for example, Werner Sombart, *War and Capitalism* [1913]), historians are now in general agreement that the nation-state in the seventeenth century was still an unusually complex field of contradictions. If we remember that every state, regardless of the historical moment, is always a fragile alliance among competing practices and institutions, it comes as no surprise that not even the absolutist monarchy of the Habsburgs was a rigidly fixed system impervious to contestation and contradiction. Numerous dramatic texts, including Guillén de Castro's *Mocedades del Cid* (1618), for example, represent the problems of a weak king confronted by a

La vida rural castellana en tiempos de Felipe II, trans. Francesc Espinet Burunat (Barcelona: Ariel, 1982), pp. 301–17.
[69] Domínguez Ortiz, *El antiguo régimen*, p. 90.

rebellious aristocracy and thus suggest the potential dangers faced by still incomplete forms of absolutism. The more general theoretical point is that all hegemonic conjunctures, while undeniably capable of dominating the social field, are nonetheless not exempt from internal conflicts and fissures.

For the purposes of tracking subjectivity in the early modern period, I am less interested in the institutional apparatus that constituted the state than in the idea of the state. The extent to which the Spanish conceived of themselves as a national community apart from others was determined in no small part by the written representations of those cultures outside the peninsula considered to be antithetical to "Spanishness." In Spain the construction of the imaginary of the nation had been deferred by Charles V's involvement in dynastic and imperial politics. That is to say, the alternative but no less totalizing myth of a universal Catholic monarchy preceded and deferred the desire for an independent and autonomous national identity. By the second half of the sixteenth century, however, the project of the nation was well under way, and it began to consolidate itself in the antagonistic decades of the 1580s and 1590s, when the Spanish imperial project ran head on into the English intervention in the world economy. The "English" functioned as one national "other" among many, but the figure of the Englishman was uniquely charged within the ideology of the Spanish ruling class as it came to be an emblem for a new and dangerous form of the subject—the individual.

As is the case with a majority of cultural materials in the period, political statements were consistently framed within a religious master code.[70] The emergent forces of capital, class, and nation continued to be articulated through the residual discourses of theology and Counter-Reformation dogma, even in cases where religious differences were of secondary importance.

[70]On the function of the religious master code in early modern culture, see Fredric Jameson, "Religion and Ideology: A Political Reading of *Paradise Lost*," in *Literature, Politics, and Theory*, ed. Francis Barker, Peter Hulme, Margaret Iversen, Diana Loxley (London: Methuen, 1986), pp. 35–56.

One of the most striking textual examples of this articulation is a representation of the English written around the time of the first Armada (1588):

> [The English] confound and pervert the order of all things, human and divine, preferring the body to the soul, civil to spiritual government, and the reign of the earth to that of heaven, the inferior to the superior, the sheep to the shepherd, and they make the head the feet and the feet the head, and give freedom to the subject so that he may judge his judge.

> ([Los ingleses] confunden y pervierten el orden de todas las cosas divinas y humanas, prefiriendo el cuerpo al ánima, el gobierno civil al espiritual, y el reino de la tierra al del cielo, el inferior al superior, las ovejas al pastor, y haciendo de la cabeza pies, y de los pies cabeza, y dando libertad al súbdito para que juzgue a su juez).[71]

The rhetorical structure of this text, written by a Jesuit and dedicated to Philip II, forces the reader to accept the rigid opposition that locates the other as antagonistic and then rapidly oscillates between two irreconcilable poles—body/soul, earth/heaven, England/Spain—suggesting that the relationship between two political entities was a rivalry based on an essential, divinely ordained alterity.

It was through this textual displacement, by which political and economic categories were refunctioned through religious language, that the new concept of the individual became intimately associated with heresy. Although the word *individual* ("individuo") as a signifier for "person" made its earliest appearance in Spain in the seventeenth century (the ideologically charged *individualism* not gaining widespread currency until the late nineteenth century), the idea of a radically self-determining subject was most often figured by *singularity* ("singularidad"). In his influential *Tesoro de la lengua castellana* (1611), for example,

[71] P. Pedro de Rivadeneira, *Historia eclesiástica del scisma del reino de Inglaterra* (1588) in *Obras escogidas*, Biblioteca de autores españoles, 60 (Madrid: Atlas, 1952), p. 320.

Covarrubias records the following entry for *singular*: "Heretics, in order to be named and known by everyone, invent singularities. . . . The heretic is recognized not by his faith but for the freedom of consciousness that he professes and by making himself singular he sows discord instead of wheat" ("Los herejes, por ser nombrados y conocidos de todos, inventan singularidades. . . . Conoceráse al hereje no por la fe sino por la libertad de conciencia que predica y por hazerse singular siembra ziçania en lugar de trigo").[72] Such ideas were deeply rooted in the ideology of the dominant groups and had been particularly useful as ideological support for the proliferation of anti-English propaganda in the final two decades of the sixteenth century. It was during those years that the renowned preacher Alonso de Cabrera was explaining to his congregation that the heretic's primary sin was to set himself above traditional ways of thinking, to try to be an individual by constructing private ideational systems distinct from those of the community: "Singularity is the property of heretics: refusing to go where others go, disseminating novelty in public places, new doctrines, opinions from their own mind, never before imagined by anyone until them" ("La singularidad es esta de los herejes: aquel no pasar por lo que pasan los otros, aquel sacar novedades a las plazas, nuevas doctrinas, opiniones de su propio cerebro, nunca por nadie hasta ellos inventadas").[73] But the English were other to the Spanish for more reasons than mere rebelliousness or unorthodoxy. Economic developments in England had produced a work force that in essence realized for the first time in history the humanist utopia (as figured in texts such as Vives' *De subventione pauperum*) in which individual freedom was directly linked to work. Writing on England in *Capital*, Marx was among the first to trace this relationship between a large work force and a massive accumulation of capital. In Spain the development of a similar work force would be deferred for several centuries. Thus in the early seven-

[72]Covarrubias, *Tesoro de la lengua.*
[73]Quoted in Alejandro Ramírez-Araujo, "El moro Ricote y la libertad de conciencia," *Hispanic Review* 24 (1956): 283.

teenth century, Englishness itself, that is the subject as Englishman, became the conceptual analogue to the subject as individual.

As the structures of absolutism became more rigidly elaborated and the threat of heresy receded, a shift occurred in the signification of the word *freedom* ("libertad"). While it retained its centrality in the discourse of orthodoxy as an attribute of otherness, it took on an additional class-based connotation and began to be associated with the secular desire of nonaristocratic groups for political and individual freedoms. As Maravall has demonstrated in his analysis of Saavedra Fajardo, the humanist praise of natural freedom which surfaces on occasion in early modern Spanish literature, most notably in Segismundo's well-known speech in *La vida es sueño* and in *Don Quixote* (2:58), by the mid–seventeenth century is set in direct opposition to obedience and the power of the state. In this new context, *libertad* now comes to signify a potentially destructive desire for autonomy; it is therefore positioned at the lower end of the hierarchy of social traits as each trait is made the exclusive property of a given rank: "the king, his dignity; the nobility, its power; the people, its liberty" ("el rey, su dignidad; los nobles, su poder y el pueblo, su libertad").[74] With the king essentially removed from the mundane conflict of the social world, the rigid dualism between the aristocracy and nonaristocratic groups was locked in place. The subordinate class's irrational desire for freedom was perceived as running head on into the containing strategies of the governing elites.[75]

[74] See José Antonio Maravall, "Moral de acomodación y caracter conflictivo de la libertad (notas sobre Saavedra Fajardo)," *Cuadernos hispanoamericanos* 257 (1971): 685.

[75] As early as 1548, the Cortes of Valladolid had warned that vagabonds and orphans, "because they were raised in freedom, of necessity must become uncontrollable people who destroy the public good and corrupt proper behavior" ("porque habiéndose criado en libertad, de necesidad han de ser cuando grandes gente indomable, destruidora del bien público, corrompedora de las buenas costumbres"). Quoted in Francisco Rico, ed., *La novela picaresca española*, vol. 1 (Barcelona: Planeta, 1967), p. xxxii.

Certainly, the early modern state was not already a political reality in the same way that its nineteenth-century descendant would be. Still, the construction of national others was crucial to the process Benedict Anderson has called the invention of an "imagined community."[76] In effect, all the discourses and practices I have traced worked to construct the idea of community, whether it be premised on blood, virtue, sexuality, genealogy, or class. Through a set of exclusionary gestures, each discursive field constituted its own limits and generated its own forms of subjectivity. The denial of subjectivity to those groups falling outside the newly imagined totality is a constant corollary to virtually all cultural enterprises of this kind, nowhere more obviously than in early modern Spain, where traditional ideologies were transformed under the pressure of trying to resolve the issue of how to appropriate previously unknown peoples and worlds. In each successive historical moment, the idea of Spain as a social body would continue to be reconceived. The rise of the nation-state, advanced forms of capitalism, the elaboration of new kinds of writing, the emergence of more complex disciplinary mechanisms—all would work to produce forms of the subject that were only barely imaginable in the early modern period.

VII

In seventeenth-century Spain the idea of the individual made its appearance in writing surrounded by a host of rival and inhospitable discourses. Almost everything in the culture worked against its further elaboration: relations of production and the institutions of aristocratic life blocked its formulation, and where it did appear, it was labeled as heretical, subversive, or mad. This is not to say, however, that the various ruling groups that governed the early modern state desired a return to a medieval concept of community in which feudal bonds held each subject

[76] Benedict Anderson, *Imagined Communities: Reflections on the Origin and Spread of Nationalism* (London: Verso, 1983).

in its proper position within the overall hierarchy. On the contrary, individuation had to take place to a limited extent if the practices of kinship and blood loyalty were to be effectively overcome. We can see this process at work, for example, in the church's attempt to redefine baptism as the entry of the individual into the religious body rather than a further enactment of clan affiliation, and it is also visible in the counterdiscourse of virtue, which, at least in theory, contradicted the hierarchy of blood. But if the tentative move toward individuation was an unavoidable development, it was quickly recognized as potentially subversive; unchecked, it could well lead to the chaos that to the Spanish mind characterized English culture. The traditional idea of the community had to be broken up, but only to be immediately reconstituted around the state itself. The myth of the individual, then, was a dangerous undecidable that had to be decentered and rewritten by the elaborate cultural machinery of the Counter-Reformation.

What is clear from the recurring tropes and figures that came together to represent the aristocratic subject in literature is that the diverse exclusionary practices of the culture at large worked to produce a gallery of "other" characters as well. In reality there were dozens of groups, some of which do not play a major role in literary texts of the period, whose alterity was crucial to the maintenance of the idea of the dominant: women, Amerindians, the religiously heterodox (Lutherans, Muslims, conversos), members of the subordinate classes, and those of other nationalities. In the case of the most conservative writers, theological discourse marked the outsider as diabolical and a threat to the entire social body: "Because a camp of gypsies is nothing more than an army of Satan. The entire Republic is the King's family. How then can one tolerate such an evil part of the family?" ("Porque no es otra cosa un aduar de Gitanos, que un exercito de Satanás. Toda la República es familia del Rey. ¿Cómo pues tolera tan mala parte de familia?")[77] An example as extreme as this,

[77] Pedro de Figueroa, *Aviso de príncipes* (1647), quoted in Caro Baroja, *Las formas complejas*, p. 509.

however, is undercut to a certain extent by more sympathetic representations of the gypsy in such secular texts as Cervantes's "Gitanilla," although it should not be forgotten that even Cervantes does not fail to reproduce the conventional opinion of that group, if only to problematize it later for his readers. The fact is that throughout the sixteenth century, racial, sexual, and national otherness determined the borders of the carnivalesque domain of figures who inspired either wonder (*admiratio*) or ridicule—thus the bunching together of such dissimilar types as "Moors, Jews, doctors, physicians, penitents, savages . . . cuckolds, pilgrims, devils . . . hermits, black men and women, Portuguese, Amazons, nymphs" in a 1555 masque presented in Toledo.[78] By the turn of the century, however, the idea that the body politic must be protected from all potential difference formed the very core of the political agenda of the ruling elites, culminating in the expulsion of the Moriscos in 1609 and dominating Spanish culture well into the eighteenth century. Differentiation based on race and blood was at the center of aristocratic subjectivity, for without differentiation subjectivity simply could not take shape.

It is a curious irony of Spanish history that the extended period known to historians as the Reconquest immediately preceded what we now know as the Conquest. That is to say, the homogenizing of Castilian society through a concentrated effort to purge the Iberian peninsula of undesirable ethnic groups ostensibly ended at the very moment at which Spain was confronted by a "new world" of previously unimagined peoples and cultures. It should not surprise us, therefore, that alterity has always played an unusually explicit role in the constitution of subjectivity in Hispanic culture. The effects of the American experience on social relations and discursive formations at home cannot be overestimated. Even as the dominant groups struggled to manage the contradictions that threatened the coherence of their own

---

[78] Rodríguez Marín's reference to this masque is noted in Maxime Chevalier, *Lectura y lectores en la España de los siglos XVI y XVII* (Madrid: Turner, 1976), p. 148.

ideologies, the intervention of such "new" subjects as those born of the union between nonaristocratic conquistadores and female members of the Indian nobility called into question the entire structure of traditional Castilian life. The very presence of the Indian supplemented the ideologies of blood and class by forcing groups previously considered to be inferior upward within the social hierarchy: in the colonies, all whites might now claim to be caballeros. But every *criollo* (Spaniard born in the colonies), according to a Jesuit father writing in the late sixteenth century, would have to be subjected to a more rigorous educational program than his peers born in Spain because of the liberty and vice in which he was reared.[79] As the *indianos* (returnees from America) began to intervene in peninsular life, it was clear that traditional categories would have to be expanded if they were to hold together. All these new forms of subjectivity were the product of nothing less than the reconfiguration of Spanish cultural practices and institutions, which continued with striking dynamism well into the seventeenth century. The texts of Cervantes and Quevedo inherit these tremendous changes.

The writings discussed in the next two chapters must not be thought of as in any way separate from or secondary to the other discourses I have outlined. On the contrary, what we now take to be the autonomous domain of "literature" was, in the wider field of seventeenth-century society, but one of the many cultural practices that contributed to the formation of subjects.[80] I do not claim, therefore, that the texts of Cervantes and Quevedo are privileged forms of writing, although I would agree that in some cases they are rhetorically more complex. Their relation to the materials discussed in this chapter is not one of reflection or allegorical representation. My sketch of the discursive field should not be considered an "outside" to the texts I want to move

[79] See Anthony Pagden, "Identity Formation in Spanish America," in *Colonial Identity in the Atlantic World, 1500–1800*, ed. Nicholas Canny and Pagden (Princeton: Princeton University Press, 1987), p. 82.

[80] See Wlad Godzich and Nicholas Spadaccini, eds., *Literature among Discourses: The Spanish Golden Age* (Minneapolis: University of Minnesota Press, 1986).

"inside" of. Rather, I am suggesting that all writing—lyric poetry and narrative but also texts about blood, the family, and class—worked to establish the boundaries of subjectivity and thus participated in the construction of material reality as it was lived by early modern Spaniards.

CHAPTER 3

Francisco de Quevedo:
Individuation and Exclusion

To what prison, to what void, to what oppression is he referring?

(¿A qué cárcel, a qué vacío, a qué opresión alude?)
—D. Alonso

Quevedo is much more complex than we think.

(Quevedo es mucho más complejo de lo que se piensa.)
—J. A. Maravall

I

My contention that in the seventeenth century literary writing was not granted a significantly higher status than other forms of writing would seem to falter most readily in the case of lyric poetry. Since the nineteenth century, no other genre has enjoyed more prestige and aesthetic autonomy than the modern lyric, and this privileged position has subsequently been read back onto the poetry of earlier historical moments. Despite the caveats issued by the New Critics and others, theories of expression continue to collapse the speaker of the poem into the biographical poet, so that the preoccupation with a fully embodied presence (in contemporary critical language: phonocentrism) still effaces the fact that the poetic voice is a linguistic construct that participates in the kind of broad discursive formations I mapped out in the previous chapter. More important, the exclusively aesthetic and private sphere into which postromantic poetry has been driven has blocked understanding of how the lyric text may have functioned in other cultural contexts. In this chapter, I am not as interested in the formal or expressive qualities of the poem as in how the courtly lyric, one form of writing among many, contributed to the discursive elaboration of early modern aristocratic subjectivity.

Few poets of any century or national literature have textualized as many of the antagonisms of their culture as did Francisco de Quevedo (1580–1645). In his opening paper at the Quevedo quadricentennial held in Boston in 1980, the respected Golden Age critic Elias Rivers proposed "to make clear at least one or two reasons why a vulgar Spanish aristocrat named Don Francisco Gómez de Quevedo Villegas should continue to obsess us, to attract and repel us, so violently."[1] The two primary reasons offered by Rivers are social criticism and daring linguistic strategies, both of which he reads as undercutting the dominant ideological and aesthetic conventions of seventeenth-century Spain. Taking a different tack, I want to argue that what continue to attract Hispanists to Quevedo are not only the issues of language and society as separate fields of experience but that construct which is the product of both—subjectivity itself.

The Quevedesque poetic text, in its struggle to represent both traditional and emerging forms of the subject and the resultant contradictions, continues to attract the attention of contemporary criticism because it presents one limited textual space in which an early form of modern subjectivity was tentatively worked out. This incipient modernity has been sensed by a number of critics, from Dámaso Alonso, who equated Quevedo with an existentialist, to Rivers, who suggested (in the same opening address) that Quevedo's sonnets somehow anticipate Sartre's *Being and Nothingness*. Although a strict historical reading must insist on the inadequacy of such comparisons, it is nonethe-

---

[1] Elias Rivers, "Language and Reality in Quevedo's Sonnets," in *Quevedo in Perspective: Eleven Essays for the Quadricentennial*, ed. James Iffland (Newark, Del.: Juan de la Cuesta, 1982), pp. 17–32.

less true that Quevedo's text gestures toward and grapples with a form of the subject (the autonomous and self-possessed individual) which I have identified as only one historically specific variant among many, but one that has enjoyed hegemony in the West at least since the nineteenth century. What still fascinates us about Quevedo, apart from the power of his language and his critique of imperial Spain, is the struggle of a writer to create voices incompatible with his own sociocultural context.

It is incumbent on us to understand Quevedo's poetry as a discursive site where multiple and competing forms of subjectivity take shape. In this sense, the courtly lyric participates in the same competition that took place among blood, virtue, class, and the other principal tropes of early modern Spanish writing. It should not surprise us, therefore, that Quevedo's texts have consistently refused to be totalized into a harmonious whole and that since the end of the seventeenth century the image of Quevedo the man has been that of a contradictory and insoluble figure. In reality, all writing produced in a specific historical period participates in the same conflictive cultural field. Our inability to see the contradictions in certain texts has to do with the ways in which the ideological subplots of those texts have been selectively effaced in order to satisfy the desires of a later universalizing and aestheticizing criticism.

The resistance of Quevedo's opus to unification, however, did not preclude the enshrinement of many of his texts within the canon of Spanish literature. Ironically, those writings that Quevedo sought to withhold from public view during his own lifetime and in some cases openly denounced (for example, the picaresque novel *El Buscón,* "renounced at the request of the author, who does not recognize it as his own" ["reprobado a petición de su autor, el cual no lo reconoce por suyo"]) are today the basis upon which we have constructed his reputation for "authenticity" and "originality," qualities undoubtedly privileged far less in the seventeenth century than in postromantic culture. Had the author's own wishes been realized—that is, if instead of the *Sueños, El Buscón,* and the moral and burlesque poetry, we were to read and teach the Quevedo of the *Introducción a la vida devota* and the *Epítome* to the life of Saint Thomas of Villanueva—the desire for a Quevedo without contradictions would surely be realized. Indeed, criticism early in this century made a convincing case for such an alternative canon. In 1917, for example, Julián Juderías complained: "Our carelessness has been the reason that Quevedo's popularity is founded upon that of which he himself was ashamed; we have ignored the most interesting, most beautiful, and most elevated part of what he composed" ("Nuestro descuido ha sido causa de que la popularidad de Quevedo se funde en aquello de que él mismo se avergonzaba, desconociéndose la parte más interesante, más bella, más elevada y más noble de cuanto compuso").[2]

But the search for the whole Quevedo is neither a practical nor a desirable enterprise.[3] Despite interesting attempts that replace the disunity and heterogeneity of the texts with a so-called unity of personality or those that have begrudgingly settled for a "split" or even schizophrenic personality, the poet continues to resist the totalizing impulse of criticism.[4] What today we might call the

[2] Julián Juderías, *Don Francisco de Quevedo y Villegas: La época, el hombre, las doctrinas* (Madrid: Jaime Ratés, 1922), p. 10. Conventional North American Hispanism has seen Quevedo as a traditional thinker (Baum) and even a "reactionary" (Beverley), although in recent years the potential subversiveness of some texts have been elucidated (Iffland; in Spain, Maravall).

[3] On this point, one wonders what is really at stake in the kind of project most recently articulated by Roger Moore: "Quevedo has been defined as a 'turbulent maelstrom of apparent contradictions' ('turbio revoltijo de aparentes contradicciones'—D. Alonso). While this is still true, *the search for the real, the genuine, the authentic Quevedo must continue.*" Review of D. Gareth Walters, *Francisco de Quevedo: Love Poet*, in *Revista canadiense de estudios hispánicos* 12 (1988): 524, my emphasis.

[4] A useful summary of critical approaches to Quevedo's complete works is Henry Ettinghausen, "Quevedo, ¿un caso de doble personalidad?" in *Homenaje a Quevedo*, ed. García de la Concha, pp. 27–44. It will be argued that my own project is an attempt to totalize Quevedo on the level of the social macrotext, and I would agree that any critical enterprise implies the construction of a unified field. My point is simply that it is society and culture at large from which we must begin to collect our materials. For an earlier sketch of the kind of method I am proposing, see Anthony N. Zahareas and Thomas R. McCallum, "Toward a Social History of the Love Sonnet: The Case of Quevedo's Sonnet 331," *Ideologies and Literature* 2 (1978): 90–99. Another premise of my book is that no historical conjuncture, even the apparently closed universe of Quevedo's Spain,

hybrid nature of the Quevedesque text cannot be reduced to a
single origin or divided between strict dualities. More specifically, within the poetry the absence of a coherent speaking voice
whose characteristics might be catalogued without contradiction
denies us access to a total vision of the Quevedesque subject, and
we are left with the frequently mentioned inseparability of the
moral poems from the burlesques; they share certain elements,
and they are enmeshed in what is not their opposite but their
partner in the production of a third, heterogeneous, and often
unstable sphere of discourse. Quevedo's attempt toward the end
of his life to create a unified image of himself based on his
religious and devotional production and the erasure of his burlesque works is only the first in a long line of responses born of the
feeling that the hybrid text is somehow threatening to both
subjectivity and the cultural body. The process of selection and
exclusion that constitutes the canon and ultimately determines
our image of the author has too often been concealed by simply
surrounding the name of Quevedo with a list of contradictions or,
perhaps even more counterproductive, suggesting that Quevedo
was less a man than a literature (Borges). What both of these
positions conceal is the complex relationship among the writer,
the text, and the social world, not a direct one-to-one correspondence but a field of powerful mediations whose effects we have
too often reduced to the domain of the aesthetic or the psychological.

His biographers have taught us that Quevedo pursued his
career as a diplomat and minor political figure no less intensely
than his literary activities, and in fact José Manuel Blecua has
maintained that writing for Quevedo was subordinate to politics.[5] Although he was born within the confines of the palace,
Quevedo directed much energy early in his life toward stepping

------

is completely free of sites of symbolic and real contestation. This concept of the
social as a field of competing discursive practices is as crucial to an understanding of Quevedo as is the idea of a subject without a stable center.

[5] According to Blecua, Quevedo's "political passions were greater than his
literary passions" ("su pasión política fue más dominante que la literaria"). See
the Introduction to Francisco de Quevedo, *Poemas escogidos* (Madrid: Castalia,
1972), p. 8.

up the social ladder; his goal, to win a position in the Order of Santiago and status as a *caballero de hábito*, was not realized until 1617. His association with Uceda and Lerma, his long-lasting relationship with Osuna, his travels with Philip IV in 1624 and 1626, even his early affiliation with the powerful favorite Olivares—all highlight Quevedo's deep involvement with the governing elites, a precarious existence marked by exile and incarceration in 1620, again in 1628, and the final imprisonment of 1639. And if we are to believe the accounts of Quevedo's brief marriage, allegedly forced on the poet by a group of courtiers led by Medinaceli, the overwhelming public and private pressures felt by the courtly writer become even more apparent.

This kind of intense overdetermination by the dominant social order would seem to belie my contention (to which I will return) that multiple concepts of the subject are being contested on the site of Quevedo's poetic text. The poet's position at court would seem to demand that his texts reproduce only traditional forms of subjectivity. I would argue, however, that the poet's biography should not be used by the critic as raw material for a psychological post-mortem in search of the "truth" of Quevedo's stance with regard to the ideology of the ruling elites. Rather, individual acts and statements are useful only insofar as they reveal how the poet is implicated in a myriad of discourses that ultimately determine (that is, delimit) the forms of subjectivity available for representation in the literary text. In the case of lyric poetry, for example, specific modes of address may function as institutionalized mechanisms through which subject positions are constituted in relation to the patron. These modes are less the consequence of the poet's desire or beliefs than a symptom of concrete social relations. In a like manner, courtly poetry might also work to construct an antiaristocratic figure who speaks as other to the titled nobleman. In both cases, the opposition poetry/society is rendered invalid since the discursive practices that constitute society are always already present in the production and reception of the poem itself.

Despite the appeal of the *servilleta* anecdote—the story that Quevedo slipped a critique of royal policy under the king's napkin—it is generally agreed that he was heavily invested in the status quo and thus displayed few attitudes that might be construed as oppositional. Although there are sufficient grounds for arguing that Quevedo, like most courtier poets, was writing more for other men than for any historically verifiable lady, it would probably be unwarranted to join Ludwig Pfandl in dismissing all the amorous poetry as "courtly affectations lacking any literary interest" ("discreteos cortesanos sin ningún interés literario"). Such summary repudiations of Quevedo's poetic "authenticity" deserve some reconsideration given the curious fact that the *Epistolario* contains virtually all Quevedo's literary voices except those of the love poems, as Raimundo Lida noted some years ago.[6] Nevertheless, I would argue against Pfandl's more general point (that Quevedo's poetry is without interest) precisely on the grounds that the constricting environment of the court and the poet's strategies for dealing with a limited range of available subject positions make Quevedo's poetry extremely interesting to literary historians. Within these texts it is possible to see how aesthetic and social determinations affect the individual poem and ultimately give rise to the representation of anguish and repression we associate with Quevedo's poetic voices. The textual figuration of psychic states does not originate solely in the author's unified psyche. Rather, these states are produced by the writing of certain genres within a context that is inhospi-

[6]Referring to the *Epistolario*, Raimundo Lida noted: "And all of Quevedo—except the extraordinary Quevedo of the love poetry—appears in those occasional pages with a violent presence" ("Y todo Quevedo—salvo el extraordinario Quevedo de la poesía amorosa—aparece en esas páginas ocasionales con presencia violentísima"). *Letras hispánicas* (Mexico: Fondo de Cultura Económica, 1958), p. 122. The statement from Ludwig Pfandl's *Historia de la literatura nacional española en la Edad de Oro* (1929), trans. Jorge Rubio Balaguer, 2d ed. (Barcelona: G. Gili, 1952), pp. 520–23, reminds us that in our own century Quevedo's poetry has not consistently been given canonical status despite high praise from writers such as Pound and Borges. As late as 1940, Dámaso Alonso (following Mérimée) was of the opinion that "this is not the genre in which Quevedo displays his most outstanding characteristics" ("no es este género donde Quevedo ofrece características más señaladas"). *Ensayos sobre poesía española* (Madrid: Revista de Occidente, 1944), p. 188. Alonso would of course radically revise his judgment some ten years later.

table on the level of ideology to forms of the subject which took shape at the birth of that genre and in fact made the invention of that genre possible (here I am thinking especially of the sonnet). This is to say, the forms of subjectivity figured by the lyric speakers in Quevedo's works are directly mediated by the entire discursive formation that produces them, the ideologies of blood and virtue as well as such related factors as the competitive environment of the court and aristocratic expectations about poetic and literary characters.

That above all else Quevedo was one of the first modern writers who wrote for the market has only recently been placed in the foreground of critical discourse.[7] Exactly what "writing for the market" might have meant in seventeenth-century Spain is still being investigated by literary historians and sociologists. Clearly, almost all the major writers of the period were implicated in one way or the other in a cultural marketplace, but very few of them were as deeply engaged in a combination of artistic, bureaucratic, and political activities as Quevedo, and few produced such a wide variety of texts, encompassing virtually all genres. Quevedo, perhaps more than any of the well-known writers of this period, was part of an elite group that devoted much of its time to the composition of occasional pieces dealing with contemporary issues, even trading regularly in what was then the strongest literary currency—the sermon. Like others, he sought to cash in on fashion by hurriedly composing manuscripts and rushing them into circulation in the belief that notoriety would increase the potential for direct commissions (*obras de encargo*) from aristocratic patrons. Quevedo is one of the few writers who courted contemporary fashion and still managed to attain canonical status, although, as I've already suggested, he made a concentrated effort near the end of his life to purge many of the "less serious" texts from his complete works. Despite such last-minute image-making gestures, Quevedo and his colleagues were acutely aware that the complex economy of literary pro-

[7] The most coherent statement is in Pablo Jauralde Pou, "La transmisión de la obra de Quevedo," in *Homenaje a Quevedo*, ed. García de la Concha, pp. 163–72.

duction and consumption afforded the writei a twofold potential for profit: first, direct monetary compensation and, second, the much more important prospect of courtly favors and continuing patronage. What this use of the literary text as symbolic capital might tell us about Quevedo's poetry is what I want to discover. As Antonio Rodríguez-Moñino and, more recently, Pablo Jauralde Pou have convincingly shown, much of Quevedo's poetry was composed for and recited at aristocratic "academies," then copied by hired assistants and circulated in manuscript form within courtly circles.[8] Although some poems may have reached a wider audience (including members of the subordinate classes) through public readings of unbound manuscripts (*pliegos sueltos*) or printed anthologies such as that of Alonso de Espinosa (Valladolid, 1605), we can safely say that the vast majority of Quevedo's public was made up of aristocratic courtiers who in many cases were themselves poets. The composition of his audience corroborates our sense that Quevedo produced his lyrics for fellow producers, that is, for a select group of colleagues in the court who on one level were in continual competition for the rewards I have described. A poetry produced for such an audience derives less from the desire for authenticity or originality than from the externally imposed pressure to be "wittier" in a context in which poetic wit is a valuable commodity. The so-called anxiety of influence which has been outlined by Harold Bloom with regard to romantic poetry, therefore, is of only secondary importance in a discussion of early modern literature. The constraints influencing the poetic text in the seventeenth century have less to do with an oedipal conflict in which the work of earlier writers now viewed as classic inhibits the creativity of the ephebe poet than with the concrete pressures generated by the rivalry with contemporaries within the courtly economy of cultural products.

---

[8]See Antonio Rodríguez-Moñino, *Construcción crítica y realidad histórica en la poesía española de los siglos XVI y XVII* (Madrid: Castalia, 1965); and Pablo Jauralde Pou, "La poesía de Quevedo," in *Homenaje a Emilio Orozco* (Granada: Universidad de Granada, 1980).

Quevedo and the coterie of which he was a member depended
not only on literary but on political patronage as well. Thus the
postures and voices of the love poetry, that is, the subjects
figured there, are intimately linked to broader social concerns. A
love sonnet directed to a "lady" may in fact represent the poet's
relationship with his aristocratic patron; and the subject positions found in the poetic text result less from inspiration or desire
than from concrete social relations and writing strategies. To cite
only one example, we know Quevedo composed the sonnet
sequence to Lisi in large part during a temporary withdrawal
from the court (1619–1620); its composition in exile would seem
to corroborate the hypothesis that in the seventeenth century the
Petrarchan sonnet was the poetry of those who had lost at the
game of courtly politics.[9] Whether or not this was so as a general
principle, I suggest that poetic strategies need to be reread in
light of the continual shifts in the poet's political status. This is
not to equate Quevedo's love poems with allegory. As Blecua has
shown, many of the moral poems contain indirect references to
contemporary personages. The transactions between the amorous verse and the courtly environment, however, are not direct
correspondences. Rather, they are negotiated indirectly through
poetic language, in constructs such as the lyric subject, and in
that subject's stance toward an implicit addressee. Through the
process of textualization, recognizable aristocratic forms of subjectivity are figured forth in ways not unlike those that made subjects visible in the discourses of blood, the body, the family, and
the nation. As the poetic text is received by a group of courtly
readers, the subjects it produces are positioned by the institutional context from which they had derived and into which
they have been returned.

In this regard Quevedo's strict insistence on a definition of the
word *patrón* which places the protégé in the position of a slave is
especially interesting. It is not enough, he argues in the 1628 *Su*

---

[9]This important idea is developed for the early modern English context in
Leonard Tennenhouse, *Power on Display: The Politics of Shakespeare's Genres* (New
York: Methuen, 1986).

espada por Santiago (His sword for Saint James), to understand the patron as one who bestows favors (as had the supporters of Teresa de Avila's elevation to co–patron saint of Spain). Quevedo proposes a more rigorous signification: "A patron is he who rescues the slave or defends him with his aid" ("Patrón se dice el que rescata al esclavo o le defiende con su amparo").[10] On this view, the aristocratic sponsor not only offers support to the dependent writer/protégé but in fact "subjects" him (bestows subjectivity) by allowing him access, no matter how limited, to the privileges of courtly existence. Toward the end of his career, Quevedo was still seeking to be subjected by the most influential members of the ruling classes. In a letter written in 1633 to the wife of Philip IV's powerful favorite, Count-Duke Olivares, he claims: "I, madame, am nothing but what the Count, my lord, has undone in me, for what I once was has no value or worth: and if today I am something it is because of what I no longer am, thanks to God Our Lord and to his excellency" (Yo, señora, no soy otra cosa sino lo que el Conde, mi señor, ha deshecho en mí, puesto que lo que yo me era me tenía sin crédito y acabado: y si hoy soy algo es por lo que he dejado de ser, gracias a Dios Nuestro Señor y a su excelencia").[11] Here, the discourse of blood is temporarily effaced by a discourse of virtue which has less to do with the intrinsic worth of an "individual" than with the constitution of a subject through its relationships to other positions within the hierarchical network of privileges.

II

The use of traditional genres in a new context bears directly on a set of alienation effects that structure Quevedo's amorous poetry, especially the detachment felt by both poet and reader

[10]Francisco de Quevedo, *Su espada por Santiago*, in *Obras completas*, ed. Felicidad Buendía, vol. 1, 6th ed. (Madrid: Aguilar, 1966), p. 419.

[11]Quoted in Gregorio Marañón, *El conde-duque de Olivares: La pasión de mandar* (Madrid: Espasa-Calpe, 1959), p. 128.

caused by a heightened awareness of and familiarity with convention. Such sensitivity to the "literariness" of a text becomes especially acute when social and cultural conditions no longer correspond to those in which the conventional discourse first arose:

> [Aesthetic] material is not abandoned because it has become automatized in the artistic construction for psycho-technical reasons, but because it has ceased to be important in the ideological horizon. . . . If the material is important and timely, it has nothing to fear from repetition. . . . When material that has lost its full weight in the ideological horizon enters art, it must somehow compensate for the loss of its direct ideological importance. This compensation takes the form of a more intense and extensive orientation toward the purely literary context.[12]

The poet's sense that the inherited poetic discourse of Petrarchism, which by the seventeenth century was linked in Spain to the relatively repressed ideology of singularity (early modern individualism), was in conflict with dominant constructions of the subject creates an ironic distancing within the text itself. Writing at the intersection of a number of aesthetic traditions (classical, Petrarchan, the *cancionero*, and so on), Quevedo found himself reproducing irreconcilable postures and strategies whose cultural messages found only a vague resonance in their new context. On one level the peculiar anguish of the Quevedesque "lover" results from the attempt to define and delineate a voice representative of the poet's own personal and historical circumstance, but more important, it is the result of practicing a genre without an ideological "home." At certain key moments, for example, in poem 368, the poetic speaker seems to wander aimlessly within the bounds of a discourse utterly foreign to him:

> ¿Qué imagen de la muerte rigurosa
> qué sombra del infierno me maltrata?

---

[12] P. N. Medvedev and M. M. Bakhtin, *The Formal Method in Literary Scholarship*, trans. Albert J. Wehrle (Baltimore: Johns Hopkins University Press, 1978), p. 156.

¿Qué tirano curel me sigue y mata
con vengativa mano licenciosa?

¿Qué fantasma, en la noche temerosa,
el corazón del sueño me desata?
¿Quién te venga de mí, divina ingrata
más por mi mal que por tu bien hermosa?

¿Quién cuando, con dudoso pie y incierto
piso la soledad de aquesta arena,
me puebla de cuidados el desierto?

¿Quién el antiguo son de mi cadena
a mis orejas vuelve, si es tan cierto
que aun no te acuerdas tú de darme pena?

(What image of ruthless death, what shadow of hell mistreats me?
What cruel tyrant pursues and kills me with its wanton and venge-
ful hand? What phantom, in the frightful night unsettles the heart
of my sleep? Who takes vengeance on me, divine ingrate, more for
my evilness than for your beautiful welfare? Who fills me with
cares as I pace the solitude of this sand with an uncertain and
hesitant step? Who returns the ancient sound of my chains to my
ears if it is true that even you have forgotten to give me pain?)

Few subjects produced by the Petrarchan tradition have been
more estranged from the lyric situation that surrounds them and
from which they attempt to speak; the tone here is overwhelming
nonreality. From the "imagen" and "sombra" of the first stanza to
the "fantasma" of the second and the "dudoso pie y incierto" of
the third, the poem suggests a psychic state completely inhospitable to the construction of a subject premised on interiority and
individual authority, that project which Petrarch's text had haltingly signaled. The key to this particular poem should not be
sought in a theory of expression or in the poet's biography but in
his implication in specific aesthetic and social practices: aesthetic
because Quevedo's "serious" lyric voices often seem constrained
by the sonnet form and social because aristocratic tradition de-
manded that the successful man of letters exercise his hand at the
sonnet form within the economy of courtly literary production.

The automatization of poetic language as well as these other, perhaps more crucial mediations gives rise to a lyric speaker who is the antagonistic and "endemoniado" subject we associate with Quevedo. Within a project that too often transformed early modern poets into twentieth-century men, Dámaso Alonso was nevertheless able to take the important step of showing us the distance separating Quevedo from a precursor such as Petrarch: "A continuous anguish essentially, radically, removes Quevedo from any Petrarchan psychology, just as it removes him from all post-Renaissance formalisms" ("Una angustia continuada, arranca esencialmente, radicalmente, a Quevedo de todo psicologismo petrarquista, lo mismo que le arranca de todos los formalismos postrenacentistas").[13] But rather than posit the existence of a different "psychology" as the ground for my analysis of Quevedo's difference, I want instead to undertake an investigation of the ideology of poetic forms.

The sonnet is of particular interest for such an exercise both because its origins were inextricably linked to the social and aesthetic realities of the late Italian Middle Ages, the context for one of the earliest configurations of the modern poetic subject, and because Quevedo's literary models held it to be the most demanding form. According to the poet-rhetorician Fernando de Herrera, for example, the sonnet carried with it a wide range of expectations, "in which any small error is a great fault and in which no license whatsoever is allowed, or anything that offends the ear; and its brevity cannot be laziness or one single vain word" ("donde es grand culpa cualquier error pequeño; i donde no se permite licencia alguna, ni se consiente algo que ofenda las orejas; i la brevedad no sufre que sea ociosa, o vana una palabra sola").[14] One of the most pressing questions for a poet of Que-

---

[13] Dámaso Alonso, *Poesía española*, 4th ed. (Madrid: Gredos, 1962), p. 576.

[14] Fernando de Herrera, *Anotaciones* (1580), in *Garcilaso de la Vega y sus comentaristas*, ed. Antonio Gallego Morell (Granada: Universidad de Granada, 1966), no. 608, p. 511. Herrera's literary conservatism (as opposed to El Brocense, for example) has been noted by Elias Rivers. See "Some Ideas about Language and Poetry in Sixteenth-Century Spain," *Bulletin of Hispanic Studies* 61 (1984): 379–83.

vedo's talents was how to "open up" or renew such an over worked and inherently restrictive genre. This technical project has been studied in recent years by a number of scholars,[15] and it is generally accepted that in his attempt to revitalize or de-automatize tradition, Quevedo created a language that broke with the norms of conventional sonneteering and gave rise to mixed modes of poetic thought.

Within the limited sphere of aesthetic concerns, these mutations can be attributed to what Rosalie Colie has called the sonnet's aspirations, that this rigid poetic form proved "hospitable to the attitudes and subjects of literary kinds normally quite removed from it."[16] The more profound issue for Quevedo, I believe, is less the adaptability of the sonnet than the textual effects produced by attempting to speak through a literary form whose new ideological content was distinct from, if not completely antithetical to, its original content. That is, in Spain the cultural residue of the initial Petrarchan message, which persists in the seventeenth-century sonnet, is nonetheless embedded at the level of aristocratic discourse in an almost exclusively hostile environment. Whereas an important element in Petrarch's original project was the desire to problematize the idea of a subject determined by blood, Quevedo's culture continued to be deeply interested in maintaining such a subject. A conflict arises within the poem, generated by this uneasy tension between the original "deep structure" of the genre, together with all prior moments in which the sonnet was practiced, and the new sociocultural context, and this conflict undoes the traditional notion of poetry as an autonomous and privileged discourse. Whatever similarities

[15] Recent book-length studies of Quevedo's poetry include Paul Julian Smith, *Quevedo on Parnassus: Allusion and Theory in the Love Lyric* (London: Modern Humanities Research, 1987); D. Gareth Walters, *Francisco de Quevedo: Love Poet* (Cardiff: University of Wales and Washington, D.C.: Catholic University of America, 1985); Julián Olivares, *The Love Poetry of Francisco de Quevedo: An Aesthetic and Existential Study* (Cambridge: Cambridge University Press, 1983); and Ana María Snell, *Hacia el verbo: Signos y transignificación en la poesía de Quevedo* (London: Tamesis, 1982).

[16] Rosalie Colie, *The Resources of Kind: Genre Theory in the Renaissance* (Berkeley: University of California Press, 1973), p. 107.

Quevedo's poetic text might share with that of Petrarch or even Garcilaso, their respective societies were undeniably different; these differences are crucial to understanding individual poetic voices and what the sonnet's exchange value might have been in Quevedo's Spain.

I do not intend to argue for a progressive evolution of a subject on its way to becoming the bourgeois individual. Instead, I want to isolate particular moments when related elements were configured differently and thus produced variations on what would only much later become the modern individual. Therefore, I will attempt to trace only partially and somewhat arbitrarily the process Fredric Jameson has called "generic discontinuity," that is, the persistence of residual and often contradictory ideological messages in the reproduction of traditional cultural forms: "When such forms are reappropriated and refashioned in quite different social and cultural contexts, this message persists and must be fundamentally reckoned into the new form."[17] My starting point is the generally accepted view that within the history of the lyric the Petrarchan project virtually surpassed all previous love poetry. In the social configuration of the fourteenth century a still-powerful landowning aristocracy was confronted with a new and ever-growing merchant class, a class whose fortunes would rise and fall according to peculiar national predicaments for the next two hundred years. Thus, as one critic has written, the Petrarchan text appears within "an ideological infrastructure that will help it to effect the unconscious break, on the one hand, between chivalric virtue and the bourgeois 'I' (thus founding the new discourse, 'poetry') and, on the other hand, between religious 'nominalism/voluntarism' and the morality of the new figure ('the subject') that Petrarch will call 'man' " ("una infraestructura ideológica que le ayudará a efectuar la ruptura inconsciente por un lado entre la virtud caballeresca y el yo burgués [fundando así el nuevo discurso, 'la poesía'], y, por otro lado, entre el 'nominalismo/voluntarismo' religioso y la moral de

---

[17] Fredric Jameson, *The Political Unconscious: Narrative as a Socially Symbolic Act* (Ithaca: Cornell University Press, 1981), p. 141.

la nueva figura [el 'sujeto'], que Petrarca denominará 'hombre'").[18] It was this particular variant of "man" that was reproduced in writing only with great difficulty in the context of seventeenth-century Castilian culture. In Petrarch's hands, the love lyric initiated the construction of a new kind of subject that drew on the aesthetic elements of the Augustinian strategy of literary self-creation. Written in opposition to notions of fixed estates and nobility of blood, the poetic text figures a form of subjectivity premised on the discourse of virtue and posits an interiority that had appeared relatively unavailable to poets of previous centuries. The Petrarchan individual is not the religious subject of the *Confessions*, nor is he the multifaceted performer of the troubadour lyric who shifts masks according to his audience. Instead, through the rhetorical construction of a psychological introspection, the Petrarchan subject reveals a wide range of emotions, desires, and thoughts as he attempts to move through possible subject positions ranging from the lover to the poet to the Christian. This "internal crisis of debating selves" ultimately is resolved when "at last all selves of the book close debate and become a single Christian self."[19]

[18] Juan Carlos Rodríguez, *Teoría e historia de la producción ideológica: Las primeras literaturas burguesas (siglo XVI)* (Madrid: Akal, 1974), p. 92. In his excellent study, José María Pozuelo writes: "The intimist individualism of Petrarch, linked to concrete strophic and expressive forms . . . and a growing influence of Neoplatonism in the sixteenth century, would come definitively to inform the nature and generic features of Quevedo's concept of love" ("El individualismo intimista de Petrarca, unido a formas estróficas y expresivas concretas . . . y una creciente influencia del neoplatonismo en el siglo XVI, vendría a informar en definitiva el talante y los rasgos genéricos de la concepción amorosa quevediana"). *La lírica amorosa de Quevedo* (Murcia: Universidad de Murcia, 1977), p. 10. Ultimately, however, the historical and ideological context of Quevedo's poetry divorces its construction of subjectivity from a strictly Petrarchan model.

[19] Mariann S. Regan, "The Evolution of the Poet in Petrarch's *Canzoniere,*" *Philological Quarterly* 57 (1978): 23. Regan sees a unity in Petrarch's text, but others consider it less binding. Robert M. Durling refers to the "essentially provisional nature of the unification of the work. Perfect integration of man's life and art comes only when the mutable and imperfect is caught up into eternity." *The Figure of the Poet in Renaissance Epic* (Cambridge: Harvard University Press, 1965), p. 86.

Thus the sonnets constitute a poetic autobiography that interpellates a subject that "discovers itself" through writing with the guidance of the lady, achieves full presence, and ultimately situates its readers in an analogous position of stability and wholeness. Even in the earliest *rime*, the poetic voice represents a confident singularity that will always remain beyond reach in Quevedo's text:

> Una donna più bella assai che'l sole
> et più lucente et d'altrettanta etade
> con famosa beltade
> acerbo ancor mi trasse a la sua schiera.
>
> Questa in penseri in opre et in parole,
> però ch' è de le cose al mondo rade,
> questa per mille strade
> sempre inanzi mi fu leggiadra altera.
>
> Solo per lei tornai da quel ch'i'era;
> poi ch'i' soffersi gli occhi suoi da presso
> per suo amor m'er' io messo
> a faticosa impresa assai per tempo,
> tal che s'i'arrivo al disiato porto
> spero per lei gran tempo
> viver, quand' altri mi terrà per morto.

(A lady much more beautiful than the sun, more bright and of equal age, with famous beauty drew me to her ranks when I was still unripe. She in my thoughts, my works, and my words, since she is one of the things that are rare in the world, she along a thousand roads always guided me, gaily and proudly. Only for her I turned back from what I was; after I endured her eyes from close by, for her love I put myself early to difficult undertakings; so that if I reach the port I desire, I hope through her to live a long time, when people will suppose I am dead.)[20]

In effect, Petrarch's text was liberating because it radically broke with the traditional notions of a subject determined by the

[20]Francesco Petrarca, *Petrarch's Lyric Poems: The "Rime Sparse" and Other Lyrics*, ed. and trans. Robert M. Durling (Cambridge: Harvard University Press, 1976), pp. 226–27.

community of blood or by family-clan relations, and objectively articulated the idea of an autonomous individual who posits virtue and interiority as the essential qualities. This "revolutionary" subject was able to appear in writing in conjunction with two other textual supports: first, the idea of a privileged community of *anime belle* which allows for communication not only with others but also with nature and with love itself—"ma pur sì aspre avie né sì selvagge / cercar non so ch'Amor non venga sempre / ragionando con meco, et io con lui" ("but still I cannot seek paths so harsh or so savage that Love does not always come along discoursing with me and I with him")—and, second, the figure of the lady as a fixed and stable center around which the singular individual can take shape. This center serves as a point of reference and of presence even after the death of Laura: "Là v'io seggia d'amor pensoso et scriva / lei che 'l Ciel ne mostrò, terra n'asconde / veggio et odo et intendo ch'ancor viva / di sì lontano, a'sospir miei responde" ("Where I am sitting in thoughts of love and writing, I see her whom Heaven showed us and the earth hides from us, I see and hear and understand her, for, still alive, from far away she replies to my sighs").[21]

The best-known offspring of Petrarch in Spain, as well as the link between Petrarch and poets who more directly influenced Quevedo, is Garcilaso de la Vega (1503–1536). In his literary production the attempt to individualize and privatize poetic subjectivity achieves a heightened intensity, although he is probably not the first poet on the Iberian peninsula to use such strategies. Indeed, within an earlier critical language, convincing cases have been made for anticipatory forms of the "individual" in the texts of both Juan de Mena and Ausias March.[22] But never before in Spanish poetry had a speaker been constructed relatively apart from discourses of blood and status. Imbued with the Neoplatonism of the reigning Italian philosophers (Bembo, Castiglione,

[21]Petrarca, poems 35 and 279, ibid., pp. 95, 459.
[22]See, for example, María Rosa Lida de Malkiel, *Juan de Mena: Poeta del prerrenacimiento español* (México: Nueva Revista de Filología Hispánica, 1950); and Karl Vossler on March in *La soledad en la poesía española* (Madrid: Revista de Occidente, 1941).

and others) and following the example of Petrarch, Garcilaso cultivated the idea of the *alma bella* who stood apart from traditional hierarchies.

> Hermosas ninfas que, en el río metidas,
> contentas habitáis en las moradas
> de relucientes piedras fabricadas
> y en colunas de vidro sostenidas:
>   agora estéis labrando embebecidas,
> o tejiendo las telas delicadas;
> agora unas con otras apartadas,
> contándoos los amores y las vidas;
>   dejad un rato la labor, alzando
> vuestras rubias cabezas a mirarme,
> y no os detendréis mucho, según ando;
>   que o no podréis de lástima escucharme,
> o convertido en agua aquí llorando,
> podréis allá de espacio consolarme.

(Lovely nymphs who, deep in the river, live happily in mansions built of shining stones and upheld by crystal columns: whether you are now busily embroidering or weaving fine fabrics, or whether in little groups you are telling one another of your loves and lives, lay aside your work for a moment, raising your golden heads to look at me, and it won't take you long, in my sad state; for either you'll be too sorry to listen, or else, changed into water by weeping here, you'll have plenty of time to console me down there.)[23]

For the lyric subject here, there is no hopeless isolation or permanent entrapment as in Quevedo's text but a continual fluidity of forms and the comforting presence of the natural world. It is the subject's interpellation by a discourse of undifferentiated nature rather than caste purity that sets him apart from his precursors in Castilian writing. In a further gesture toward a Petrarchan subjectivity, the speaker's unique identity in the eclogues is articu-

---

[23] Garcilaso de la Vega, sonnet 11, in Gallego Morell, *Garcilaso de la Vega*, p. 92, hereafter cited in the text. Translation by Rivers, *Renaissance and Baroque Poetry*, p. 36.

lated not through blood or clan affiliations but through the community of shepherds, who imagine a different kind of solidarity founded on the idea of personal suffering.

Even when the comfort provided by the community is lacking in Garcilaso, and the speaker is perceived to be "imprisoned and captive and alone in foreign lands" ("preso y forzado y sólo en tierra ajena"), the communicative power of writing or desire itself liberates him and grants him a kind of heroic subjectivity:

> Un rato se levanta mi esperanza.
> Tan cansada de haberse levantado
> torna a caer, que deja, mal mi grado,
> libre el lugar a la desconfianza.
> ¿Quién sufrirá tan áspera mudanza
> del bien al mal? ¡Oh, corazón cansado!
> esfuerza en la miseria de tu estado,
> que tras fortuna suele haber bonanza.
> Yo mismo emprenderé a fuerza de brazos
> romper un monte, que otro no rompiera,
> de mil inconvenientes muy espeso.
> Muerte, prisión no pueden, ni embarazos,
> quitarme de ir a veros, como quiera,
> desnudo espiritu o hombre en carne y hueso.
>
> (sonnet 4)

(My hopes are raised for a while. Exhausted from having been raised, they fall again, and against my will give rein to suspicion. Who could withstand such a shocking change from good to evil? Oh, weary heart! In the misery of your condition be strong, for after a storm there is usually fair weather. I myself will attempt by force of arms to destroy a mountain, thick with a thousand impediments, that no one else can destroy. Neither prison, death, nor obstacles can stop me from seeing you, whether it be as pure spirit or as a man of flesh and blood.)

The two quatrains, with their fluctuating emotional states, remind us of the play of contrarieties which afflicts most lyric subjects in the Petrarchan tradition, including those associated with the name of Quevedo. But it is the hopeful note of line 8 that

marks one of the major differences between Quevedo and Garcilaso. The tercets, in which the speaker declares his willingness to
overcome any obstacle, emphasize this difference to an even
greater degree. Despite Quevedo's best-known speaker, who,
following Propertius, is consumed by desire, yet continues to
love as "enamored dust" ("polvo enamorado"), more often than
not Quevedo's poetic subjects are overwhelmed by insurmount-
able obstacles. In Garcilaso, however, desire for the beloved,
within the Neoplatonic system of the movement of souls, precludes inescapable entrapment even if the attendant struggle at
times produces a "corazón cansado." In a sense, Garcilaso's lyric
subject is the prisoner of love we met in Petrarch's text: the lady
functions as the source of pain and thus is the other, the object
against which the construction of subjectivity takes place. But
for the voice in Garcilaso there always exists "the force of desire
as much as the desperate conviction to break any obstacle that
opposes itself to fusion, whatever blocks departure, the need
to 'open the way to seeing'" ("tanto la fuerza del deseo como
la convicción desesperada de romper cualquier obstáculo que
se oponga a la fusión, cualquier cosa que impida la salida, la
necesidad de 'abrir camino' para 'ver'").[24] It is precisely when
the function of the poetic speaker is premised on a stable self-
consciousness as in the previous poem ("pure spirit or man of
flesh and blood") or through a unified vision that a fixed point of
reference is produced within the text. Such a reference point
engages the world from its position of full presence and thus is
prerequisite to any construction of an imaginary individualism.

In contrast, one of the distinguishing marks of Quevedo's
canonical poetry is the lack of a center and the relative absence of
a stable consciousness within the textual economy of the poem.
Thus the powerful resonances produced by rereading Garcilaso's sonnet 36 in the shadow of Quevedo:

> A la entrada de un valle, en un desierto,
> do nadie atravesaba ni se vía

[24]Rodríguez, *Teoría e historia*, p. 191.

vi que con estrañeza un can hacía
estremos de dolor con desconcierto;
ahora suelta el llanto al cielo abierto,
ora va rastreando por la vía;
camina, vuelve, para, y todavía
quedaba desmayado como muerto.
  Y fué que se apartó de su presencia
su amo, y no le hallaba, y esto siente;
mirad hasta dó llega el mal de ausencia.
  Movióme a compasión ver su accidente;
díjele: Lastimado, ten paciencia,
que yo alcanzo razón, y estoy ausente.

(At the entrance to a valley in a desert where no one traveled or was seen, I saw with wonder that a dog in confusion unleashed his pain; now he lets loose his cry to the open sky, now he drags himself along the road; he walks, turns, stops, and still he remained stunned as if he were dead. It so happened that his master had abandoned him, and the dog suffers not finding his master. Look how extreme the pain of absence can be. His predicament moved me to compassion; I said to him: Pitiful one, have patience, for I too am absent and remain sane.)

Garcilaso's sonnet can be read as an account of two distinct moments in the history of Spanish poetry; it brings together the poetic subjects of Garcilaso and Quevedo in a relationship of alterity that marks the ideological difference between their respective cultures. The first voice, entering the deserted and barren space where Quevedo's speaker habitually dwells, happens on a dog who has been separated from his master. For the purposes of a comparative reading, let us say that the figure of the dog functions as a representation of the majority of Quevedo's voices. Complaining to the open sky and not receiving any response, running, stopping, turning in circles, finally freezing in total desperation ("quedaba desmayado como muerto"), the dogs feels the complete absence of his master (the reference point upon which his identity is predicated) and panics. The speaking subject of Garcilaso's text views this behavior with a sense of "wonder" ("extrañeza") because, although he too suffers from the

122 Contradictory Subjects

absence of his lady, he is able to "remain sane," and so he counsels the terrified animal to have patience. The Quevedesque subject, however, has no patience. He is the "pitiful one" ("lastimado") of Garcilaso's poem made human, who, having "in confusion unleashed his pain" ("hacía estremos de dolor con desconcierto"), ultimately succumbs to the profound "pain of absence" ("mal de ausencia").

As one of the last poets of the generation bridging the eras of Garcilaso and Quevedo, Fernando de Herrera (1534–1597) stands as both model and antimodel to Quevedo's project. Despite surface similarities, the two poets were separated by fundamental differences in historical context and aesthetic intention, Herrera being one of the last Spanish poets whose literary career was in effect made possible by a Renaissance-style court and patron, the count of Gelves. Much of Herrera's poetry is therefore an elaboration of certain of Garcilaso's poetic gestures. To cite only one example, if we recall the "corazón cansado" of Garcilaso's sonnet 4, we are immediately struck by the resonances in Herrera's first elegy:

> al lloroso exercicio del cuidado
> buelvo, de mis trabajos perseguido;
> de vida sí, no de passión cansado.[25]

(I return to the tearful practice of suffering, persecuted by my cares, exhausted not by passion but by life.)

Here, the speaker is no longer tired of desire's trials but of life itself. Covarrubias defines *cansado* as "fatigued and broken in body" ("fatigado en el cuerpo y quebrantado") and considers it a corruption of the Latin *quatio*, "to shatter."[26] Herrera's speaker, then, is both tired and shattered by existence. Quevedo's subject, however, presents us with an even more fragmented identity.

---

[25]Fernando de Herrera, *Poesía castellana original completa*, ed. Cristóbal Cuevas (Madrid: Cátedra, 1985), p. 362.
[26]Covarrubias, *Tesoro de la lengua* (1611).

Oreste Macrí has described how the center (whether it be the lady or art, as in Petrarch and Garcilaso, or nature, as in Francisco de la Torre) tends to recede in the poetry of Herrera. In many of the lyric situations, the kind of confusion and psychological chaos associated with Quevedo's subject is evident, a textual effect produced by the intensification of certain poetic conventions,

> exacerbating at the ground of the senses and the intellect the impressions and feelings of the primitive "prison of love." . . . The poet always remains doubtful in his confused state. Without light, without a guide, lost in confusion, he begs desire for a moment of truce in the commotion of his confused life, fearful of so much confusion; a Light offers him aid from afar, but it disappears when he approaches.

> (exacerbando en las raíces de los sentidos y del intelecto las impresiones y los sentimientos de la atávica "cárcel de amor." . . . El poeta siempre permanece dubitante en su confuso sentir. Sin luz, sin guía, perdido en la confusión, implora un instante de tregua al deseo en las revueltas de su confusa vida, temeroso de tanta confusión; una Luz le presta ayuda desde lejos, pero desaparece cuando se acerca.)[27]

This analysis by one of Herrera's most insightful commentators traces the formation of subjectivity through verses such as "I am full of doubt in my confused feelings" ("dudoso estoy en confuso sentimiento"), "I lived a long while lost in confusion" ("Viví gran tiempo en confusión perdido"), and others, suggesting that Herrera's subject continues the tradition of the "prisoner of love," which locates the source of the lover's anguish in a fixed center figured by the lady. Just as Petrarch's Laura is always implicitly present even after her death, the beloved in Herrera (Luz) acts as the reference point that makes possible both the subject in pain and the subject redeemed. More generally, the omnipresence of Luz gives Herrera's text its "lightness" in contrast to the foreboding darkness and heaviness of Quevedo's love lyrics. If the

[27] Oreste Macrí, *Fernando de Herrera*, 2d ed. (Madrid: Gredos, 1972), p. 478.

speaker is comforted by Luz only to have her withdraw when he approaches, he nevertheless has the knowledge that subjectivity can be constructed around the potential for a relationship with the beloved. Indeed, the subject in Herrera is always seen in connection with an absolute (the lady) and cannot be considered fully realized until he is inserted into that imaginary realm. The constructive power of the speaker's fixed subject position in relation to the other produces the same kind of erotic heroism we have seen at work in Garcilaso's sonnet 4. Herrera's subject, who articulated a variation of such heroism in his well-known patriotic poetry, persists in his desire against all odds:

> Sigo al fin mi furor, porque mudarme
> no es onra ya, ni justo que s'estime
> tan mal de quien tan bien rindió su pecho.
>
> (sonnet 1)

(I pursue my fury to the end because to waver is dishonorable, nor is it just that one who surrendered himself so fully should be esteemed so low.)

> Mas ya tarde mis lástimas contemplo.
> Pero si muero, porque osé, perdido,
> jamás a igual empresa osó algún ombre.
>
> (sonnet 43)

(Yet later I contemplate my sorrows. But if I die lost because I dared, no other man has ever attempted such a feat.)

> No temo, i oso todo libremente,
> porqu' es al coraçón desesperado
> la ostinación impenetrable escudo.
>
> (sonnet 51)

(I fear not and freely dare all because to the desperate heart obstinacy is an impenetrable shield.)

Here the lover is able to defy the afflictions that persecute him, because they always emanate from a known source that once physically located offers the possibility of union. Despite those rare situations in which the speaker is alone or surrounded— "fear and ice surrounded me" ("me cercó el temor i el ielo") (sonnet 37)—the lady's name is always implicitly centering the text even if it is in absentia:

> Bolví; halléme solo i entre abrojos,
> i, en vez de luz, cercado de tiniebla,
> i en lágrimas ardientes convertidos.
>
> (sonnet 14)

(I turned and found myself among thorns and surrounded by darkness instead of light and transformed into burning tears.)

The "luz" situated in the very center of the tercet establishes a palliative reference point rarely found in Quevedo's text. The more typical lyric subject in Herrera, however, is not under siege; he is a wandering lover in search of the center to which I have been referring. The Neoplatonic emphasis on movement as a positive force by which the soul liberates itself from its captivity is figured in Herrera's text by the speaker's continual traversing of the "passos," "vías," "camino," and "senda" of the poetic landscape. This contrasts sharply with the retreating toward empty spaces of the Quevedesque subject. The so-called "frénésie du mouvement" noted by Mas and others in Quevedo's later prose works, a language-based action that works to destroy the referent, is effectively contained by the poetic form, which forces the speaker in on himself instead of allowing him access to the world.

In general, the Quevedesque "lover" displays little of the rich interiority and self-determination of previous poets in the sonnet tradition. In fact, he seems to lack a clear understanding of love's language. Instead of being a man to whom a benign universe speaks directly (as it had in the texts of Garcilaso, Herrera, and others), Quevedo's speaker openly admits his ignorance:

Esta fuente me habla, mas no entiendo
su lenguaje, ni sé lo que razona;
sé que habla de amor, y que blasona
de verme a su pesar por Flori ardiendo.
(poem 351)

(This fountain speaks to me, but I do not understand its language,
nor do I know what it proposes; I know that it speaks of love and
that it boasts of seeing me burning for Flori.)

Yo confieso de mí que no entendía
el secreto lenguaje de los ojos.
(poem 386)

(I confess I did not understand the secret language of the eyes.)

This sense of being out of place within the very discourse in
which he is inscribed, of being incapable of recapturing a lost
presence, seems to produce extreme physical and psychological
suffering in the speaker. In reality, the opposition at work here
is between the speaking voice and the very discourse through
which it is constituted. By means of a relatively simple stylistic
exaggeration of inherited commonplaces, the poem figures forth
complex discursive antagonisms and in so doing produces a new
kind of subject that is markedly singular in comparison to those
of earlier and even contemporary poets:

Dejad que a voces diga el bien que pierdo
si con mi llanto a lástima os provoco,
y permitidme hacer cosas de loco:
que parezco muy mal amante y cuerdo.

La red que rompo y la prisión que muerdo
y el tirano rigor que adoro y toco,
para mostrar mi pena son muy poco,
si por mi mal de lo que fui me acuerdo.

Oiganme todos: consentid siquiera
que, harto de esperar y de quejarme,
pues in premio viví, sin juicio muera.

De gritar solamente quiero hartarme.
Sepa de mí, a lo menos, esta fiera
que he podido morir, y no mudarme.

(poem 360)

(If I provoke you with my painful lament, let me proclaim the good
I am losing and allow me to act like a madman, for I make a poor
sane lover. The net I tear and the bonds I gnaw and the harsh chain
I adore and touch are unable to reveal my pain when I sadly recall
what I once was. All of you listen: since I lived without reward and
am now tired of hoping and complaining, permit me to die insane.
I want only to exhaust myself screaming. Let this beast at least
know that I was able to die without wavering.)

The alienation of this speaker seems readily apparent, and love,
which in the Petrarchan sonnet mitigates all pain, here has lost
its healing powers. The use of the imperative (lines 1, 3, and 9)
aggravates the sense of separation not only from the beloved but
from the implicit reader as well; the plural form (especially the
"Oiganme todos" of line 9) vividly conveys the speaker's aggressive posture toward his potential public. This, in fact, is a lyric
subject who reaches the limits of his own frustration, rejects the
possibility of any salutary camaraderie (for example, Garcilaso's
shepherds), and simply asks to be allowed to go mad. That he
feels compelled to confront and request the permission of some
unspecified authority underscores what I have been saying about
the pressure of the ideological content of inherited forms and
their potential for generating contradictions within contemporary poetic discourse.[28]

[28] With regard to Góngora's *peregrino*, John Beverley has written: "Like Cervantes' hero, the pilgrim represents a strategy of invention, the vehicle for the
creation of a possible discourse in a moment of history in which all models and
canons have suddenly become obsolete and no longer serve to represent the
writer's own contingencies and contradictions, much less the shape and mean-

What is clear from this brief genealogy of the lyric subject in Spain is that, rather than a progressive evolution toward the figure of the individual, there was variation and mutation according to the conjuncture of discursive elements and the writer's place within them. This pattern has a direct effect on our understanding of Quevedo's lyric speaker, for if a poet is constrained by a literary inheritance that can be spoken only haltingly in the contemporary situation and also by a dominant discourse that allots emotions according to one's status in a hierarchy, he finds himself drawing poetic speakers from a severely limited pool of subject types. In seventeenth-century Spain, the notion of individual autonomy which Renaissance humanism had struggled to elaborate is repressed both within textualization and through cultural practices—hence the trapped and solitary figure associated with much of the art of the period, "an individual of unknown or negated intimacy (the total lack of intimacy in the literary creations of the Baroque was clearly pointed out by Tierno Galván); an individual anonymous to others, closed off and without ties" ("individuo de intimidad desconocida o negada (la total falta de intimidad en las creaciones literarias del Barroco fue agudamente señalada por Tierno Galván); individuo anónimo para los demás, cerrado y sin vínculos").[29] Put another way, the subject that appears in Quevedo's poetic discourse is hopelessly reduced to a solitude rooted in forms of social containment, not metaphysical malaise. We can only imagine the destructive effects of an aristocratic ideology that discredited any textual

---

ing of his culture and society." *Aspects of Góngora's "Soledades"* (Amsterdam: John Benjamins, 1980), p. 69. The makeup of the Quevedesque "lover," although fundamentally a product of the same problematic that informs the texts of other writers of the period, strikes us as qualitatively different because of the poet's participation in a number of unusually varied cultural and political practices.

[29] Maravall, *La cultura del Barroco*, pp. 413–14. Elsewhere Maravall adds: "Man can be realized only through strict compliance with the obligations of one's position in aristocratic society, not by being faithful to an intimate consciousness" ("sólo en el acatamiento a las obligaciones de su puesto en ese sistema de la sociedad aristocrática, se realiza el hombre; no en la fidelidad a una conciencia íntima"). *Teatro y literatura*, pp. 97–98.

representation of individuality (*singularidad*) or of a strictly private sphere, especially for a love poet in the Petrarchan tradition. Thus Quevedo's "lover" sings in the overcrowded chorus of Petrarchism in a voice that is significantly off-key, precisely because the Petrarchan mode directly contradicts the hegemonic discourse of the ruling social groups to which the poet aspired and which constituted his public. Petrarch's notion of a "free" and virtuous individual now attempts to survive within a cultural context whose investment in the ideology of blood and status programmatically blocked the construction of such a figure. It is not so much that "the [multifaceted and autonomous] subject does not appear anywhere; it is difficult for an ideological matrix to produce what it does not contain" ("el sujeto no aparece por ninguna parte y difícilmente una matriz ideológica puede producir lo que no tiene").[30] Rather, the problem is that the traces of an emergent form of subjectivity now functioned in a hostile environment. The rearticulation of those traces might well produce alternative forms of the subject, and indeed some of these were represented in other literary texts of the period (for example, by Cervantes). In the field of poetry, however, the pressure to adhere to traditional subject positions while reproducing a literary form such as the sonnet gives rise in Quevedo's case to lyric voices caught in a network of contradictory codes. Predictably perhaps, Quevedo expressed this profound sense of entrapment most strongly not in a sonnet but in the popular form of the *jácara*:

> Todo este mundo es prisiones;
> todo es cárcel y penar;
> los dineros están presos
> en la bolsa donde están;
>   la cuba es cárcel del vino,
> la troj es cárcel del pan,
> la cáscara, de las frutas,
> y la espina, del rosal.

[30] Rodríguez, *Teoría e historia*, p. 122.

> Las cercas y las murallas
> cárcel son de la ciudad;
> el cuerpo es cárcel de l'alma,
> y de la tierra, la mar;
> del mar es cárcel la orilla,
> y en el orden que hoy están,
> es un cielo de otro cielo
> una cárcel de cristal.
> Del aire es cárcel el fuelle,
> y del fuego, el pedernal;
> preso está el oro en la mina;
> preso el diamante en Ceilán.
>
> (poem 856)

(All this world is chains, all is prison and sorrow; money is imprisoned in the purse in which it lies; the barrel is the wine's
prison, the bin that of bread, the skin encloses the fruit, and the
thorn the rosebush. The walls and ramparts are the city's prison,
the body the prison of the soul, and the sea that of the land; the
shore is the ocean's jail, and in the order they are in today, one
heavenly sphere is the crystalline prison of the other. The bellows
is a prison to the air, and the flint that of fire; gold is imprisoned in
the mine, the diamond imprisoned in Ceylon.)

The extended metaphor essentially amplifies the condition of the
Quevedesque poetic subject to include all of everyday life, eventually enclosing the four elements themselves. The moral commonplace of line 11 plays a relatively insignificant role against
the more striking images of the sea entrapping the land, the shore
the sea, and ultimately the concentric spheres of the Aristotelian
universe containing one another.

The consequences of this "writing against oneself" (Raimundo
Lida's phrase "Quevedo contra Quevedo, siempre" is especially
suggestive here) are the contradictory nature of the Quevedesque
"lover" and the continuing frustration of the desire for a totalized
portrait of the poet himself. That the subject seems to be lost
within his own lyric situation cannot be attributed solely to the
dominance of paradox and oxymoron in the poetry of the period
or to individual psychology alone. Rather, the pressures of the

cultural market and especially the obligatory use of genres that lacked ideological foundation inhibited the representation of alternative subject positions and gave rise to the exaggerated figures of hyperbole, metonymy, and what Dámaso Alonso once called an "affective boldness" or ripping apart (*desgarrón afectivo*). In Quevedo's text, the conventional anguish of the Petrarchan lover is rewritten as an ontological problem since suitable replacements for now-unsuitable concepts of the subject are simply unavailable in the present context: "I am a was, a will be, and an exhausted is" ("Soy un fue, un será, y un es cansado"). At best, at those points where new forms do struggle to take shape, they are dismissed by the ruling elites as inferior, heretical, or insane. But the problem of Quevedo's "other" voices leads us away from the sonnet and toward those poetic forms such as the *jácara*, which moved from popular discourse to the foreground of aristocratic culture in the crucial moment of the 1590s and ultimately gave shape to the marginal "new" subjects of the satirical and burlesque verse. [31]

III

As I have shown in my discussion of blood and the body, physiological discourse positioned women in a space (inferior and "to the left") separate from that occupied by the masculine. This was a cultural strategy designed less to create distinctions based on gender than to mark the differences between males. Through a process of inversion, the Petrarchan mode as it was handled by Quevedo reproduced this strict hierarchy by increasing the distance between the female addressee and the male

[31] By claiming that Quevedo's obsession with the construction of the emergent individual is figured most clearly in the noncanonical picaresque poems, I follow Gramsci's insight that a writer's "truth" often resides in the most improbable texts: "In every personality there is one dominant and predominant activity: it is here that his thought must be looked for, in a form that is more often than not implicit and at times even in contradiction with what is professly expressed." *Selections from the Prison Notebooks*, p. 403.

speaker. Lyric subjectivity in Quevedo depends almost exclusively on the speaker's inability to make contact with the lady who is seen as source of all suffering, for the drive toward interiority could not be accomplished without the agonistic relationship determined by her unattainable presence. By paraphrasing Don Quixote's explanation of why courtly poets invent ladies ("to give subject to their verses") and employing both meanings of the Spanish *sujeto* ("topic" and "subject"), we can say that the poetic subject could not appear without the opposition of an alterity within the text. For the aristocratic poet, the extratextual reality of the female addressee, on which nineteenth-century critics speculated, was a relatively unimportant issue. In the seventeenth century, even an impoverished hidalgo understood the function of the "lady":

> Do you think that the Amaryllises, the Phyllises, Sylvias, Dianas, Galateas, Phyllidas, and all the rest that books and ballads and barbers' shops and theatres are so full of, were really flesh-and-blood ladies, and the mistresses of the writers who wrote about them? Not a bit of it. Most of them were invented to serve as subjects for verses, and so that the poets might be taken for lovers, or men capable of being so.

> (¿Piensas tú que las Amariles, las Filis, las Silvias, las Dianas, las Galateas, las Alidas y otras tales de que los libros, los romances, las tiendas de los barberos, los teatros de las comedias, están llenos, fueron verdaderamente damas de carne y hueso, y de aquellos que las celebran y celebraron? No, por cierto, sino que las más se las fingen, por dar subjeto a sus versos, y porque los tengan por enamorados y por hombres que tienen valor para serlo.) (*Don Quixote*, 1:25)

The figure of woman, then, was constructed as an other against which the "individual" (male and aristocratic) could take shape. A similar process is at work in the picaresque poetry, but the new object of desire, the picaro, stands in a marginalized and excluded position with regard to dominant culture precisely because he represents qualities associated with emerging forms of the subject.

Carlos Blanco Aguinaga's insight is of fundamental impor
tance for a project such as my own, despite its existentialist
language:

> A clearly structured world view cannot run unnecessary risks
> produced by the violence of a passing delirium. Only words re-
> main from that inexplicable moment: "My eyes may be closed by
> the final..." But in these words we clearly see man's vibrant effort
> to create himself, or to find once again his place in the World.
> Against every restriction. A senseless resistance perhaps; an an-
> guished affirmation of the value of the realm of Time.
>
> (No puede una visión del mundo claramente estructurada correr
> riesgos innecesarios frente a la violencia de un delirio pasajero. De
> aquel momento inexplicable sólo quedan palabras: "Cerrar podrá
> mis ojos la postrera..." Pero en ellas—los vemos claramente noso-
> tros—el vibrante esfuerzo del hombre por crearse, o volver a
> encontrar, su sentido en el Mundo. Contra cualquier ley severa.
> Rebelión quizá insensata; angustiosa afirmación del valor de las
> cosas del Tiempo.)[32]

As I have been claiming all along, what in an earlier critical
moment was viewed as "man's vibrant effort to create himself" is
better understood in Quevedo's poetry as the effect of competing
forms of subjectivity at work within the text. What we must
consider now is that the poet's various attempts to break with
traditional forms and modes of thought, his emphasis on mate
rial reality, all constituted much more than a "passing delirium."
What seems to be a short-lived delirium in the poetry is in fact a
gesture toward alternative forms of the subject, a gesture produced by profound contradictions in the thinking of the poet and
in aristocratic culture as a whole. In a dual ideological operation,

[32]Carlos Blanco Aguinaga, "Dos sonetos del siglo XVII: Amor-locura en
Quevedo y Sor Juana," *Modern Language Notes* 77 (1962):153. Blanco also refers
to "the suspicion that a dark and perhaps all too conventional force sought to
break the limits of an ideology otherwise firmly established in Quevedo's epoch
and in Quevedo himself" ("la sospecha de que una fuerza oscura y quizá
demasiado convencional quisiera romper los moldes de una ideología por lo
demás fuertemente establecida, en la época de Quevedo y en Quevedo mismo").

Quevedo's poetry employs the picaresque figure to refine the boundaries of the aristocratic subject as it simultaneously foregrounds and potentializes (that is, gives voice to) those qualities condemned and excluded by dominant forms of subjectivity. This dialectical movement, which was understood by an essentially romantic criticism as a question of psychological depth (hence the attribution to the author of a "split personality" or even schizophrenia), is in fact a kind of warfare being fought on the sociocultural battlefield of subjectivity itself.

Pérez de Montalbán retells a story, now part of Golden Age lore, of Lope de Vega as a child running away from home to live the life of a picaro. In a curious way, Quevedo the poet often strikes us as another aristocratic writer attracted to the kind of existence represented by his picaresque characters. The anguished entrapment of the speaker we have seen in the amorous verse is alleviated by recasting subjectivity in the nonaristocratic forms of the *letrilla* and the *jácara*. The latter term signified not only a poetic form but an entire subgroup of society, the *jaques*, or picaros. The immense popularity of the *jácara* in the early 1600s, whose influence, according to Rafael Salillas, rivaled that of the chivalric novel on an earlier period, has yet to be satisfactorily explained by literary historians.[33] What we can say with certainty is that all forms of the so-called *poesía rufianesca* were widely received by virtually every level of society and that the genre itself constituted a heteroglossia that drew on a diverse field of cultural products ranging from the *zéjel* to the *villancico*.

Some years ago Amédée Mas noted the paradoxical appeal for a courtly public and for Quevedo himself of the marginal figures who inhabit these texts. At first dismissing the sympathy with which Quevedo treats his picaros as merely the poet's indulgence of his own creations, Mas goes on to suggest that there is something more serious at work: "The attraction is none other than that which an author may feel toward his character when it is colorful and lends itself to lively scenes. This attraction on the artistic level can be compatible with the most complete contempt

[33] Rafael Salillas, "Poesía rufianesca," *Revue hispanique* 13 (1905): 21.

on the human level. It is true, on the other hand, that this contempt can be reconciled in turn with sensual enjoyment... all this leads one to believe that the pleasure involves a certain affinity."[34] Early in the seventeenth century Juan Valladares had referred to "the agreeable picaro" ("el agradable pícaro"). The potential irony in such a remark does not efface its underlying ambivalence. Lázaro Carreter's contention that the picaresque underworld (*el hampa*) "offers great attractions to its observer" ("ofrece grandes atractivos para el contemplador") is corroborated by the historical facts Bataillon reports: at the turn of the seventeenth century this subculture attracted members from all levels of society and "even exercised its irresistible seduction over the youth of the upper class" ("ejercía incluso su irresistible seducción sobre jóvenes de la buena sociedad").[35] Within the field of literature, we need only recall the anonymous poem "La vida del pícaro" of 1601 or the strangely deironized praise of alternative life-styles found in Mateo Alemán's *Guzmán de Alfarache*. It is certainly true that Quevedo offers the picaresque figure to his courtly audience as an object of derision—a strategy even more explicitly at work in *El Buscón*. And it is no less the case that the reality of so-called picaresque freedom was more often than not a brutal, physically deprived existence on the margins of society. But it must also be said that those qualities represented in an extreme form by the picaro could not help but appeal to a writer intensely aware of the limitations on what the subject could be within aristocratic social practice and literary discourse.

---

[34] Amédée Mas, *La caricature de la femme, du mariage, et de l'amour dans l'oeuvre de Quevedo* (Paris: Hispanoamericanas, 1957), pp. 333–34.
[35] F. Lázaro Carreter, *Estilo barroco y personalidad creadora: Góngora, Quevedo, Lope de Vega*, 3d ed. (Madrid: Cátedra, 1977), p. 94; Bataillon, *Pícaros y picaresca*, p. 176. Bataillon records the following quotation from the spurious continuation (1602) of the *Guzmán*: "I saw it clearly in my picaresque life with many who professed it, the sons of good parents, parents who later tried to get them back, but were unable to do so because freedom and self-will are so intoxicating" ("Bien lo eché de ver en mi vida picaresca, que muchos hijos de buenos padres que la profesaban, aunque después los quisieron recoger, no hubo remedio, tal es el bebedizo de la libertad y propia voluntad"). *Pícaros y picaresca*, p. 176.

It is not surprising, therefore, to find that in many cases the marginal figures who represent an unconventional existence in the poetry are themselves prisoners, speaking from either prison or the galleys. The process by which the dominant social groups exclude and contain subordinate groups yet at times represent in writing many of the qualities of those groups in a kind of cultural play-acting produces a poetry that voices what is otherwise denied by the dominant culture. Quevedo, while perhaps attracted to or even "haunted" (as Mas would have it) by his picaresque speakers, nevertheless makes certain that their potential for representing alternative subject positions is inscribed within established social institutions:

> Zampuzado en un banasto
> me tiene su majestad,
> en un callejón Noruega,
> aprendiendo a gavilán.
> . . . . .
> Yo, que fui norte de guros,
> enseñando a navegar
> a las godeñas en ansias,
> a los buzos en afán,
>   enmoheciendo mi vida,
> vivo en esta oscuridad,
> monje de zaquizamíes,
> ermitaño de un desván.
>
> (poem 856)

(His majesty has me hidden away in a basket [jail] in a dark alley, learning the hard way. . . . I, who was the greatest of con men, teaching the picaresque life to prostitutes and to thieves, now live in this darkness, my life becoming moldy, a monk in a cell, a hermit in a hole.)

> Embarazada me tienen
> estos grillos la persona;
> mas, encarcelada y presa,
> sólo a tus rizos les toca.

En casa de los bellacos,
en el bolsón de la horca,
por sangrador de la daga
me metieron a la sombra.
Porque no pueda salir,
me engarzaron en las cormas,
y siempre mandan que siga.
¿Quién entenderá las ropas?
(poem 860)

(These chains have me imprisoned, but in jail and captive only your ropes suffer. They threw me into the darkness of the house of criminals on the prison's death row, accused of being a pickpocket. So that I could not escape, they put me in shackles and always command me to keep on. Who knows the reason why?)

What is striking about texts such as these is the overall tone of lighthearted defiance which gently mocks the social powers that have incarcerated the speaker. In the first example, the picaro recounts his former life, in which he was both the scourge of the rich and the envy of his fellow thieves. In the second, the singular "su majestad" of the first poem as the agent of the law has become the impersonal third-person plural: "me metieron," "me engarzaron," "siempre mandan." The variation suggests the diffused power of the social order in general. In both cases there is the strong sense of place and positioning. Whether in a "banasto," a "desván," or as the "norte de guros," the speaker physically situates himself in relation to others within the social context. This strategy stands in direct contrast to the preoccupation with time and the impossibility of finding a stable subject position which dominates the so-called serious poetry: "Yesterday is gone, tomorrow has not arrived," "I am a was, a will be, and a weary is" ("Ayer se fue, mañana no ha llegado," "Soy un fue, un será y un es cansado"). Ironically, the effect of the speaker's marginality and its consignment to the repressed side of aristocratic experience ("oscuridad," "sombra") is to construct a space from which the other can speak.

To better understand how the suggestion of rebellion and

relative autonomy characteristic of these marginal speakers is produced even when they are physically contained, we must look closer at the language of the poem, for it is through the use of *germanía* (thieves' jargon) that Quevedo undercuts the despair we have seen in the speakers of the more traditional genres. In the same way that the picaro as speaker subverts and implicitly challenges the dominant aesthetic and social order, so too does his language inherently undermine the dominant linguistic code. We know that the cultural project of a Góngora, for example, designed to further aestheticize and distance aristocratic discourse from everyday language, had its inverted double in the *jerga* (thieves' jargon) of the *jacaradinos*. Whether or not Quevedo had firsthand experience of this semantic otherness (during his reportedly "scandalous" early years in Valladolid) or was acquainted with it only through books such as Juan Hidalgo's compilation *Romances de la germanía y vocabulario desta lengua* (1609) is less important than that he was more willing than many of his contemporaries to make use of it within both his poetic and narrative texts.

The obvious problem here is that the voice speaking from within the poems is not really that of a picaro at all but the invention of a highly literate aristocrat, Quevedo himself. This is not to say, however, that the *germanía* used by the poet is nothing more than an invented dialect comparable to the *sayagués* in Lope and elsewhere in the *comedia*. Although it probably could not be considered "reported speech," the picaresque slang of the text is nonetheless drawn from the actual language of a functioning subculture, and Quevedo's decision to give that marginal group a voice would have important consequences for the delineation of subjectivity in the seventeenth century. Once textualized, such language would simultaneously be divested of its original function as cryptic speech and inserted into aristocratic cultural production as other.

Some years ago Salillas perceived that such an insertion might have numerous unforeseen consequences. Although his was a conspicuously class-bound reading, more easily imaginable at the turn of the century than in our own period ("the common people, whose nature is inclined toward awe-inspired musings that derive from their ignorant and simple spirit" ["el pueblo, cuyo natural se inclina a ponderaciones maravillosas, emanadas de su espíritu ignorante y sencillote"]), Salillas did sense the uncontrollable nature of the reception of the picaresque poems: "Even though there is neither the intention nor the commitment to dwell on lowly actions and even though the satirical mode is applied to them, the indirect dwelling and the recreation it produces constitute a kind of familiarity between the event and the reader" ("Aunque no haya empeño ni intención en ponderar las bajas acciones y aunque se les aplique un modo de sátira, la ponderación indirecta y el recreamiento que produce constituyen una especie de familiaridad entre el asunto y el lector").[36] While it is not my intention to reconstruct what an aristocratic reader's response might have been to Quevedo's burlesque poetry (an impossible task), it must nonetheless be said that a line such as "Hidden away in a basket" ("Zampuzado en un banasto") forces the courtly reader to enter a world considered socially inferior and exposes him to a speaker who defiantly speaks for a large sector of society which is denied a voice by the ideologies of the ruling elites. In his study of Velázquez, Ortega made a case for the potentially contestatory effect of *bodegones*, realistic portraits of members of subordinate social groups, which around 1615 constituted an attack on the traditional codes of aristocratic painting and self-representation.[37] But in the end, we are faced with the probability that the figuring forth of an unruly picaro in a poetic text destined to be read by a limited courtly audience almost always worked to contain alterity. In the end, the aristocrat's own sense of social and moral superiority was reinforced. In saying this, I am not negating what to my mind is the more important point: the picaro and the subcultural language through which he takes shape could also problematize a text by forcing the reader to "see" himself from the outside. Thus specific areas

[36] Salillas, "Poesía rufianesca," pp. 22–23.
[37] José Ortega y Gasset, *Papeles sobre Velázquez y Goya* (Madrid: Revista de Occidente, 1950), pp. 80–81.

considered problematic for the culture as a whole, especially subjectivity, were exposed as the site of discursive antagonisms and contradictions.

In the well-known romance that depicts a meeting between Alexander the Great and the cynic Diogenes, we hear one of the most searing attacks against courtly values in all of Quevedo's poetry:

> que, yo, vestido de un tiesto,
> doy dos higas a la Parca,
> pues tengo en él sepultura,
> después que palacio, y capa.
> Tiende redes por el mundo,
> mientras yo tiendo la raspa:
> que en cas de las calaveras
> ambos las tendremos calvas.
> . . . . .
> El no tener lisonjeros
> lo debo al no tener blanca;
> y si no tengo tus joyas,
> tampoco tengo tus ansias.
>
> (poem 745)

(For I, covered up by a planter [in jail], could not care less about Fate since it [the cell], rather than a palace or a cape, serves as my tomb. Fate weaves webs throughout the world while I take a nap, for in the house of skulls we are both bald. . . . I have no hangers-on because I have no money, and although I lack your jewels, I also lack your worries.)

The desire to be free from externally imposed restrictions based on blood, convention, or class is what most vividly separates Quevedo's speakers from the more traditional lyric subjects of the period. In Quevedo's text much more is at stake in freedom from the "ansias" of social obligations than the traditional court/country opposition ("menosprecio de la corte/alabanza de la aldea"). What we are confronted with here is the articulation of an alternative form of subjectivity produced from within an antiaristocratic language linked to a concrete and subordinate social group.

In the most extreme examples of Quevedo's artificial picaresque world, the speakers glory in their own marginality:

> Con testa gacha toda charla escucho;
> dejo la chanza y sigo mi provecho;
> para vivir, escóndome y acecho,
> y visto de paloma lo avechucho.
> Para tener, doy poco y pido mucho;
> si tengo pleito, arrímome al cohecho;
> ni sorbo angosto ni me calzo estrecho:
> y cátame que soy hombre machucho.
> Niego el antaño, píntome el mostacho;
> pago a Silvia el pecado, no el capricho;
> prometo y niego: y cátame muchacho.
> Vivo pajizo, no visito nicho;
> en lo que ahorro está mi buen despacho:
> y cátame dichoso, hecho y dicho.
>
> (poem 529)

(With head bowed I listen to all talk; I lay off the jokes and seek my profit. To live, I hide and observe and drape a sheet over unpleasantness. To have, I give little and ask a lot; when I get into trouble, I depend on a bribe; I don't drink too much or walk too close: watch out, for I'm a clever one. I reject all haughtiness, I disguise my heritage[?]; I give Sylvia money for sex, not for her whims; I make promises and don't deliver: watch out, boy. I live humbly and don't frequent shrines; my well-being is in what I save: consider me fortunate in word and deed.)

Within the semantic field of thieves' jargon, everyday signifiers are detached from their conventional meanings, so that within the alternative world of the poem an implicit challenge is aimed at the dominant social groups. But the speaker's self-fulfillment, so heavily laden with irony when read from an aristocratic position, reminds us of the conclusion of *Lazarillo de Tormes* and Lázaro's empty boast that he is at the height of his good fortune.

This in fact was González de Salas's point when in editing Quevedo's poetry he attached the following title to this text: "Cheap and artificial happiness of the poor man" ("Felicidad barata y artificiosa del pobre").

Still, the many dispossessed characters within the burlesque poetry construct a figure comprising all those qualities considered either immoral or heretical or both by courtly society, a figure who in his limited but undeniable individuation shares an uncanny resemblance to the autonomous subject of earlier texts (Montaigne, Cervantes) and who is thus distantly related to later philosophical discourse as it was developed through the writings of Descartes. Free of external restrictions, the speaker is no longer forced to live for others but now lives "for himself" and rejects the concept of social climbing (*medrar*):

> Pues que vuela la edad, ande la loza;
> y si pasarse tragos, sean de taza;
> bien puede la ambición mondar la haza,
> que el *satis est* me alegra y me remonta.
>   Ya dije a los palacios: "Adios, choza."
> Cualquiera pretensión tengo por maza;
> oigo el dácala y siento el embaraza,
> y solamente el libre humor me goza.
>   Menos veces vomito que bostezo:
> la hambre dicen que el ingenio aguza,
> y que la gula es horca del pescuezo.
>   El pedir a los ricos me espeluza,
> pues saben mi mendrugo y mi arrapiezo,
> y darme saben sólo en caperuza.
>
>   (poem 572)

(Since time flies, let gaiety reign, and if there are to be troubles (drinks), let them be by the cupful; ambition can make the land barren but *satis est* makes me soar and be happy. I've already told the palaces: "Farewell, hut." I consider any pretension to be a chain; I hear "Take this," and I feel obligation; only freedom pleases me. I vomit less than I yawn: they say hunger sharpens the mind and that gluttony is the neck's noose. Begging from rich men makes me sick, for they see my crumbs and my rags and will only strike me in the head.)

The enchained and encircled speaker characteristic of the amorous verse, who is unaware of the identity of his persecutors, is here replaced by a speaker who has located the origin of his imprisonment: "Cualquiera pretensión tengo por maza." *Pretensión* in this context must be understood as those forms of established behavior considered proper for specific social groups and estates, forms that constrict the potential for alternative subject positions in the same way that the "maza," or chain, restrains the trained monkey.

In another example dealing with a similar theme, the speaker nostalgically recalls his life of picaresque freedom and rejects conventional modes of courtly behavior:

¡Oh santo bodegón! ¡Oh picardía!
¡Oh tragos, oh tajadas, oh gandaya!
¡Oh barata y alegre putería!
Tras los reyes y príncipes se vaya
quien da toda la vida por un día,
que yo me quiero andar de saya en saya.
(poem 595)

(Oh holy tavern! Oh picaresque life! Oh drinking, oh drunkeness, oh idleness! Oh cheap and happy whore-mongering! Let those who would sell their life cheaply chase after kings and princes, but I want to chase skirt after skirt.)

In the third line of the same poem, the speaker's ideal is revealed: "navegar en ansias." R. M. Price and others have pointed out that this phrase had multiple meanings in the seventeenth century. The conventional rendering is "to follow one's base desires."[38] A secondary meaning, "to be condemned to the galleys," is especially useful for my reading because it conveys the negative consequences imposed by the social order on this kind of unmediated subjectivity. Nevertheless, the speaker of poem 596

[38] R. M. Price, "A Note on Three Satirical Sonnets of Quevedo," *Bulletin of Hispanic Studies* 40 (1963): 84. Mas cites this poem as an example of a lyric subject whose trespassing of social limits destroys the reader's sympathy: "The degradation can go too far" (*La caricature*, p. 335).

openly declares his indifference to condemnation by the authorities:

> Volver quiero a vivir a trochimoche,
> y ninguno me apruebe ni me tache
> el volver de privado a moharrache,
> si no lo ha sido todo en una noche.
> Mesa y caricia, y secretillo y coche
> trueco yo a quien me sufra y me emborrache,
> y ruéganme con este cambalache
> los que saben decir "aroga" y "zoche."
> Con la fortuna el ambicioso luche,
> y a los malsines y a la envidia peche,
> y para otro mayor ladrón ahúche;
> que yo, porque la vida me aproveche,
> por si hay algún bellaco que me escuche,
> tanto estaré contento cuanto arreche.

(I want to go back to living recklessly, and let no one approve or censure as unthinking my return to a wild life since the decision was not made in one night. Food and luxury, court gossip and a coach: I would trade all for her who puts up with me and gives me a drink; those who know how to say "aroga" and "zoche" are urging me to make the change. Let the ambitious man fight with fortune and put up with gossip and envy and hide away from other more successful thieves, for I, in case some fool is listening, will take advantage of life and will be all the more content the more I fuck.)

The most interesting section of this text for my argument are lines 7 and 8, in which the *germanía* is linked to a marginal social group that entices the speaker to embrace its way of life. As Price noted, one possible reading of these verses might be "and those who can speak the rough language of freedom are appealing to me with this change."[39] The so-called language of freedom is nothing less than a discourse within which forms of subjectivity excluded by aristocratic ideologies could take shape. Although he is contained and ultimately subordinated, the antiaristocratic

---

[39] Price, "A Note," p. 87.

subject is given a voice in the burlesque poetry and thus takes his place in the gallery of cultural products. Nowhere is this voice heard more clearly than in the character known as King Palomo:

Yo me soy el rey Palomo:
yo me lo guiso y yo me lo como.
Después que de puro viejo
caduca ya mi vestido,
5   como como un descosido,
por estarlo hasta el pellejo.
No acierto a topar consejo
que pueda ponerme en salvo
contra un herreruelo calvo
10   y una sotana lampiña,
que, cuando mejor se aliña,
me descubre todo el lomo.
Yo me soy el rey Palomo:
yo me lo guiso y yo me lo como.
15   Si va a decir la verdad,
de nadie se me da nada,
que el ánima apicarada
me ha dado esta libertad.
Sólo llamo majestad
20   al rey con que hago la suerte.
No temo en damas la muerte
tanto como en un doctor:
que las cosas del amor
como me vienen las tomo.
25   *Yo me soy el rey Palomo:*
yo me lo guiso y yo me lo como.
Para mí no hay demasías
ni prerrogativas necias
de los que se hacen Venecias
30   sólo por ser señorías.
En mi mesa las Harpías
mueren de hambre contino;
pídola para el camino,
si me despide mi dama;
35   mas, si a mi ventana llama,
después de comer me asomo.

Yo me soy el rey Palomo:
yo me lo guiso y yo me lo como.
   Entre nobles no me encojo,
40   que, según dice una ley,
       si es de buena sangre el rey,
       es de tan buena su piojo.
       Con nada me crece el ojo,
       si no es con una hinchazón.
45   Más estimo un dan que un don;
       y es mi fuerza y vigor tanto,
       que un testimonio levanto,
       aunque pese más que plomo.
       Yo me soy el rey Palomo:
50   *yo me lo guiso y yo me lo como.*
               (poem 644)

(I am King Palomo [fool]: I cook it and I eat it. After my clothes fall apart from sheer age, I eat like someone unraveled [lunatic] since I am one to the bone. I can't follow advice that might save me from a bald cape [nobleman?] and a beardless cossack [priest?], for when things seem to go well my whole back is laid bare [flogged]. I am King Palomo: I cook it and I eat it. If the truth be told, I don't care what anyone thinks, for the picaresque spirit has given me this freedom. I only call majesty the king with which I gamble. I have not as much fear of ladies as of a doctor. I take affairs of love as they come. I am King Palomo: I cook it and I eat it. For me there are no insults or foolish privileges as for those who dissemble merely for a title. At my table Harpies die of constant hunger; I ask for food for the road when I leave my lady, but when she calls at my window I come out only after eating. I am King Palomo: I cook it and I eat it. I do not bow around nobles since, as a law states, if the king has good blood so must his louse. Nothing makes my eye big [astounds me] unless it's a swelling. I respect a handout more than a title, and my strength and vigor are such that I can raise evidence [give false testimony] even if it weighs more than lead. I am King Palomo: I cook it and I eat it.)

Positing a subject constituted by its direct opposition to the dominant social order effectively resolves the malaise characteristic of the speaker in the love poetry. Mas has correctly called the refrain of this poem "a program for life" and "a complete way of life," stating further that "this freedom is the rejection of all the sentimental and social conventions that submit men to civility, to women, to the powerful; in a word, it is picaresque freedom."[40] The so-called freedom of the picaresque, although it is marked as immoral and mad by aristocratic discourse, nonetheless makes visible in writing a form of subjectivity completely at odds with those authorized by the dominant ideologies.

Several years ago in his study of Olivares, Marañón pointed out that the myth of Quevedo the rebellious intellectual was an invention of nineteenth-century liberalism and had little to do with the actual historical figure. On this view, it would be a mistake to overestimate the range of what Mas called "picaresque freedom," and I myself would not want to be misunderstood as attempting to make a case for a "subversive" Quevedo. Despite the representation of antiaristocratic values in his poetry, Quevedo's literary practice was not about to unsettle the ruling classes enough to bring about radical social change, and he himself would probably have considered such a goal either heretical or mad. No purely discursive transgression can ever produce results in the social world as long as the sites of the production of discourse are left unchallenged.[41] Although I balk at the construction of a so-called progressive Quevedo, however, I nevertheless insist that the otherness in the picaresque poems figures a form of subjectivity struggling to take shape in early modern culture but everywhere repressed by aristocratic ideologies. Put another way, a potential utopian space is posited in the poetic text, which, once inserted into a new socioeconomic conjuncture, becomes much more than a "delirio pasajero." The non-

[40]Mas, *La caricature*, p. 334. Mas's reading of poem 644 underscores the articulation of a new kind of subject: "It is difficult to find in as few words so many affirmations of self: besides the three verbs in the first person, the triple usage of the two pronouns, subject and object: the *yo* marking the subject and the *me* for the me." We sense in Quevedo an early form of what would later become the self-possessed, unmediated individual of bourgeois ideology.

[41]For a discussion of the political power of carnival or cultural transgression, see Peter Stallybrass and Allon White, *The Politics and Poetics of Transgression* (Ithaca: Cornell University Press, 1986).

aristocratic form of the subject figured forth in the burlesque poetry remains undeniably linked to dominant forms insofar as it presses to the foreground those qualities that the dominant either represses or cannot know; still, its emergence announces certain alternatives that in a new context will no longer be containable either by the strategies of courtly poetry or by aristocratic culture at large. It is not surprising that in later historical moments and contexts Quevedo's name would become a sign for the intellectual who challenges the established order or, in an even more radical appropriation, the rallying point for the striking miners in the Asturian rebellion of 1934.

IV

The marginalization of the picaro is an unstable way station on the road to individualism, and individualism (or the myth of autonomy), as we have been told, is one of the founding principles of the capitalist state. Among the effects of the crisis of the seventeenth century was a new conjuncture of social conditions which made possible the idea of the "bare individual" in ways as yet so unintelligible or unspeakable that a thinker as immersed in the authorized tradition as Quevedo felt compelled to turn to the other for advice. Maurice Molho's contention that Quevedo merely represents the fearful reaction of the aristocracy faced with the rising power of the underclass may be an accurate reading of the picaresque novel *El Buscón*, but it is less convincing for the poetic texts in which the poet does not "punish" the picaro (as he does the novel's protagonist, Don Pablos) but gives him a voice and a certain autonomy.[42]

At one level, Quevedo participated in the growing aristocratic fascination with the picaresque which Bataillon was among the first to point out. The account of an evening festival held at court in June 1605 is especially instructive because it reveals how

___
[42]Maurice Molho's discussion is in "Cinco lecciones sobre *El Buscón*," in *Semántica y poética* (Barcelona: Crítica, 1977).

traditional divisions of class and sexuality were often trans-gressed, in this case by one group of courtiers "disguised as picaros" ("disfrazado a lo pícaro") and "some members of the military orders dressed as women and others as dandies" ("visti-éndose los caballeros de hábito de mugeres y otros de galanes").[43] Such rehearsals of alternative forms of the subject were not mere idle play; the shifts in cultural and socioeconomic conditions produced a crisis in subjectivity which informed not only the literary texts of the period but everyday life as well. It must also be said, however, that Quevedo's working out of emergent forms of the subject cannot be attributed in any simple way to the tran-sition from one mode of production to another. Both poetry and prose drew heavily on residual articulations of interiority asso-ciated with neostoic ideologies; Quevedo's later projects were in large measure designed to reconcile stoical ideals with Catholic dogma. But even those of his works we now consider part of the religious discourse of the period are strangely secularized, as Tierno once argued: "The *Introduction to the Devout Life* has bourgeois intimacy as its social basis" ("La *Introducción a la vida devota* tiene como presupuesto social la intimidad burguesa").[44] Thus stoicism in Quevedo is significantly refunctioned and comes to have an uneasy relationship to other contemporary discourses produced by the new alignment of economic and class practices. The well-known poems in which Quevedo's speakers comment on the increasing intrusion of money into traditional areas of aristocratic life represent some of these new contradic-tions. In a poem attributed to Quevedo (poem 726), titled "In-structions and papers for the new man at court" ("Instrucción y documentos para el noviciado de la corte"), the novice is told:

[43] Recorded by Bataillon, *Pícaros y picaresca*, p. 189 n. 17.
[44] Tierno Galván, "Notas sobre el Barroco," p. 125. Maravall describes a similar process in the works of Luis Vives in which Augustinian interiority and bourgeois intimacy combine to create a private space, so that "each may retreat to an intimate personal space into which neither the powerful nor other mem-bers of society can enter" ("cada uno pueda retirarse a un íntimo reducto personal, en el que ni los que ejercen el poder ni los demás miembros de la sociedad puedan penetrar"). *Utopía y reformismo*, p. 372.

> Mas si allá quieres holgarte,
> hazme merced que en la venta
> primera trueques tus gracias
> por cantidad de moneda.
> No han menester ellas lindos,
> que harto lindas se son ellas:
> la mejor facción de un hombre
> es la bolsa grande y llena.

(But if you want to enjoy yourself there, do me the favor of first exchanging your personal graces for a sum of money at the inn. They [at court] have no need for good-looking men, for money is attractive enough: a man's best feature is a large and full purse.)

The allusions to money in the burlesque poetry remind us that in a wide variety of social practices the subject was being increasingly rewritten as the individual, an atomized entity in continual competition with others and relatively unimpeded by traditional restrictions. Even the lack of pure blood might be overcome by reinscribing oneself through the category of the economic:

> Alguno vi que subía,
> que no alcanzaba anteayer
> ramo de quien descender,
> sino el de su picardía.
> Y he visto sangre judía
> hacerla el mucho caudal
> (como papagayo real)
> clara ya su vena oscura.
> *Pícaros hay con ventura*
> *de los que conozco yo,*
> *y pícaros hay que no.*
>
> (poem 648)

I have seen some rise who yesterday could not find a branch [genealogy] from which to descend except that of their roguishness. And I have seen great wealth transform (like a peacock) Jewish blood from impure to pure. *Of the pícaros I have known, some have good luck and others do not.*)

What I am asserting here about the picaresque poetry would seem to be in direct conflict with conventional readings. Molho, for example, correctly argues that in general the ideology of classic picaresque literature, such as the *Guzmán de Alfarache*, is profoundly anticapitalist.[45] All the great novels of the picaresque condemn the new systems of exchange and idealize traditional modes of production. But the function of the picaro in Quevedo's burlesque poetry is decidedly different. That it is should not surprise us since Quevedo's writings are nothing if not the representation of nearly every contradiction that made up seventeenth-century Spanish culture. After all, it was Quevedo who defended traditional class divisions in a two-part political handbook based on the life of Christ (*La política de Dios*, part 1 [1626]), only to write shortly afterward (ca. 1635) the following passage: "Let the rich man not impede the poor man's becoming rich, or the poor man gain wealth by stealing from the powerful. Let the nobleman not despise the common man, or the common man abhor the noble; and let the government take care that the poor are motivated to become rich" ("Que el rico no estorbe al pobre que pueda ser rico, ni el pobre enriquezca con el robo del poderoso. Que el noble no desprecie al plebeyo, ni el plebeyo aborrezca al noble; y que todo el gobierno se ocupe en animar a que todos los pobres sean ricos").[46] Potentially conflicting discourses were also juxtaposed within a single text with seemingly little concern for ideological consistency. Thus in *La hora de todos*

---

[45] Maurice Molho, *Introducción al pensamiento picaresco* (Salamanca: Anaya, 1972), p. 154. With regard to Quevedo, however, I am in agreement with Maravall: "It would be absurd to try to discover in Quevedo's world a properly capitalist perspective, even that of an early form of capitalism. But, in some ways, there are breathing in the atmosphere of his time many ideas, aspirations, problems, fears, peculiar to the society in which capitalism begins to develop" ("Sería absurdo intentar descubrir en el mundo quevedesco una perspectiva propiamente capitalista, ni aun de un primer capitalismo. Pero, de algún modo, respira en la atmósfera de su tiempo muchas ideas, aspiraciones, problemas, temores, propios de la sociedad en que éste comienza a crecer"). "Sobre el pensamiento," p. 91.

[46] Quevedo, *La hora de todos y la fortuna con seso* (written ca. 1635; published 1650), ed. Luisa López Grigera (Madrid: Castalia, 1975), p. 213.

Quevedo, although he is one of the great ideologues of *limpieza* (purity) elsewhere in the text, could allow an African character to claim: "There is no other cause of our slavery but color, and color is an accident and not a crime" ("Para nuestra esclavitud no hay otra causa sino la color, y la color es accidente, y no delito"). In a similar textualization of antagonistic ideological figures, Quevedo's burlesque poetry, by inserting the voice of marginalized groups into aristocratic literary discourse, produced a subject that shared many of the elements at work in the configurations of subjectivity emerging in Spanish culture. These new cultural configurations called into question nothing less than the primary categories of aristocratic discourse: virtue, genealogy, status, and even blood.

CHAPTER 4

Miguel de Cervantes:
Deindividuating Don Quixote

I answered him, "It seems you haven't noticed, sir, that I have no cape."

(Bien parece, señor, que no se advierte, le respondí, que yo no tengo capa.)

—Cervantes, *Viaje del Parnaso*

I

In the preceding chapter we have seen how two seemingly contradictory modes of writing in Quevedo's poetry work to delineate the boundaries of aristocratic subjectivity. In effect, the picaresque speaker reaffirms the metaphysics of the blood by sketching out an alternative subject position—an emergent form of the individual—which in the final analysis is considered monstrous and unspeakable by the traditional ideologies of seventeenth-century Spain. The uneasy attraction of Quevedo for such a figure, however, despite his overt opposition to what it signified for the culture at large, invokes the new forms and in the end makes space for alternative positions that potentially challenge the dominant order.

Within the field of early modern literature, one variant of this emergent subjectivity is evident in the narrative fiction of Cervantes, specifically the *Don Quixote* of 1605. Whereas a part of Quevedo's poetic production constructs those forms of the subject excluded by aristocratic discourse and ultimately contains them, Cervantes's first *Don Quixote* develops such forms more fully and sets them in opposition to those sanctioned by the hegemonic social groups. The more important point, however, is that in his 1615 sequel Cervantes retreats from most of the contestatory gestures of his earlier text. To understand how and why he retreats, it is necessary to dismantle the unity of *Don Quixote*, for we are unquestionably dealing not with a single novel but with two very different literary projects.[1]

To a great extent, the rivalry critics have imagined between the figures of Cervantes and Quevedo has depended on striking differences in their biographies. If Quevedo is the courtier par excellence, Cervantes is the ex-soldier, whose life story consists of one hardship after another. It is certainly true that the author of the original *Don Quixote* failed in all his attempts to participate in aristocratic practices, even in their most marginalized forms. In other words, Cervantes possessed no cape, that synecdochic sign of noble status. From his earliest petitions for a commission in Madrid in 1582 to his failed attempt at the age of sixty-three to win a position in the count of Lemos's newly formed Neapolitan court, Cervantes would know little of the intimate association with power that was an essential part of Quevedo's daily life. Other than his brief service in Rome with Cardinal Acquaviva (ca. 1570), Cervantes' relationship to the governing elites would be tenuous and primarily literary in nature: the patronage of the count of Lemos and the duke of Béjar; his activities in the Congregation of the Most Holy Sacrament, a quasi-religious intellectual circle; his participation in literary academies founded by wealthy citizens of Madrid.

Quevedo and Cervantes, then, shared the desire that motivated virtually all writers in early modern Spain, the wish to be somehow associated with the aristocracy, but Cervantes began his career with serious disadvantages. The suspicion of Jewish

---

[1] The 1615 sequel would not enjoy the popularity of the 1605 *Don Quixote*. Fourteen editions of the original were published in Spain between 1605 and 1650, compared to only seven editions of the sequel before 1650. See Maxime Chevalier, "Don Quichotte et son public," in *Livre et lecture en Espagne et en France sous l'ancien régime: Colloque de la Casa de Velázquez* (Paris: AOPF, 1981).

ancestry haunted him throughout his life and may have been the reason for a delay in his admission to a Sevillian confraternity in 1593, despite repeated declarations as to his *limpieza de sangre*. His lack of university training was another factor that distanced him from the majority of his literary colleagues and rivals. In the previous chapter, I argued that Quevedo's investment in literature may have been less important than his interest in politics. For Cervantes, too, writing may have been of secondary importance, at least in terms of his economic survival. We know that his *curriculum*, filed around 1593 as part of a solicitation of employment in the Indies, makes no mention whatsoever of his accomplishments as a writer. This omission was assuredly not due to humility, for in another context (the preface to his collected plays) he was not reticent about his literary accomplishments. Indeed, he touted himself as an innovator of theatrical practice. What seems to us a glaring omission arose in fact from Cervantes's understanding that in the seventeenth century writing possessed less exchange value than did an illustrious military record, especially when one's aim was to reposition oneself within the hierarchies of status and service. Ultimately, however, it was Cervantes's extended contact with all levels of Spanish society during his travels throughout Andalusia and Castile, his exposure to the new economic and cultural dynamics of a city like Seville, his imprisonment in Spain and North Africa, even his nearly twenty-year absence from intellectual circles (ca. 1585–1605)—it is all this biographical raw material that contributed to the construction of the alternative subjectivities figured in the two versions of *Don Quixote*.

To understand the cultural logic against which Cervantes conceived his first novel, I want to look closely at a different kind of text. In 1614 one of Cervantes's most aggressive rivals published a *Don Quixote* under the pseudonym Alonso Fernández de Avellaneda. This text mounts a ruling-class reaction to the emergence of an autonomous subject premised on singularity. The battlefield was writing; the stakes were nothing less than identity and the structure of society.

In the prologue to his *Don Quixote*, which purported to be a

follow-up to the misadventures of the Manchegan knight, Avellaneda launched a scathing personal attack against Cervantes.
Thus he set off the most infamous and mysterious literary rivalry
in all of Spanish literature. Just who was this Avellaneda who
chose to hide behind an obvious pseudonym? Why did he decide
to write a spurious sequel and rush it into print a year before
Cervantes could complete his own continuation? More important (at least since the beginning of the last century), what was it
about the imitator's treatment of Don Quixote that was so dis-
turbing and so unlike the original? Why, in other words, did
Avellaneda situate his own text in direct opposition to that of
Cervantes?

The riddle of Avellaneda's true identity has never been solved,
nor have the origins of his personal dislike for Cervantes been
entirely recovered.[2] It seems likely, however, that the author was
a Dominican friar, who, not surprisingly, filled the first few
pages of his text with references to Aquinas, Saint Gregory,
Saint Paul, the *Flos sanctorum*, and other religious writings. The
precise identity of the author is of less interest to me, however,
than how the text itself functioned in Spanish culture. Clearly, it
speaks from a dominant ideological position, but the Spanish
reading public received it with relative indifference. It won new
life in René Lesage's French adaptation, published ninety years
later, but by the nineteenth century the canonization of Cervantes's two texts had decided the fate of the "false" *Don Quixote*,
consigning it to the realm of cultural oddities deemed both
unreadable and undesirable.

Banishing the other Quixote served to dehistoricize the Cervantine text, creating the impression that Cervantes was the
anomalous "inventor of the modern novel" and granting him the

---

[2]On these and other matters, the superior study of Avellaneda continues to be
Stephen Gilman, *Cervantes y Avellaneda: Estudio de una imitación*, trans. Margit
Frenk Alatorre (Mexico City: Fondo de Cultura Económica, 1951). Other critics
who have understood Avellaneda's text as a hostile response to that of Cervantes
are E. C. Riley in the "Avellaneda's Quixote" section of *Cervantes's Theory of the
Novel* (Oxford: Clarendon Press, 1962), pp. 212–25; John G. Weiger, *The Substance of Cervantes* (Cambridge: Cambridge University Press, 1985).

status of virtually the only Spanish author to be allowed into the canon of world literature. The rejection of Avellaneda's Quixote also worked to limit our understanding of power and subjectivity in the early modern period. Avellaneda may be the most important of the early readers of *Don Quixote* precisely because his text inserts the emergent subject figured by Cervantes's 1605 novel into a textual environment no less hostile than was Quevedo's aristocratic culture to the "free individual" of the Petrarchan love sonnet.

The Cervantes-Avellaneda rivalry is not the only duel between competing texts, competing notions of subjectivity. Such intertextual debates were relatively common, and they had less to do with strictly literary resonances or oedipal rivalries than with specific political and ideological oppositions. The feud between Mateo Alemán, for example, and the author of a spurious continuation (1604) of his *Guzmán de Alfarache* (1599) was a contemporary antecedent of the Cervantes-Avellaneda dispute. Still another case of this kind of competition in early modern Spain involved Quevedo's picaresque novel *El Buscón* (1626, but probably written ca. 1604) and the anonymous *Lazarillo de Tormes* (1554). It could be argued that Quevedo wanted to cash in on the popularity of Aleman's text; certainly, he seems to have intended to undercut the social criticism and suggestion of mobility implicit in the humanist-influenced *Lazarillo*. He does so by punishing the protagonist (the picaro) who fights to improve his status and thus to shift subject position within the limited range of possibilities available. This "punishment" or disciplining is accomplished with the representation of physical violence directed against the hero, together with an attack mounted through language that transforms everyday objects into strange and grotesque emblems of the supposed depravity of the subordinate class. The battle that would be waged between Avellaneda and Cervantes over *Don Quixote* shares many of the strategies of the picaresque debates, but the stakes were much higher, for the Cervantine project was ultimately more challenging to the established order than was that of the unknown author of *Lazarillo de Tormes*.

As I have shown, a rival ideology of virtue competed with that of blood for the status of determinant "in the final instance" of aristocratic subjectivity. Given his humanistic education, it should not surprise us that one of the guiding axioms (if not the central principle) of Cervantes's first *Don Quixote* is the concept "Each man is the child of his deeds" ("Cada uno es hijo de sus obras"). This idea, as it had been carefully theorized by Huarte de San Juan and many others writing within the humanist tradition, cannot be separated from the process through which the subjectivism of the 1605 protagonist is figured. Despite Don Quixote's status as a minor nobleman (*hidalgo*, "child of something"), the discourse of virtue is set in direct opposition to that element considered central to the determination of identity within aristocratic discourse—inherited nobility. In the Cervantine text, with the exception of an occasional remark by Sancho Panza followed by Don Quixote's rebuke, there are virtually no references to the category of blood, and as we listen to Avellaneda's Quixote, Cervantes's conscious omission is clear: "Indeed, gentlemen, I think it would be hard to find three people like us to travel from Zaragoza to this spot, for each of us is deserving of honor and fame because, as we know, one of three things in this world assures us of them: blood, arms, or letters, virtue being common to all three, making a perfect combination" (215–16). ("Por cierto, señores, que entiendo verdaderamente que a duras penas se podrán hallar tres sujetos tales como los tres que habemos caminado desde Zaragoza hasta aquí, pues cada uno de nosotros merece por sí grande honra y fama; porque, como sabemos por una de tres cosas se alcanzan en el mundo las dos dichas: o por la sangre o por las armas, o por las letras, incluyendo en sí cada una dellas la virtud, para que sea perfecto cumplimiento") (309).[3]

---

[3] The Spanish is quoted from Alonso Fernández de Avellaneda, *El ingenioso hidalgo Don Quijote de La Mancha que contiene su tercera salida y es la quinta parte de sus aventuras* (1614), ed. Fernando García Salinero (Madrid: Castalia, 1971). English versions are from the fine translation by A. W. Server and J. E. Keller, *Don Quixote de La Mancha (Part II): Being the Spurious Continuation of Miguel de Cervantes' Part I* (Newark, Del.: Juan de la Cuesta, 1980). Both are cited hereafter by page number in the text.

Cervantes's privileging of virtue and deemphasizing of blood firmly situates the first *Don Quixote* in a counterdiscourse with a long history in humanist Europe and even in Spain itself.[4] As Sancho is about to make the radical shift in subject position from peasant to governor, Don Quixote offers him the following advice: "Remember, Sancho, that if you take virtue for your means, and pride yourself on performing virtuous deeds, you will have no reason to envy those who were born princes and lords. For blood is inherited but virtue acquired, and virtue has an intrinsic worth, which blood has not" ("Mira, Sancho: si tomas por medio la virtud, y te precias de hacer hechos virtuosos, no hay para qué tener envidia a los que los tienen príncipes y señores; porque la sangre se hereda, y la virtud se aquista, y la virtud vale por sí sola lo que la sangre no vale") (2:42).

In the new situation of the early seventeenth century, such a gesture could only be viewed as potentially subversive by the Spanish ruling class. Carried too far, the suggestion that inherited social position or lineage had little or nothing to do with the subject's status could conceivably have brought down the entire cultural apparatus that sustained Spanish absolutism: aristocratic privilege, the exclusion of impure ethnic groups (Jews and Muslims) and their descendants, the ability of the community to employ shame as a controlling device, the "cleansing" of the blood through revenge (a ritual act crucial to an understanding of Calderonian theater), and so on. I do not intend to exaggerate Cervantes's position with regard to the category of blood. Those readers familiar with his other writings will immediately recall the function of inherited nobility and genealogy in texts such as "La fuerza de la sangre" and "La gitanilla." The movement away from the counterdiscourse of virtue in some of the *Novelas ejemplares* (1613) is already suggestive of Cervantes's settlement in the

---

[4]Of the rival discourses of blood and virtue, Domínguez Ortiz writes: "In practice they intersected, giving rise to . . . a variety of nuances that crisscrossed confusedly and even to *palpable contradictions within a single author*" ("en la práctica se mezclaron, originando . . . variedad de matices que se entrecruzan confusamente, cuando no *palpables contradicciones en un mismo autor*"). *Las clases privilegiadas*, p. 186 (my emphasis).

1615 novel with more traditional ideologies. Still, the mention of blood in the 1605 *Don Quixote* is undeniably understated; when it does appear, as in Dorotea's account of her family, it is presented as a perfunctory gesture toward conventional values: "In short they are farmers, simple people without any taint of ignoble blood, and what are generally called 'rusty old Christians'" ("Ellos, en fin, son labradores, gente llana, sin mezcla de alguna raza mal sonante, y, como suele decirse, cristianos viejos ranciosos") (1:28).

What we see in Avellaneda's version of *Don Quixote* is in part a reaction to Cervantes's problematization of aristocratic subjectivity. This reaction is realized by disciplining Cervantes's character through two complementary modes of violence: shame and revenge. Although I will stress the importance of shaming strategies in Avellaneda's novel, I do not want to imply that direct corporal punishment no longer formed the basis of the law in seventeenth century Spain. On the contrary, the techniques made infamous by the Inquisition from its founding in 1480 were only the most dramatic examples of a well-oiled disciplinary machinery that functioned at all levels of Spanish society. But in the Spanish context the experience of violence designed to reposition the anomalous subject within the social body, an act necessary to the maintenance of order at all levels, was almost always informed by a powerful ascetic inheritance that targeted the individual consciousness as the domain of control to an equal if not greater extent than the body. Foucault has spoken in passing of shame as part of the economy of punishment, but the seductive descriptions of public torture in his *Discipline and Punish* have tended to make us forget the importance of this no less dramatic attempt to refunction and thus reinterpellate the subject. For Avellaneda, since his protagonist is written as little more than a caricature and a representative of madness who produces his own spectacles, it is not necessary to make Don Quixote suffer any pain beyond that inherent in the humiliating situations in which he is inscribed. On every occasion that Avellaneda does punish his protagonist, he is indirectly punishing Cervantes's character as well and, by extension, repudiating the forms of subjectivity represented in the 1605 text.

II

It is no accident that the Avellaneda Quixote's first act as a "reactivated" knight-errant is to interfere with a public punishment.[5] Newly arrived in the city of Zaragoza, he is almost immediately confronted with the reality of power as it is practiced by the absolutist state: "It so happened that as Don Quixote was going up the street, giving everybody who saw him looking as he did plenty to talk about, the law was bringing in a man riding on a donkey. His back was naked from the waist up, there was a rope around his neck, and he was being given two hundred lashes for being a thief. Three or four constables and notaries were accompanying him, with more than two hundred boys following them" (73). ("Sucedió, pues, que yendo don Quijote la calle adelante, dando harto que decir a toda la gente que le veía ir de aquella manera, traía la justicia por ella a un hombre caballero en un asno, desnudo de la cintura arriba, con una soga al cuello, dándole docientos azotes por ladrón, al cual acompañaban tres o cuatro alguaciles y escribanos, con más de docientos muchachos detrás") (140). Don Quixote attempts to free the thief since in his madness he believes him to be a knight who has been unjustly accused, but soon finds himself overwhelmed by the representatives of the law: "They took him off Rocinante and, to his grief, tied his hands behind his back; gripped firmly by five or six constables he was dragged off to jail. . . . They put his feet in the stocks and handcuffed him after having taken away all his armor" (76). ("Le abajaron de Rocinante, y, a pesar suyo, se las ataron ambas atrás; y agarrándole cinco o seis corchetes le llevaron a empellones a la cárcel. . . . y le metieron los pies en un cepo,

---

[5] The resonances of Cervantes's own episode of Don Quixote and the galley slaves (1:22) are strong here, yet there is not the same discussion of liberty or the final unhindered dispersal of all the participants. Ginés and his colleagues do not punish Don Quixote but rather attack him for attempting to limit their newfound freedom: "It is my will that you bear this chain which I have taken from your necks and immediately take the road to the city of El Toboso, there to present yourselves before the Lady Dulcinea del Toboso" ("Y es mi voluntad, que, cargados de esa cadena que quité de vuestros cuellos, luego os pongáis en camino y vais a la ciudad del Toboso, y allí os presentéis ante la señora Dulcinea del Toboso").

con unas esposas en las manos, habiéndole primero quitado todas sus armas") (142).

Don Quixote's lawlessness is quickly controlled, and he is rapidly put in the same position as the thief he had attempted to liberate. This is only one of the many occasions in which Avellaneda's Quixote finds himself in chains—a condition not experienced by Cervantes's hero in either the 1605 or the 1615 novel. Physical imprisonment in the original text, with the exception of the open cage in the final chapters, is displaced by images designed to represent the inescapable, complex, and often tenuous mediations between material conditions and the subject (ropes, strings, nets, and so on).[6] In Avellaneda's novel, on the other hand, he whose behavior is judged to be a product of unorthodox subject positions must be held forcibly in place so that he can be refunctioned by state violence and the shame produced by exchanges with the community: "All the people at the jail door were saying, 'The poor knight in armor well deserves the lashes that await him, because he was so stupid that he meddled with the law'" (78). ("Toda aquella gente estaba a la puerta de la cárcel diciendo: 'Bien se merece el pobre caballero armado los azotes que le esperan, pues fue tan necio que metió mano sin para qué contra la justicia'") (144–45). Here, the condemnation of Don Quixote by the subordinate classes underscores the extent to which Cervantes's character is refigured as other by Avellaneda and attests to the success enjoyed by the Spanish elites (in this case, with Avellaneda as their spokesman) in their drive for ideological homogeneity. In this text, unlike that of Cervantes, there is no willing participation in the quixotic project by innkeepers, serving girls, or galley slaves. As we have seen in the chapter on Quevedo, the specter of the "individual" may have haunted the Spanish ruling class, but it was consistently contested wherever it appeared in discourse.

Despite Avellaneda's desire to castigate Cervantes's character

---

[6]For a discussion of this kind of imagery, see Helen Percas de Ponsetti, "Authorial Strings: A Recurrent Metaphor in *Don Quijote*," *Cervantes* 1 (1981): 51–62.

and thus counter an emergent form of the individual, the other Don Quixote is not disciplined through an orchestrated attack on the body. He does incite a spontaneous beating by the jailer, vividly described for us by the narrator as "half a dozen punches in the face, making blood stream from his nose and mouth" (76) ("media docena de mojicones en la cara, haciéndole saltar la sangre por las narices y boca") (143)—Avellaneda's Quixote is rescued from the hands of the civil authorities ("el Justicia") by Don Alvaro, the aristocrat who will later trick him into the madhouse. Don Alvaro's is by no means a humanitarian gesture; he "rescues" Don Quixote only to subject him to a different kind of discipline, the efficacy of which originates in public humiliation and the manipulation of sexuality. The reader's experience of this process begins soon after Don Quixote's departure from the asylum. Left alone by Don Alvaro in order to rest, he imagines that he is addressing the judges at a jousting tournament:

> At this loud shouting a page and Sancho Panza came upstairs; entering the room they found Don Quixote with his breeches down, talking to the judges and looking at the ceiling. Since his shirt was a little short in front, it didn't fail to reveal a bit of ugliness. When Sancho Panza saw this he said, "Cover your etcetera, loveless sir! Sinner that I am! There are no judges here intending to take you prisoner again or give you two hundred lashes or take you out to be shamed, even though you are only too well uncovering your shame with no reason, you can be sure!
>
> Don Quixote looked around, and as he lifted the breeches to put them on with his back turned he bent over slightly and revealed from the rear what he had revealed from the front as well as something more repulsive. Sancho, who saw it, told him, "Confounded be my breeches, sir!" It's worse than it was before; what you are doing is trying to salute us with all the unmentionable things God has given you. (85)

> (A la voz grande que dio, subieron un paje y Sancho Panza; y entrando dentro del aposento, hallaron a don Quijote, las bragas caídas, hablando con los jueces, mirando al techo; y como la camisa

era un poco corta por delante, no dejaba de descubrir alguna fealdad; lo cual visto por Sancho Panza, le dijo:
—Cubra, señor Desamorado, ¡pecador de mí!, el etcétera, que aquí no hay jueces que le pretendan echar otra vez preso, ni dar docientos azotes, ni sacar a la vergüenza, aunque harto saca vuesa merced a ella las suyas sin para qué; que bien puede estar seguro.
Volvió la cabeza don Quijote, y alzando las bragas de espaldas para ponérselas, bajóse un poco y descubrió de la trasera lo que de la delantera había descubierto, y algo más asqueroso. Sancho, que lo vio, le dijo:
—¡Pesia a mi sayo! Señor, ¿qué hace? Que peor está que estaba: eso es querer saludarnos con todas las inmundicias que Dios le ha dado.) (153)

Besides the explicit humiliation of the protagonist informed by an ascetic ideology in which the human body is abhorrent, this passage contains a relatively minor linguistic detail that is nonetheless crucial to my argument. Sancho's pun on *vergüenza* is important here because it reminds us that within the semantic field of seventeenth-century Spanish this word signified public punishment, shame, and the genitals. Covarrubias clarifies this connection among sexuality, shame, and punishment: "VER-GÜENÇAS and shameful parts in men and women, *latine pudenda a pudore*. To take someone out for public shaming is a sentence and punishment that is usually given for some crimes, and these offenders are usually placed in the pillory for some time so that they are ashamed and affronted" ("VERGÜENÇAS y partes vergon-çosas en el hombre y la mujer, *latine pudenda a pudore*. Sacar a uno a la vergüença, es pena y castigo que se suele dar por algunos delitos, y a estos tales los suelen tener atados en el rollo por algún espacio de tiempo, con que quedan avergonçados y afrenta-dos").[7] The word *vergüenza* and its multiple significations are strikingly present in Avellaneda's text, particularly throughout the section following Don Quixote's arrest: "They found the good hidalgo Don Quixote being unchained so he could be taken out for public punishment" (80). ("Hallaron al buen hidalgo don

---

[7] Covarrubias, *Tesoro de la lengua*.

Quijote, que le estaban desherrando para sacarle a la vergüenza") (146). It reappears during his rescue by the nobleman: "Don Alvaro said, 'They would undoubtedly have put you to public shame if your good fortune, or better said, if God, who settles all things smoothly, had not arranged my arrival'" (80). ("'Sacá- ranle a ella [pública vergüenza] vuesa merced,' dijo don Alvaro, 'sin duda, si su buena fortuna, o por mejor decir, Dios, que dispone todas las cosas con suavidad, no hubiera ordenado mi venida'") (147).

Insofar as these scenes represent ways of reconstituting the subject through long-standing social practices, it is clear that within the economy of punishment shame was just as powerful a tool as physical pain, perhaps more powerful.[8] The particular effects of such practices on the "criminal" or deviant himself was perhaps less crucial than the overall scene in which the commu- nity (in the case of early modern narrative, a community of listeners or readers) marked the person to be shamed as deserving of ridicule and reasserted its values over against individualized behavior. It would seem that this kind of spectacle had less to do with the display of the unrestrained power of the sovereign, as Foucault would have it, than with the complicity and participa- tion of the entire social body in the containment of what was considered an anomalous form of subjectivity, that is, *singulari- dad*.[9]

Avellaneda's repositioning of Don Quixote takes another turn moments later. Having been asked to dine with Don Alvaro, Don Quixote is visited by a small group of nobles: "They had been invited in order to decide on the livery each was to wear and

[8]An essential part of inquisitorial proceedings was the undressing of the accused prior to actual torture. See Haim Beinart, ed., *Records of the Trials of the Spanish Inquisition in Ciudad Real* (Jerusalem: Israel National Academy of Sci- ences and Humanities, 1974).

[9]Paradoxically, the reconstitution of the aberrant subject through the tech- nique of shaming would seem to contribute simultaneously to individuation. At least for a moment, the guilty party might be set apart from the community. Foucault in fact has spoken of an inversion by which the subject being punished, having been temporarily detached from the social body, is transformed into a hero.

to enjoy Don Quixote as though he were a private performance, so they went straight up to his room and, finding him half-dressed and looking as has been told, they laughed heartily. . . . He [Don Quixote] used such extraordinary names that at each one the guests gave a thousand retches of suppressed laughter" (87). ("A los cuales había convidado para dar orden en las libreas que cada uno había de sacar en ella, y para que gustasen de don Quijote como de única pieza; y así se subieron derechos a su aposento, y hallándose medio vestido y con la figura que queda dicho, rieron mucho. . . . [don Quijote] diciendo uno nombres tan estraordinarios, que con cada uno dellos daban mil arqueadas de risa los convidados") (155–56). This new humiliation replaces the peasant spectators of the first scene of shame (Sancho and the page) with those drawn from a more powerful social group, so that in a dual operation Don Quixote can be punished even as each member of the aristocratic audience (both inside and outside of the text) is made secure in his own sense of superiority. The translator's rendering of "mil arqueadas de risa" as "a thousand retches of supressed laughter" is a trifle inaccurate; there is no sign of middle-class politeness in this passage. The laughter in the original text is not suppressed but open and uninhibited. In effect, the grotesque body of the other is set in opposition to the grace and decorum associated with a nobility of blood in order to be ridiculed. Thus, for those who "rescue" and subsequently mock him, Don Quixote's mental infirmity is far less important than his inferior social status as a hidalgo, the lowest rank within the minor nobility, and the belief that it is the aristocracy's privilege, not the state's, to discipline a member of any social group who acts outside the range of conduct acceptable to that group. This feeling has little to do with a reenactment of feudal relations (that is, the humbling of a peasant by an aristocrat), for Don Quixote is not a character drawn from the subordinate classes. His exposure before Don Alvaro and his colleagues is less a sign of the struggle between estates than it is an example of the conflict between subgroups within the same social formation. In this case, the wealthy urban nobility's "correction" of an impoverished and unruly hidalgo from the countryside works to undercut the potential for individuation which had been figured in Cervantes's 1605 novel.

As we have seen, the process of subjection in Avellaneda's text consists primarily of shaming techniques designed to refunction the subject in relation to the categories of aristocratic practice. When the offense is sufficiently grave, however, shame is supplemented by personal revenge and a direct physical attack on the offender. Despite humanist and Counter-Reformation denunciations of revenge, Spanish literary production of this period continued to be the site of numerous textual representations of personal vengeance, symptoms of the incompleteness of Spanish absolutism as well as the Spanish aristocracy's continuing investment in the ideology of blood, a powerful cultural trope well into the late seventeenth century. Although the transition to a more complete state monopoly on institutional practices and hence on the discursive construction of subject positions was clearly under way, this process could not as easily be figured within literary discourse and had to be displaced back onto the earlier cultural model of revenge. In the first interpolated tale, which Avellaneda situates at the center of the text in structural imitation of Cervantes's 1605 novel, the reader is shown how the transgression of traditional subject positions can lead not only to public disgrace but in extreme cases to physical and moral destruction.

Briefly told, the story concerns a Flemish aristocrat, M. de Japelin, who is inspired by a Dominican friar to enter the priesthood. After doing so, Japelin is suddenly overcome by doubt and decides to leave the order and marry. Soon after his first child is born the couple receives as a houseguest a Spanish soldier who immediately falls in love with Japelin's wife (herself a former novice). Through a series of deceptions and mistaken identities, the Spaniard succeeds in having sex with her. Overcome with shame and fear, he flees the house only to be pursued and murdered by an enraged Japelin. His wife having already committed suicide, Japelin returns home to kill both his newborn son and himself.

What is striking about this otherwise typical exemplary tale is the violence with which all the main characters are punished.

The Spanish soldier who forces himself on the unknowing wife (only days after she has given birth) is depicted as immediately regretting his act: "[He] returned to his room and bed, quite grief-stricken over what he had done. Since guilt is followed by repentance and sin by shame and worry, he was at once so overwhelmed by his evil that he cursed his lack of reasoning and patience" (144). ("Se volvió a su aposento y cama, harto apesarado de lo que había hecho, que, en fin, como se consigue a la culpa, el arrepentimiento y al pecado la vergüenza y pesar, túvole tan grande luego de su maldad, que maldecía por ello su poco discurso y sufrimiento y su maldita determinación") (224). Nevertheless, the soldier becomes the object of Japelin's merciless vengeance. After running the Spaniard through with his lance, "he dismounted, pulled the javelin out of the corpse and stabbed it again five or six times, hacking its head to pieces. . . . The soldier remained there, trampled in his own blood, food for birds and beasts, as an example to bold decisions" (149) ("se apeó del caballo, y sacando el venablo del cuerpo del cadáver, le volvió a herir con él cinco o seis veces, haciéndole pedazos la cabeza. . . . [El soldado] quedando allí revolcado en su propia sangre para ejemplo de temerarias deliberaciones y comida de aves y bestias") (230). The murder of the infant and Japelin's own suicide are no less graphic.

Any reader familiar with Cervantes's first *Don Quixote* will recognize such passages as utterly foreign to the original novel, but Avellaneda's project is significantly different from that of his precursor. In a text constructed on the twin constraints of shame and revenge, Avellaneda, in this interpolated tale, drives home his point that any attempt at individualized behavior, especially if it involves the abandonment of one's social position, can lead only to death and damnation. As Avellaneda's priest says on hearing the story of Japelin: "The sad end of all the main characters in that tragedy is very much to be feared, but the principal actors could expect nothing better (morally speaking), since they had given up the religious orders which they had started to join" (153). ("Porque muy de temer es el fin triste de todos los interlocutores desa tragedia; pero no podrán tenerle mejor (moral-

mente hablando) los principales personajes della, habiendo dejado el estado de religiosos que habían empezado a tomar")
(235).[10] The emergent concept of subjectivity as the product of
individual will which was being generated by the discourses of
virtue and deeds (a tentative project of the Cervantine text) was
judged to be subversive by a culture founded on the maintenance
of aristocratic and clerical privilege. The application of what
would have been considered poetic justice within the text and,
more important, the use of physical violence in everyday life
were twin options available to the ruling class should inter-
nalized controls fail.

Perhaps it will be said that these are purely fictional accounts
of how the struggle over subjectivity was waged, having more to
do with the aesthetic strategies of literary writing than with the
historical reality of Habsburg Spain. I do not subscribe to the
notion that writing is somehow different from the real, however,
nor do I believe that literature simply reflects social reality.
Japelin's revenge is personal insofar as it was not widely repeated
in daily life. Still, the historical record is replete with similar
attempts to test the status quo. In a letter written in 1635, for
example, a Jesuit reports that in the village of Piedrahita an
elderly nun, having fallen in love with an elderly gentleman, had
abandoned the convent to run off with him. Fleeing toward

---

[10]The priest's remarks, with the explicit warning about leaving the priesthood, as well as the content of the second interpolated tale, seem to support the
hypothesis that Avellaneda's audience was initially a clerical one and that he
himself was a Dominican. Although Avellaneda's second interpolated tale is less
concerned with the issues germane to my argument, it too exemplifies the extent
to which elements of an earlier theological discourse are reworked for a seventeenth-century audience. The story of a prioress who leaves the convent to
pursue a life of secular debauchery, is abandoned, and finally is forced to
prostitute herself is drawn from the miraculous discourse of Mariolatry more
common to the fourteenth century in Spain. After returning to her convent, the
nun discovers that the Virgin has protected her good name by playing the role of
prioress in her absence. As far as the congregation is concerned, the nun has
never been gone. Subjugation and order, which had been disrupted by the nun's
abandonment of social position and vows and which in the story of Japelin could
only be reinstated through violence, is achieved here by the direct intervention
of the sacred.

Portugal, they reached Ciudad Rodrigo: "There the police of Avila (under whose jurisdiction Piedrahita is) came up with them and took them; she returned to her convent where she will die imprisoned or immured; he was taken to Avila, where today he was executed."[11] In this case, it is the state that is responsible for the elimination of dislocated subjects, and it is expeditious in placing firm limits on individual agency.

Avellaneda, in his attempt to rewrite and contain the Cervantine experiment, allows Don Quixote to live, albeit with significant preconditions. If personal vengeance supplements shame in the example of Japelin and if the direct force of the law ends the lives of the wayward nun and her companion, confinement that must mark the final resting place of the other Quixote. The series of public humiliations that seek to discipline him in lieu of direct physical punishment culminates in the final scene of the novel, set in the Toledo madhouse, a space in which the chorus of dissonant voices can be more easily subjected to indoctrination and readjustment.

In *Madness and Civilization*, Foucault tells of the public nature of Renaissance madness. Not yet confined within the fortress of reason, unreason was free to drift effortlessly back and forth across the still-unguarded border of the public sphere before the shift in epistemes that would inaugurate the new age. According to this view, Don Quixote traversed a landscape as yet unmarked by institutional enclosures designed to control those who were thought to be insane. The strong sense of mobility and relative freedom reminds us that Foucault's Quixote is but one more variation on Burckhardt's notion of the Renaissance individual, itself a product of individualism's triumphs in nineteenth-century literary and legal practices.

---

[11]Letter of Father Juan Chacón, Dec. 2, 1635. Quoted in Julio Caro Baroja, "Honour and Shame: A Historical Account of Several Conflicts," in *Honour and Shame: The Values of Mediterranean Society*, ed. J. G. Peristiany (Chicago: University of Chicago Press, 1966), p. 113. Four years after Father Chacón's letter, Sebastián Coto would devote an entire text to such problems: *Discurso médico y moral de las enfermedades por que seguramente pueden las religiosas dejar la clausura* (1639).

With Avellaneda's Quixote out in the open, however, we see that by 1614 there were already strategies for the containment of madness, effective strategies that revealed a strong desire on the part of some sectors of society to remove the "madman" from public view and to erase the figure of the individual from public discourse. Foucault's account of Renaissance madness falters on two fronts: it overly privileges the humanist tradition represented by Erasmus, Cervantes, and Shakespeare in order to make more dramatic the moment of the "Great Confinement" of the later seventeenth century, and it attributes a later period's myth of the individual to early modern culture. What is completely silenced in Foucault's narrative is the countertradition of ascetism, which, in its open hostility to the mad as monstrous and inhuman, continued to thrive throughout the European Renaissance. In Spain it culminates in the satirical writings of Quevedo and others. On the level of Spanish institutions, this other view of madness contributed to the early dismantling of the Ship of Fools; its rotting timbers were rapidly transformed into the rafters of the urban madhouse. Indeed, the first asylum in western Europe devoted specifically to the mentally ill was the one founded in Valencia in 1409 (Lope de Vega set his play *Los locos de Valencia* there), and throughout the fifteenth century, mental institutions were established in most of the major cities of Spain: Zaragoza (1425), Seville (1436), and Valladolid (1489). Avellaneda's Quixote, then, although not a subject constituted by the bonds of classical reason which would be forged in the eighteenth century or refunctioned on the nineteenth-century model in order to increase his economic productivity, is nonetheless made docile by recognized forms of domination underwritten by the social powers of the age: the aristocracy and the church.

It is no accident that in Avellaneda's novel Don Quixote is led by Don Alvaro Tarfe, a nobleman from Granada, to the Casa del Nuncio, the Toledo asylum founded in 1483 by a representative of the Holy See and infamous for having the worst conditions of any asylum in Spain. As Don Quixote waits patiently in the courtyard, unaware that he is about to be committed, one of the inmates tells him: "These thieving guardians are bringing you to throw a heavy chain on you and give you a thorough trouncing until you recover some sanity whether you like it or not. They've done the same thing to me" (339). ("Que le traen engañado estos ladrones guardianes, para echalle una muy buena cadena y dalle muy gentiles tundas hasta que tenga seso, aunque le pese, pues lo mismo han hecho conmigo") (455–56). Despite the obvious illness of Quixote, the clarity of the inmate's warning suggests that the issue of sanity has become secondary to what are ultimately political concerns. Avellaneda imprisons his protagonist because he is mad, but his more pressing ambition is to refunction the alternative forms of subjectivity which Cervantes's first novel had figured forth. Cervantes's representation of a radically autonomous individual runs head on not only into the traditional constraints of shame and revenge but finally into the twin powers of early Spanish absolutism (with Avellaneda as their literary spokesman), which work to suppress it.

Transporting the new subject into an urban environment, then, situates its harmless meanderings in an economy of violence, punishment, and confinement, and reinvigorates the network of far-reaching institutional practices that aimed to control all radically individual behavior. It should not surprise us that Avellaneda's novel is set primarily in cities, and Cervantes's in the country. As one of the characters in Lope de Vega's *Fuente Ovejuna* says: "In the cities there is God's justice / and speedy [secular] punishment" ("En las ciudades hay Dios / y más presto quien castiga").[12] It is not until the 1615 *Don Quixote* that Cervantes would take his protagonist into the courtly society of the duke and duchess and the properly urban setting of Barcelona. In the prologue and first chapter of his own sequel, Cervantes prepares the reader for the new landscape in which his Don Quixote will move, giving three accounts of madness, two in the streets of Seville and Cordoba, one in the asylum in Seville. At no time is Cervantes's Quixote exposed to the horrors of the mad-

---

[12] Lope de Vega, *Fuente Ovejuna*, ed. Alonso Zamora Vicente (Madrid: Espasa-Calpe, 1978), p. 131.

house, and even though the literary experience of confinement in Cervantes reveals the same sources of power we see at work at the end of Avellaneda's version (church and state), there is none of the physical violence that marks Avellaneda's description of an attack by one of the inmates on Quixote: "A sudden rage came over the lunatic and he bit him viciously two or three times, ending by seizing his thumb between his teeth in such a way that he almost lopped it off" (343–44). ("Cuando sobreviniéndole al loco una repentina furia, le dio tres o cuatro bocados crueles en ella, asiéndole a la postre el dedo pulgar con los dientes, de suerte que faltó harto poco para cortársele a cercen") (461). Opposing his text to that of his imitator, Cervantes presents us with a madman who, having convinced the archbishop of his sanity through a series of letters, in essence (since in reality he continues to be mad) mocks the traditional knowledge offered to Avellaneda's Quixote as he was being committed to the Toledo madhouse.[13] The undecidable status of the graduate who thought he was Neptune and Don Quixote's response to the barber's story suggest that in Cervantes's text the character's sanity or madness is not a condition to be decided by external judges but an act of will inherent in the concept of radical subjectivism on which the 1605 text is founded.

In the end, the pressure of traditional values alienates both Don Quixotes, yet only Cervantes's hero is possessed of sufficient agency to be able to realize his intolerable position vis-à vis the elites who seek to manipulate him. Avellaneda's Quixote in fact displays a strong desire to be subjugated by the dominant order.

[13] Alvaro Tarfe's page tells Don Quixote: "Take care of your soul and realize God's mercy in not permitting you to die on those roads in the disastrous situations in which your madness placed you so many times" (344) ("Mire por su alma, y reconozca la merced que Dios le ha hecho en no permitir muriese por esos caminos a manos de las desastradas ocasiones en que sus locuras le han pusto tantas veces") (462). In the barber's story of Cervantes's 1615 text (2.1), the madman of Seville decides that "by the mercy of God he had recovered his lost wits"; the recovery is refuted a few pages later when he proves that he has only played at being sane and is led back to his cell. In Cervantes's version, God's mercy seems to have less to do with the illness or the cure than does individual will and self-determination.

Early in the novel we are told that his ultimate goal will be determined by the limits of aristocratic society: "He intended to go to the court of the King of Spain to make himself known by his exploits. 'And,' added good Don Quixote, 'I shall make friends with the grandees, dukes, marquises, and counts who help in the service of his royal person' " (30). ("Y que de allí pensaba después ir a la corte del rey de España para darse a conocer por sus fazañas. Y trabaré amistad—añadía el buen don Quijote—con los grandes, duques, marqueses y condes que al servicio de su real persona asisten") (86). His stated intention, to provoke and kill the majority of the noblemen he meets, is merely a variation on aristocratic rivalries that push incessantly toward the source of all power, the monarch himself. In effect, Avellaneda's Quixote lacks any subjectivity at all until he has been interpellated through the symbolic order of courtly society—("His Catholic Majesty will be forced to extol me as one of the best knights in Europe") (30). ("Es fuerza que Su Majestad Católica me alabe por uno de los mejores caballeros de Europa") (87)—and thereby incorporated into the body politic. This position for subjectivity stands in sharp contrast to Cervantes's 1605 character, who virtually never speaks of the Spanish ruling classes and at no time expresses the wish to gain their favor or serve their interests. The refusal to subject himself to any of the hegemonic forces at work in his society underscores the strong motif of wandering which has been noted by critics ranging from Lukács to Foucault. Moving along the margins of the dominant culture, Cervantes's Don Quixote is not the romantic rebel many traditional critics have wanted him to be; nonetheless, he works to clear a space in which modern forms of subjectivity would later appear.[14]

If the protagonist of Cervantes's 1605 novel had not posed a threat to the dominant order that surrounded it, even if only on

---

[14]A similar case has been made for the character of Hamlet. The fragile interiority of Shakespeare's prince at once emerges and recedes from view; its potential for disrupting the social whole is recuperated through the dispersal of its power into other characters, who destroy Hamlet's claim to singularity. See Francis Barker, *The Tremulous Private Body: Essays on Subjection* (London: Methuen, 1984).

the symbolic level, there would have been little need for swift and hostile rebuttal from Avellaneda and his ideological brethren. Francisco de Avila, to name only one further example, staged the following scene in "El entremés famoso de los invencibles hechos de Don Quijote de la Mancha" (1617), denigrating both Sancho and his companion in ways similar to those used by Avellaneda:

> ([Don Quixote] enters dressed as a picaro . . . as ridiculous as possible)
> INNKEEPER: To what is he who takes himself for a noble knight obliged?
> DON QUIXOTE: To many things.
> SANCHO: Not to pay what he owes,
>   To waste his inheritance,
>   To gamble, chase whores, and give himself to vices,
>   And never to undertake good deeds.

> ([sale a escena vestido a lo pícaro . . . lo más ridículo que ser pudiera]
> VENTERO: ¡A qué se obliga el noble caballero
>   que se tiene por tal?
> DON QUIJOTE: A muchas cosas.
> SANCHO: A no pagar jamás lo que debiere
>   a gastar mal gastado el mayorazgo
>   a jugar, a putear, a darse a vicios
>   y no emplearse nunca en buenas obras.)[15]

By no means had Cervantes written a revolutionary concept of the individual or even a fully developed bourgeois concept. These possibilities simply were not available to him in the historical conjuncture in which he was situated. The fact of the matter is that the 1615 novel contains several changes in the quixotic project similar to those Avellaneda had made: the suggestion that knights-errant might serve the king (2:1), the disper-

---

[15] Francisco de Avila, *El entremés famoso de los invencibles hechos de Don Quixote de la Mancha* (Madrid: Enciclopedia Moderna, 1905).

sal of Don Quixote's singularity by the introduction of Sansón Carrasco as the agent of Don Quixote's "cure" (2:3), the subtle display of state-sponsored revenge (2:60), and the spectacle of public humiliation in Barcelona (2:62). In addition, the novel's final scenes emphasize that Cervantes felt compelled to convert the subjectivist Don Quixote of 1605 to the more traditional Christian of 1615, who dies a conventional death well within the bosom of the church. But Avellaneda could not have foreseen these developments. Sufficiently disturbed by the gesture toward a new kind of subject in Cervantes's first text, he responded quickly to punish and correct it. What this literary rivalry brings into view is a struggle that would be carried out on diverse cultural backgrounds for decades to come. In Spain, the emergent form of the individual sketched out in Cervantes's 1605 text would be locked away in the gloomy dungeons of Avellaneda's madhouse at least until the early nineteenth century. In other parts of Europe, the Cervantine Quixote would ride at the vanguard of bourgeois individualism and the new forms of freedom and containment it authorized.[16]

III

Cervantes's own response to the first Don Quixote was in many ways no less dramatic than Avellaneda's. The 1615 *Don Quixote* moves away from the extreme subjectivism of the origi-

[16]Within the field of Hispanism, the various historical appropriations of Don Quixote have given rise to what in contemporary Cervantes criticism is referred to as the "hard" and the "soft" approach to the novel, the former maintaining that the original creator of Don Quixote meant to portray him negatively, the latter sympathetically. Ultimately this is but one more false opposition not unrelated to others this book seeks to undo. Proponents of the hard school, openly concerned with authorial intention, want the novel to be read strictly as a burlesque, and accuse the soft or "romantic critics" of idealizing the hero, relating the text to either the "human spirit" or Spanish history or forcing twentieth-century values on it. See Anthony Close, *The Romantic Approach to "Don Quixote": A Critical History of the Romantic Tradition in "Quixote" Criticism* (Cambridge: Cambridge University Press, 1978).

nal text by reconstructing the individual through a complex economy of alterity, spectacle, and resubjectification. This is not to say that Cervantes incorporates Avellaneda's critique into his own continuation. On the contrary, in chapter 62 of the 1615 text he directly rejects his anonymous rival's transformation of Don Quixote and has the knight defiantly proclaim: "I have heard of this book already, said Don Quixote, but truly, on my conscience, I thought it had been burnt by now and reduced to ashes for its presumption. But it will get is Martinmas like every hog" ("Ya yo tengo noticia deste libro—dijo don Quijote—, y en verdad y en mi conciencia que pensé que ya estaba quemado y hecho polvos, por impertinente; pero su San Martín se le llegará, como a cada puerco"). More important, in chapter 72, Cervantes rewrites one of Avellaneda's most significant characters, Alvaro Tarfe, the aristocrat who had manipulated Don Quixote into the madhouse. In a scene that powerfully textualizes the ideological struggle between the two authors, the name Alvaro Tarfe is recognized by the real Don Quixote, who had noticed it in Avellaneda's novel in a Barcelona printshop. In their discussion of the confusing existence of the two Quixotes and two Sanchos, Tarfe perceives the vast difference that separates the man he had met from the one he now faces:

> There's no doubt in my mind that the enchanters who persecute Don Quixote the Good have been trying to persecute me with Don Quixote the Bad. But I don't know what I'm saying, for I dare swear that I left him shut up in the madhouse at Toledo for treatment, and here starts up another Don Quixote very different from mine.
> I do not know, said Don Quixote, whether I am good, but I can say that I am not "the bad." And to prove it I would have you know, Don Alvaro Tarfe, that I have never been in Saragossa in all the days of my life. On the contrary, when I was told that the fictitious Don Quixote had taken part in the jousts in that city I decided not to go there, and so to proclaim his lie to the world. . . .
> In short, Don Alvaro Tarfe, I am Don Quixote de la Mancha, the same of whom fame speaks, and that miserable man who sought to usurp my name and take the credit for my designs is not he. I beg

your worship, as you are a gentleman, to be so kind as to make a declaration before the mayor of this place that you have never seen me in all the days of your life till today, and that I am not the Don Quixote written of in the second part, nor is this Sancho Panza, my squire, the man your worship knew.

I'll do that with very great pleasure, replied Don Alvaro, for it's very surprising to see two Don Quixotes and two Sanchos at the same time, alike in their names yet how different in their deeds. Let me affirm once more that I didn't see what I did see, and that what happened to me didn't happen.

(Y tengo por sin duda que los encantadores que persiguen a don Quijote el bueno han querido perseguirme a mí con don Quijote el malo. Pero no sé qué me diga; que osaré yo jurar que le dejo metido en la casa del Nuncio, en Toledo, para que le curen, y agora remanece aquí otro don Quijote, aunque bien diferente del mio.

—Yo—dijo don Quijote—no sé si soy bueno; pero sé decir que no soy el malo; para prueba de lo cual quiero que sepa vuestra merced, mi señor don Alvaro Tarfe, que en todos los días de mi vida no he estado en Zaragoza; antes, por haberme dicho que ese don Quijote fantástico se había hallado en las justas desa ciudad, no quise yo entrar en ella, por sacar a las barbas del mundo su mentira. . . . Finalmente, señor don Alvaro Tarfe, yo soy don Quijote de la Mancha, el mismo que dice la fama, y no ese desventurado que ha querido usurpar mi nombre y honrarse con mis pensamientos. A vuestra merced suplico, por lo que deba a ser caballero, sea servido de hacer una declaración ante el alcalde deste lugar, de que vuestra merced no me ha visto en todos los días de su vida hasta agora, y de que yo no soy el don Quijote impreso en la segunda parte, ni este Sancho Panza mi escudero es aquel que vuestra merced conoció.

—Eso haré yo de muy buena gana—respondió don Alvaro—, puesto que causa admiración ver dos don Quijotes y dos Sanchos a un mismo tiempo, tan conformes en los nombres como diferentes en las acciones; y vuelvo a decir y me afirmo que no he visto lo que he visto ni ha pasado por mí lo que ha pasado.)

Don Quixote's self-defense and its invocation of "vuestra merced" reminds us of Lázaro de Tormes's "autobiography" even as it looks forward to the transformation of Don Quixote into Alonso

Quijano the Good. More important, the erasure of Avellaneda's character through legal discourse marks the moment in which Cervantes asserts ownership of his creation and further distances his own text from the forms of subjectivity figured in that of his rival. It is not that Cervantes seeks to defend the radical individuation of his first *Don Quixote* since in the continuation of 1615 he alters the makeup of his protagonist in significant ways. But even as he modifies his own project through deindividuating textual strategies, he makes a point of calling our attention to the disjuncture between his new Don Quixote and Avellaneda's insistence on the traditional categories of blood and status.

In the 1615 *Don Quixote*, the emergent individual of 1605 is refunctioned through a series of encounters not so much with the representatives of traditional culture as with the complex social practices of early modern Spanish society. But before Don Quixote's conversion can occur, the idea of the subject as individual undergoes an uncanny transference onto the character who will precipitate Don Quixote's return, Sansón Carrasco. Carrasco is one of the first readers of Don Quixote. The university-trained scholar, who is perhaps best known for being the physical cause of Don Quixote's demise, has the additional distinction of being among those privileged readers given the opportunity to come face to face with a literary hero. Given this doubly unique status, Carrasco proves to be much more than a passive receiver of a fictional or even historical narrative; on the contrary, not unlike Don Quixote himself, he too is "converted" through chivalric discourse and becomes one of Don Quixote's most devoted (and hence most destructive) followers. The contradictory desires of Carrasco to publicize, participate in, and ultimately destroy Don Quixote's project are central to the development of Cervantes's 1615 novel and are an important symptom of the contradictory forms of subjectivity at work in seventeenth-century literary discourse.

The figure of Carrasco has traditionally been seen as relatively passive, either the willing tool of other characters (the priest and the barber) thought to be intimately linked to the hegemonic ideology that struggles to contain the idea of singularity or, in a more properly psychological view, as a device by which Don

Quixote comes to achieve self-knowledge. Critics have agreed that despite his active participation in the attempt to make Don Quixote "return to his senses," Carrasco has little understanding of what Don Quixote is really about. Américo Castro, for example, maintained that Carrasco is "a stubborn and earthbound individual, [who] neither understands nor puts up with the chimerical complexity of quixotic life."[17] On this view, Carrasco becomes a sophisticated variation on Sancho Panza, the realist other to Don Quixote's idealist and idealistic vision. But unlike Sancho's complementarity, Carrasco's otherness must be regarded as decisively "antiquixotic." Joaquin Casalduero in fact reads the final defeat of Don Quixote at Carrasco's hands as the passage from one world to another, from one historical moment to the next: "It is an epoch, a style, an illusion that is ending, even as it is still unknown what the world of the Knight of the Mirrors and of the White Moon will be like" ("Es una época, un estilo, una ilusión que se acaba, cuando todavía no se sabe cómo será el mundo del Caballero de los Espejos y de la Blanca Luna").[18] I will have occasion to return to this idea later. For now, I would only say that Casalduero underestimates the power inherent in the subjectivism of the 1605 text. The world of the Knight of the White Moon is less a rupture with the world of Don Quixote than its logical continuation.

Castro's remark that Carrasco fails to understand the complexity of Don Quixote's project presents a number of problems since it is clear that, despite his incomplete comprehension, Carrasco is anxious to sign on as a knight-errant. Castro himself says elsewhere: "Here we are faced with a character who participates in what I have called the quixotic project, in the presence of Don Quixote!" ("henos aquí en presencia de un personaje que se aventura en la que he llamado serie quijotesca, ¡frente a Don

---

[17] Américo Castro, "An Introduction to the *Quijote*," in *An Idea of History: Selected Essays of Americo Castro*, trans. Stephen Gilman and E. L. King (Columbus: Ohio State University Press, 1977), p. 99.

[18] Joaquin Casalduero, *Sentido y forma del Quijote (1605–1615)* (Madrid: Insula, 1966), p. 371.

Quijote!").[19] That he does is not so surprising, perhaps, if we begin to analyze Carrasco's behavior as a result of Don Quixote's powerful influence on him. Arthur Efron makes a case for viewing Carrasco as an extremely hostile opponent to Don Quixote's project, yet points out the depth of the bachelor's ambivalent desire: "Sansón Carrasco, seen very literally, is the most determined of those who oppose Quixote, because he is the man who rides out and finally defeats the knight in combat and forces him to return home. But Carrasco as poet is invited by the Knight to compose verses in honor of Quixote's departure from Dulcinea . . . [and] he is glad to agree to go into the pastoral life with Quixote."[20] To these last two, seemingly unimportant details, which readers often ignore inasmuch as Carrasco is ultimately the agent of Don Quixote's demise, I would add that Carrasco also offers to replace Sancho as Don Quixote's squire (2:7).

Clearly, Carrasco is willing to put his own talents at the service of Don Quixote. Some have claimed that Carrasco does these things only to achieve Don Quixote's cure, but his interest goes far beyond mere altruism and his function in the novel is complex. From their earliest meeting, we sense the importance of this new character who is brought into Don Quixote's circle by Sancho Panza. The narrator's insistence in chapter 7 that Carrasco is a "famous rascal" ("socarrón famoso") and a "great rascal" ("gran socarrón") underscores his being "in a malicious state" ("de condición maliciosa") or, in a more accurate translation, "of a malicious nature." Indeed, the word *socarrón* connotes negative qualities and the kind of repressed resentment that will motivate Carrasco later in the novel. According to Covarrubias, the *socarrón* is "the dissembling scoundrel who only feigns interest and when speaking with you *is secretly raging against you*" ("el bellaco dissimulado, que sólo pretende su interés, y quando

[19]Américo Castro, *El pensamiento de Cervantes* (Barcelona: Noguer, 1972), p. 140.
[20]Arthur Efron, *Don Quixote and the Dulcineated World* (Austin: University of Texas Press, 1971), p. 103.

habla con vos os *está secretamente abrasando"*).²¹ What Carrasco
might be raging about is something that will concern us later. For
now, I want to insist that despite an underlying animosity, the
bachelor is one of the characters most attracted to Don Quixote
and his peculiar activity; throughout the novel we are reminded
that Carrasco thinks highly of Don Quixote, "for he has an
excellent brain, if he can only be freed from the follies of chivalry" ("un hombre que le tiene bonísimo [el juicio], como le dejen
las sandeces de la caballería") (2:65). And, at the same time, the
implicit trust Don Quixote seems to invest in Carrasco is the
kind usually reserved for only one's closest followers. Not long
after the narrator has reminded us of Carrasco's "socarronía" he
refers to him simply as "el gran Carrasco," the irony of which is
weakened by the surprising detail that follows: "who was their
oracle from that time on" ("que por entonces era su [Don Quixote's] oráculo") (2:7). The undecidability of the term *oráculo* is
important because it suggests the ambiguity of Carrasco's relationship to Don Quixote. The oracle is at once a guiding principle and a harbinger of disaster and death. If we adhere to the
conventional seventeenth-century understanding of the word,
however, we are drawn to an exclusively negative reading of
Sansón. Covarrubias tells us: "Oracle, according to the Gentiles,
was the answer, always mistaken and ambiguous, given by de-
mons and their false gods" ("Oráculo, cerca de los gentiles, era la
respuesta que davan los demonios y sus falsos dioses, que siempre eran equívocas y ambiguas").²² As both *socarrón* and *oráculo*,
the bachelor is clearly much more than the errand boy for Pero
Pérez, the priest.

Don Quixote's transformation from a strictly comic to a more
complex character has traditionally been marked at the point at
which Quixote enters the Sierra Morena (1:23). But there are
indications of the shift as early as chapter 19. With the terrifying
sight of blazing torches, forms in white surplices, and a litter
laden with a corpse approaching in the night, the narrator draws

²¹Covarrubias, *Tesoro*, my emphasis.
²²Ibid.

his most positive portrait yet of Don Quixote: "So without more ado he couched his lance, steadied himself in the saddle, and with exquisite bearing and courage took up his position in the middle of the road along which the white figures would have to pass" ("y, sin hacer otro discurso, enristró su lanzón, púsose bien en la silla, y con gentil brío y continente se puso en la mitad del camino por donde los encamisados forzosamente habían de pasar"). In this brief charismatic episode, even the pathetic figure of Rocinante is endowed with special powers: "He then turned on the others, and the speed with which he attacked and routed them was a wonder to see, for Rocinante seemed in that moment to have sprouted wings, so swiftly and proudly did he move" ("Y revolviéndose por los demás, era cosa de ver con la presteza que los acometía y desbarataba, que no parecía sino que en aquel instante le habían nacido alas a Rocinante, según andaba de ligero y orgulloso"). Although this momentary apotheosis ends in the condemnation by Alonso López, whose leg Don Quixote has broken, the reader's initial reaction might not be unlike that of Sancho Panza, who "looked on all this, admiring his master's dauntless courage and saying to himself, 'There's no doubt that my master is as valiant and mighty as he says'" ("Todo lo miraba Sancho, admirado del ardimiento de su señor, y decía entre sí: Sin duda este mi amo es tan valiente y esforzado como él dice").

The kind of personal authority displayed by Don Quixote at this point in the novel, ephemeral as it might be, is a surface manifestation of a more complex appeal that draws Carrasco into the quixotic project to a greater degree than any other character but Sancho. By the time Carrasco appears on the scene, Don Quixote already possesses an additional level of renown, since, as Carrasco himself is the first to tell us, the published version of his exploits now enjoys a large reading public. The bachelor, then, is not only one of the first readers of *Don Quixote* but also the first historian of its reception (2:3). As such he is intensely aware of the fame that surrounds the first part and the envy that fame produces in other would-be writers: "Renowned men of genius, great poets and famous historians are always, or generally, envied by such as make it their pleasure and particular pastime to judge the writings of others, without having published any of their own" ("Los hombres famosos por sus ingenios, los grandes poetas, los ilustres historiadores, siempre, o las más veces, son envidiados de aquellos que tienen por gusto y por particular entretenimiento juzgar los escritos ajenos, sin haber dado algunos propios a la luz del mundo") (2:3). Sansón, the ephebe-poet and amateur critic, is caught up in a peculiar anxiety of influence which creates both literary and personal rivalries.[23] The emergent form of the individual, now textualized in the first *Don Quixote*, problematizes his subjectivity even as it had disturbed Avellaneda's ideological universe.

Carrasco's function as a sign of the desire for alternative subject positions is revealed in the contradictory space between two statements he makes in reference to himself. Early in the novel (2:4), when Don Quixote requests that Carrasco compose a poem on Dulcinea, "The Bachelor replied that, although he was not one of the most famous poets in Spain . . . he would not fail to write the verses" ("el bachiller respondió que puesto que él no era de los famosos poetas que había en España . . . que no dejaría de componer los tales metros"). Some time later, however, when Don Quixote is home and Sansón is enthusiastically seconding the pastoral project that would have figured yet another kind of subject, the bachelor pridefully proclaims, "As all the world knows by now, I am a most famous poet" ("Como ya todo el mundo sabe, yo soy celebérrimo poeta") (2:73). Of course, apart from a few attempts at poetry, Don Quixote is not really an author anyway. Why then should Carrasco envy Don Quixote's celebrity, especially when Carrasco suggests that he is actually in contact with Cide Hamete, the real author of the first part? "I will take care . . . to warn the author of this history," he says, "not to forget what our good Sancho has said should he print it

---

[23] Luis Murillo was among the first to note that "Sansón Carrasco . . . recognizes the knight famed in and out of his history. . . . Sansón is the first of a line of celebrators of [Don Quixote's] prowess." *The Golden Dial* (Oxford: Dolphin, 1975), p. 65.

again" ("Yo tendré cuidado . . . de acusar al autor de la historia que si otra vez la imprimiere, no se le olvide esto que el buen Sancho ha dicho") (2:4). What increases Don Quixote's prestige in Carrasco's eyes is not the celebrity of an author or even the fame of the text itself, which has been symbolically transferred to its protagonist. Rather it is the setting apart of Don Quixote, his individuality (*singularidad*), that the bachelor comes to covet. In a complex process involving alterity and desire, the transference of cultural power to an individual produces both the disciple and its opposite. In essence, Sansón Carrasco is one of the first modern assassins in literature.

The economy of the relationship between Sansón and Don Quixote, then, is founded on more than the traditional concept of fame or the hero. Carrasco's sense that Don Quixote is somehow in touch with a vital and active source of power compels him to become the Knight of the Wood, of the Mirrors, and of the White Moon, for his overriding desire is to participate in this power at any cost. I would not want to be understood as saying that Don Quixote possesses some magical or mysterious ability to dominate others; on the contrary, his gifts of persuasion are more often than not pitifully ineffectual (his speech on the Golden Age, for example). In his actualization of certain cultural values of both the past and present, however, Don Quixote appears to Carrasco as someone set apart from the community, who thus embodies a specific alternative to traditional forms of the subject. As the Knight of the Wood, Carrasco explains how he has defeated the famous Don Quixote de la Mancha in battle and how "since I have conquered him, his glory, his fame and his honour are transferred and have passed to my person" ("abiéndole yo vencido a él, su gloria su fama y su honra se ha transferido y pasado a mi persona") (2:14). Although at this point in the novel Carrasco has not yet accomplished what he claims, he is in effect foretelling what he seeks to achieve later as the Knight of the White Moon.

Edward Shils's reworking of Weber's theory of charisma is useful here because it provides us with a model that is at once secular and devoid of the kind of psychologism that reduces individual authority to the effects of the pathological. The bearer of charisma, according to Shils, can be perceived either as somehow in contact with a profound ordering principle or as challenging the existing order, thereby anticipating a new configuration superior to the old. The extraordinary quality of such a figure lies in his ability to intensify and bring to the foreground values that are either repressed or as yet not fully realized within the structures of everyday life. Or to put the matter another way, the charismatic individual disrupts the status quo by figuring a form of subjectivity constituted by discursive practices that are still only emergent; thus he claims an authority derived from sources that seem remote in time and space. It is especially in periods of social upheaval that such figures arise: "Their demand for the right order of things is intensified; their sensibility to the divergence between this right order and the actually existing state of affairs is heightened."[24] Even seventeenth-century readers, who for the most part probably saw little else in Don Quixote than a burlesque figure, did not hesitate to make him the symbol of contemporary worthy causes such as defenses of the Virgin or even the purity of the Castilian language: "I want to sally forth like a Don Quixote de la Mancha to defend the beauty of the princess Dulcinea of our Language." ("Quiero salir como un Don Quijote de la Mancha a defender la hermosura de la princesa Dulcinea de nuestra Lengua").[25]

The resonances of messianic and prophetic thought are unavoidable here, and I want to dissociate my reading of Don Quixote's charismatic power from others that have made it explicitly religious in nature (Unamuno's is the best-known example), especially since Don Quixote's one opportunity to play the role of savior in the Cave of Montesinos is a complete failure. The possibility that Don Quixote represents a higher spiritual order does not interest me as much as his figuration of emergent

[24]Edward Shils, *Center and Periphery: Essays in Macrosociology* (Chicago: University of Chicago Press, 1975), p. 132.
[25]Juan de Robles, *El culto sevillano* (1631).

social relations—in other words, a form of subjectivity that stands in contradiction to the traditional forms of seventeenth-century Spanish life. But what are the principal ideological currents that traverse the figure of Don Quixote as he rides across the Spanish landscape?

Don Quixote's charismatic authority originates in two distinct and seemingly antithetical ideological centers: first, the imaginary moment, now past, of the harmonious *Gemeinschaft*, a utopian community founded on Christian virtues, and, second, the incipient figure of an autonomous subject (the individual) relatively free of the inherited determinants of blood and caste. That both of these principles functioned essentially as myths of desire (the first could not be realized in the real world, the second continued to be contradicted by the Castilian legal system) does not diminish their effect on the social world in which they were invoked. On the contrary, despite the fact that one would seem to cancel out the other, their combined appeal is what makes Don Quixote such a formidable figure, a figure Carrasco feels compelled to follow and ultimately to destroy. On one level, Don Quixote's appropriation of the Golden Age as the organizing principle of his project may be read as a backward-looking act designed to avoid the harsh realities of contemporary life. This in effect is how the utopian myth functions in most pastoral discourse: a primitive economy forms the basis for the simple and virtuous existence of a rustic population; the nostalgic glance of the reader is directed back to a time in which "all was peace then, all amity, all concord" ("todo era paz entonces, todo amistad, todo concordia") (2:11). According to one school of critical thought, Cervantes's purpose is antipastoral, insofar as he uses his protagonist to deconstruct a myth that he felt was responsible for the contemporary state of affairs in Spanish society. Maravall has written, for example: "Cervantes needs to explain that utopia in all its breadth and in all seriousness in order to demonstrate how it leads to one failure after another (therefore, despite its element of humor, the *Quixote* seems a serious book)" ("Cervantes necesita explanar en toda su amplitud y con toda seriedad esa utopía, para hacer ver cómo arrastra de fracaso en fracaso [por eso, pese a su dosis de burla, el *Quijote* parece un libro serio])."²⁶

According to this view, Sansón Carrasco, as agent of Don Quixote's "cure," would be the character most likely to reject the ideology of the pastoral (and thereby become the novel's "hero"). As I have suggested, however, the bachelor is eager to follow Don Quixote in the final scenes of the novel and to subject himself to pastoral discourse as the shepherd Sansonino Carrascón. What is insufficiently developed in Maravall's argument is the idea that Cervantes's treatment of the pastoral, here and in "The Dogs' Colloquy" ("El coloquio de los perros"), reveals not only the deficiencies of the ideology that informs it but the tremendous appeal of that ideology as well. Cervantes debunks the ways in which certain sectors of Spanish society had sought to appropriate the Golden Age myth, but he also calls attention to the desire of many to invest in its promises. Carrasco's eagerness to follow Don Quixote yet again derives from the ability of pastoral discourse to interpellate subject positions that appear more powerful than those available in contemporary social relations. Or put into the language of Barthean textual pleasure, the 1605 Don Quixote's radical subjectivism, his "otherness," is admired by Carrasco, one of his earliest readers, for its coherence and apparent unity. As a result, a *coexistence* occurs in which the kind of subject invoked in the quixotic text functions as a citation, or better yet a neologism, which, once received by Carrasco and others, disrupts the seemingly calm surface of Spanish culture.²⁷ This effect would explain in part why Avellaneda reacted so quickly and why so many of the characters in Cervantes's own novels (from the innkeeper on) are willing to participate in the quixotic project.

Don Quixote's enactment of potentially subversive new sub-

---

²⁶José Antonio Maravall, *Utopía y contrautopía en el Quijote* (Santiago de Compostela: Pico Sacro, 1976), p. 209. See also Javier Herrero, "Arcadia's Inferno: Cervantes' Attack on the Pastoral," *Bulletin of Hispanic Studies* 55 (1978): 289–99.

²⁷Roland Barthes describes *coexistence* in his preface to *Sade/Fourier/Loyola*, trans. Richard Miller (New York: Hill and Wang, 1976), and in *The Pleasure of the Text*, trans. Richard Miller (New York: Hill and Wang, 1975).

ject forms, however, both attracts and frightens Carrasco as it had fascinated and disturbed Cervantes himself. To what may we attribute the bachelor's apparently sincere response to the knight's recantation at the end of the 1615 text—"No more of that, I pray you. Return to your senses and cease your idle tales!" ("Calle por su vida, vuelva en sí, y déjese de cuentos")—if not to his desire to partake of the possibility of alternative subject positions which Don Quixote had figured forth? The uncanny parallels between Sansón's behavior and certain events in our own recent history (the celebrity-fan-assassination nexus) should not be discounted out of hand—the acolyte's obsession to be near (to become?) the object of his desire leads to the unavoidable moment when he must kill that object-person. With Don Quixote gone, Carrasco in essence loses the ground on which his own subjectivity is precariously constructed.

Carrasco deforms the quixotic project not because of some spiritual deficiency in himself (as Castro would have it) but because he fails to see that chivalry is less important than the new context in which it is being enacted. Don Quixote does not act out Amadis's adventures as much as he speaks an "Amadisian" language on the stage of seventeenth-century Castilian social life. Given what we have learned about the limited forms of subjectivity in the period, it is clear that Don Quixote's behavior opened up a new discursive space through which alternative subject positions could be imagined and enacted. In my reading, chivalric discourse, rather than an all-encompassing false consciousness as René Girard has claimed,[28] was a vehicle through which resistance might take shape. Put another way, the dis-

---

[28] Girard's notion of triangular desire is explained in his *Deceit, Desire, and the Novel: Self and Other in Literary Structure* (Baltimore: Johns Hopkins University Press, 1965). I want to make clear that my analysis of Carrasco's narrative function diverges fundamentally from Girard's theory of desire. Whereas Girard uses phenomenological language and describes the relationship between "self" and other as "a bizarre marriage of two lucid consciousnesses" (p. 4) which incapacitates one or both of the parties, my claim is that material practices (especially writing) give shape to multiple subject positions that do not collapse into one another but actively compete for dominance.

course of chivalry, which had originated in an earlier hegemonic formation (the feudal mode of production in strictly economic terms), now functions as both a residual and a (re)emergent practice. By refusing, as it were, the situation of hidalgo which was prescribed for him and answering the call of knight-errantry, Don Quixote sets the stage for other forms of agency which will be carried out by his fellow characters in the 1615 novel. I have already argued that the practical consequences of this process are perhaps best exemplified by Sancho who, far from being a simpleton, acts out of the dual motivation that more properly characterizes that moment in the history of subjectivity in the West—an increasing economic determinism and the resultant desire to *medrar* (to become upwardly mobile). It is Sancho in fact who with his performance as governor disrupts all expectations based on class and blood. The others who were exposed early on to *quijotismo*, either inside or outside of the text—that is, both characters and critics—saw only the mechanical reenactment of an anachronistic chivalric code. Hence the dead-end preoccupation with Don Quixote's madness. One possible solution to this critical impasse is to recontextualize the novel in its sociocultural milieu. Only then can the potential threat to the dominant order posed by the early stages of Cervantes's project come into sharp focus. Avellaneda's violent response is our best indication that the 1605 text was in fact received as a challenge by certain contemporary readers. Somewhere between Cervantes's position and Avellaneda's stands Carrasco who, in an ambivalent posture not unlike Quevedo's when confronted by the picaro, is both fascinated by and committed to repressing those subject forms only beginning to emerge.

IV

My reading of the episode of the duke and duchess from Cervantes's 1615 *Don Quixote* shares many of the suppositions underlying what I have said about Carrasco and therefore differs substantially from the so-called antiromantic approach. When

Oscar Mandel claimed some thirty years ago, "On the whole, then, even the ducal pair and Sansón can be counted among the centers of normalcy," he succinctly restated an argument that only recently has begun to lose its appeal.[29] My principal objection to this argument is that it dilutes the ironic force of the text and merely offers us another version of Cervantes the writer of slapstick comedy. The fundamental issues of society and social organization which inform the entire 1615 text and are in the foreground of the protagonist's first speech on "principles of statecraft and methods of government" ("razón de estado and modos de gobierno") has been too often neglected by a traditional criticism that for the most part has preferred to discuss only the earliest stages of Don Quixote's chivalric project. Such a preference is not surprising, considering that the earliest readers of the first novel who later appear in the second are themselves blind to the substantial changes that have taken place in the quixotic enterprise. The Bachelor Sansón's reading, for example, is limited because he sees only the consequences for the emergent individual; that this focus on autonomous subjectivity produces Carrasco's ambivalence, which combines a desire to "play" with the wish for personal vengeance, is a logical extension of his narrative function. And given what we know about Cervantes's negative attitude toward revenge (as illustrated in "La gitanilla," throughout *Persiles and Sigismunda*, and elsewhere), it is difficult to accept the portrayal of Carrasco as a wholly positive character. Like Carrasco, the duke and duchess react to the extreme subjectivism of the first text; unlike Carrasco, they do not attempt to destroy it but to manipulate it for their own entertainment. The government of the ducal pair, which might have served as a model for enlightened social organization, instead turns out to be an ethically bankrupt space in which spectacle is degraded and the individual subjugated.

As José Antonio Maravall taught us, the term *razón de estado* signified a number of related, yet often contradictory practices,

---

[29] Oscar Mandel, "The Function of the Norm in *Don Quixote*," *Modern Philology* 55 (1958): 160.

not the least important of which was the interpellation of subject positions conducive to maintaining the state.[30] What the ducal pair exemplifies, however, is a highly intensified desire to manipulate for no other reason than personal diversion. To them, it seems in no way extreme to convert their entire court and holdings into a stage on which their subjects are asked to act out the script they have written. In these two characters Cervantes raises the issues of power, control, and the subject's ability to resist manipulation in unexpected ways. Central to the entire mechanism of constructing subjectivity is the *afecto*, or passion, of wonder. According to seventeenth-century thought, wonder is the only objective passion. It is the moment at which the body, summarily dismissed from the stage of experience by Descartes in the *Meditations*, reinserts itself and involves the subject in commitments that in turn implicate the subject in the larger structures of culture and society. Wonder, then, leads to an ethics or a way of behaving in the world, and it should not surprise us that Don Quixote's career as a knight-errant proceeds from the awe inspired by the deeds of Amadis. Don Quixote, in turn, exercises at certain key points in the text a charismatic influence over those with whom he comes in contact (Juan Palomeque, Carrasco, and most important Sancho) and through the resulting *admiratio* they are transformed. The inevitable dialectic involving wonder, violence, and ethics is a structural constant in Cervantes's second *Don Quixote* and in my opinion has yet to be adequately investigated.

On the wider stage of history, the appropriation of wonder by the absolute monarchy and the church was a mechanism central to diverse cultural practices ranging from the colonization of America to the later *comedia*. If the moment of *admiratio* could be the catalyst for a new subjectivity, could it not also be the foundation for the refunctioning of entire populations? Spectacle, then, became a mass form of wonder insofar as it sought to astonish large groups of people, reduce them to momentary passivity, and ultimately subjugate them (that is, make them

[30]Maravall, "Moral de acomodación."

subjects). The ethical imperative underlying this project was crucial because the well-being of the empire, the body-politic that now stretched out across the Atlantic and beyond, depended on the proper functioning of each of its parts. Disconnected from its ethical base, spectacle could decline into the kind of degraded activity that already in the reign of Philip III had come to be associated with a morally bankrupt ruling class. In a culture as intrinsically theatrical as that of the early modern Spanish aristocracy, misreadings of imaginary situations could often produce very real results. In February 1604, for example, the enactment of a fake Moorish invasion for Philip III's entertainment wounded the pride of one nobleman and led to multiple casualties:

> The duke of Tursi . . . wanted His Majesty to be entertained on his journey, so he let him know that first he would put a galley off the coast near where he had to pass, so that soldiers dressed as Moors might disembark from it and approach the passing courtiers; and it so happened that Don Luis Henriquez, the chief steward, was traveling in a litter with his servants . . . and upon seeing the people who approached him, thinking they were Moors, rushed to get out of the litter and mount one of the horses that pulled it and went fleeing, with his servants after him, to where His Majesty was. [The king], seeing the steward pale and realizing what was happening, laughed heartily at the joke as did those who were with him. Don Luis was embarrassed and remained with his servants; although they say that some men who were on guard in a nearby tower came down and attacked the imaginary Moors, wounding two or three, not realizing who they were.

> (El duque de Tursi . . . quiso hacer con que se entretuviese S.M. en el camino, haciéndole saber primero que pornia una galeota cerca de la costa por donde habia de pasar, para que de ella saliesen soldados en hábitos de moros á los cortesanos que pasasen cerca de la mar; y sucedió que don Luis Henriquez, el mayordomo, iba en una litera con sus criados . . . y viese salir la gente que se encaminaba para él, pensando que eran moros, se dió priesa á salir de la litera y subió sobre uno de los machos que la llevaban y fuese corriendo y sus criados tras él, hacia donde estaba S.M., que como

lo vió mudado de color, y sabia lo que era, riyó mucho de la burla y
los que con él iban, quedando muy corrido don Luis con sus
criados; aunque dicen que de una torrecilla cerca de allí bajaron los
que la guardaban, y dieron en los moros fingidos, de los cuales
hirieron dos ó tres, no sabiendo el efecto para que habian salido.)[31]

In Cervantes's 1615 *Don Quixote*, the duke and duchess are
lovers of spectacle, and the novelist surrenders his hero to them
and their spectacular productions. Cervantes's duke, in fact, in
his almost sadistic pursuit of entertainment, is remarkably similar to the duke described in the anecdote just quoted. Even after
Don Quixote's defeat at the hands of Carrasco (now refigured as
the Knight of the White Moon), there is one final play to be
staged and we are told that it is nothing less than the "rarest and
strangest adventure that befell Don Quixote in the whole course
of this great history" ("más raro y más nuevo suceso que en todo
el discurso desta grande historia avino a don Quijote"). The
mock funeral of Altisidora (2:69) is a theatrical piece designed to
produce wonder, but it lacks any redeeming ethical base since it
is the product of a collaboration between Carrasco and the duke,
the disciple-assassin and the superfluous practitioner of wonder-
for-wonder's-sake. As the characters file into the elaborate noc-
turnal scenario lighted by a hundred torches and five hundred
lamps, the narrator inquires "Who would not have been amazed
at this?" ("¿Quién no se había de admirar con esto?") and proceeds to inform us that paradoxically neither Sancho nor Don
Quixote are terribly impressed by what surrounds them, the
squire donning the inquisitorial garb without fear, the knight
"fearful" but laughing to himself nonetheless: "Don Quixote also
gazed at Sancho, and though fear kept his senses numbed he
could not stop laughing at his squire's appearance" (my translation) ("Mirábale también don Quijote, y aunque el temor le tenía
suspensos los sentidos, no dejó de reírse de ver la figura de
Sancho"). The suspension of the senses reminds us of mystical
practice and the *admiratio* produced by Feliciana de la Voz's song

---

[31] Cabrera de Córdoba, *Relaciones de las cosas sucedidas*, p. 207.

in *Persiles y Sigismunda*. What is strikingly different here is that Don Quixote (and to a lesser extent Sancho) is relatively detached from the effects of wonder, so much so that the reader understands that Don Quixote is amused not only by Sancho's remarks but by the lack of verisimilitude of the entire charade that has been perpetrated by aristocratic whim.

This is not the first time that the plans of the duke and duchess have not led to the intended results, and although Cervantes might not have been willing to say outright that their behavior was sadistic, he nonetheless gives every indication that it is anything but "good fun." The mockery instigated by the duke is only a symptom of his own moral imperfections (Descartes would write in *Les passions de l'âme* [1649]: "Because the most incomplete people are usually the greatest tricksters"), and whatever fear the knight might experience as a result of his astonishment only further condemns the aristocratic misuse of *admiratio*: "In fact Cide Hamete says that he considers the mockers were as mad as their victims, and the Duke and Duchess within a hair's breadth of appearing fools themselves for taking such pains to play tricks on a pair of fools" ("Y dice más Cide Hamete: que tiene para sí ser tan locos los burladores como los burlados, y que no estaban los duques dos dedos de parecer tontos, pues tanto ahínco ponían en burlarse de dos tontos") (2:70).

Whether or not Don Quixote is mad or even stupid (*tonto*) and thus intended as an object of ridicule by his author is a perennial question in Cervantes studies and is not about to be resolved here. If "Don Quixote's adventures must be honoured either with wonder or with laughter" ("los sucesos de Don Quixote, o se han celebrar con admiracíon, o con risa") (2:44), we know that the seventeenth century opted for laughter, as have contemporary critics from Erich Auerbach to Anthony Close; these critics have claimed that the desired effect of the quixotic text is first and foremost laughter and that any further critical attribution will only lead to overinterpretation.[32] Yet the narrator himself

---

[32]Close's argument, to cite a more recent and influential case, hinges precariously on notions such as "art for art's sake," the "individual artistic person-

tells us that Don Quixote's deeds should be met with *either* laughter or wonder, and given the complex variety of functions carried out by wonder in the period, we must once again consider the possibility that Cervantes, an exemplary author in the early modern sense of the term, viewed laughter as only the preliminary step toward a complete understanding of the novel. If so, we are led to the other face of *admiratio—lo verosímil*. Renaissance theorists were quick to warn that the former without the latter soon degenerates into humor; hence El Pinciano's "wonder at something becomes laughter" ("la admiración de la cosa se convierte en risa").[33] I suggest that it is an improper (that is, ethically empty) or artistically ineffective use of spectacle that produces nothing more than laughter—as Altisidora's "funeral" provokes Don Quixote's mirth. This idea also begins to explain the almost (?) total lack of humor in an otherwise surprise- and wonder-filled text such as *Persiles y Sigismunda*.

And so we return to a fundamental issue—the relationship between wonder and social class. If, as I suggested earlier, aristocratic arrogance precluded the proper use of *admiratio* and the lack of refinement attributed to the subordinate classes led only to stupefied astonishment, then the morally salutary effects of wonder were available primarily to an educated elite located somewhere in the middle of the social field. The subject posi-

---

ality," and "the self-renewing tree of the human spirit." It claims that any reading of *Don Quixote* that goes beyond the readily apparent elements of comedy and satire is anachronistic. Terry Eagleton has discussed other examples of this critical move in which, for example, we are urged to give up the "tediously zealous search for moral, symbolic and historical meanings in Dickens and acknowledge instead that he is really just rather funny." "Liberality and Order: The Criticism of John Bayley" in *Against the Grain: Essays, 1975–1985* (London: Verso, 1986), p. 188 n. 19. Francisco Rico's remarks about *Lazarillo de Tormes* seems to me to be even more applicable to Cervantes's texts: "Is this all the author intended—that we merely laugh? The explanation is particularly attractive, but still does not satisfy me" ("¿Sólo eso pretendería el autor, que nos riéramos, sin más? La explicación me es particularmente simpática, pero no acaba de satisfacerme"). *La novela picaresca*, p. 52.

[33] Alonso López Pinciano, *Philosophia antigua poética*, vol. 2, ed. Alfred Carballo Picazo (Madrid: Consejo Superior de Investigaciones Científicas, 1953), p. 104.

tions of such groups were not necessarily fixed by the category of blood or determined by strictly economic factors, on the contrary, because these groups were constituted by a set of previously secondary discourses (knowledge for the *letrados*, money for the *mercaderes*, and so on), there was a certain flexibility in their situation which was potentially threatening to the established order. This threat made the proper employment of wonder-inciting strategies all the more important for any cultural activity aimed at such an audience. In effect, the emergence of a new kind of subject signaled the production of "new" kinds of passions, which, instead of originating in aristocratic concepts of blood, the genealogical family, or virtue, were the consequences of hybrid positions intersected by a number of contradictory discourses. The crisis instituted by the clash between traditional religious codes and capitalism, for example, made for a different kind of passionate subject who had to be carefully controlled and directed. Wonder was the first and most important step in the ethical refunctioning and repositioning of this peculiarly early modern individual.

In the final pages of the 1615 novel, Don Quixote recants and in essence declares that the subject position he had previously enacted is no longer functional since he himself is no longer Don Quixote but Alonso Quijano. Earlier in the text, however, it had been Avellaneda's character, Don Alvaro, who had definitively established the singularity of Don Quixote: "Many civilities and offers of service passed between Don Alvaro and Don Quixote, in which the great Manchegan showed so much good sense that Don Alvaro Tarfe was convinced that he had been deceived. He even suspected that he must have been enchanted, since he had touched two such different Don Quixotes with his own hands" ("Muchas de cortesías y ofrecimientos pasaron entre don Alvaro y don Quijote, en las cuales mostró el gran machego su discreción, de modo que desengañó a don Alvaro Tarfe del error en que estaba; el cual se dio a entender que debía de estar encantado, pues tocaba con la mano dos tan contrarios don Quijotes") (2:72). This confession by the aristocrat who had manipulated Avellaneda's Quixote into the madhouse of Toledo is crucial to the identity of the Cervantine Quixote not merely because as a literary device it heightens the "reality" of the latter for the reader but because it simultaneously denies the impostor's existence and declares the rights of Don Quixote as an individualized subject. As I argued earlier, Avellaneda's project had proposed to reinterpellate the original character through traditional disciplinary practices and the dominant ideology of blood. Although Cervantes himself had moved away from the extreme subjectivism of his own earlier project, the calm sobriety with which the real Don Quixote disabuses Tarfe of his mistake ("I beg your worship, as you are a gentleman, to be so kind" ("A vuestra merced suplico, por lo que debe a ser caballero, sea servido")— and his insistence on a publicly declared statement before a clerk and the village mayor suggest that he continues to claim his status as a "distinct individual." The difference is that he now no longer does so as the radically autonomous figure of the 1605 text but as an individual constituted through the practices of socially acceptable conventions and through legal discourse.

Avellaneda could not be allowed to have the last word since his essentialist notion of the subject contradicted the principles of the entire quixotic project. Ironically it is Carrasco, the character who, like Avellaneda in real life and many other characters in the novel, had worked to deindividuate Don Quixote, who has the final say. Of the many epitaphs written for Don Quixote's tomb, only the one composed by his earliest disciple and ultimate rival is recorded:

> Here lies the gentle knight and stout
> Who to such height of valour got
> That, if you mark his deeds throughout
> Death over his life triumphed not
> With bringing of his death about.
> The world as nothing he did prize
> For as a scarecrow in men's eyes
> He lived, and was their bugbear too
> And had the luck, with much ado
> To live a fool, and yet die wise.
>
> (Yace aquí el Hidalgo fuerte
> que a tanto estremo llegó

de valiente, que se advierte
que la muerte no triunfó
de su vida con su muerte.
Tuvo a todo el mundo en poco;
fue el espantajo y el coco
del mundo, en tal coyuntura,
que acreditó su ventura
morir cuerdo y vivir loco.)

The emphasis on time and process here is striking. "To die wise and live a fool," as the original Spanish has it, suggests the kind of transformation I have discussed. But the shift in subject positions, the passage from ignorance to knowledge, has less to do with psychological or intellectual states than with the movement from a radically individuated subjectivism to a subjectivity more directly determined by the residual and dominant discourses that constituted the social field.

In his 1615 text Cervantes retreated from his earlier project by deindividuating his protagonist through a complex series of encounters with both disciples and representatives of the governing elites. From the prolonged contact with the duke and duchess to the procession through Barcelona to the final encounter on the beach with Carrasco, Don Quixote is repositioned within the social order until he is finally reinterpellated by what undoubtedly was the master discourse of seventeenth-century Spanish society—Catholicism. As he receives the sacraments at the end of the novel, the figure who had been singular now fulfills his obligations within the wider community of believers and is thereby converted into a sign for another kind of subject produced by the ideology of Christian morality. The emergent autonomy of the 1605 character, on which modern secular criticism continues to focus its attention, by the end of the 1615 text is effaced by the more properly early modern issue of the subject's relationship to a transcendent reality. It is the appearance of Alonso Quijano the Good that forces us to understand Cervantes not as a reflection of ourselves but as a writer fully engaged with the most pressing problems of *his* culture.

The Exigencies of Agency

Men make their own history, but they do not make it just as they please.

—Marx, *The Eighteenth Brumaire*

Every man's the son of his own deeds; and since I'm a man, I can become pope, let alone governor of an isle.

(Cada uno es hijo de sus obras; y debajo de ser hombre puedo venir a ser papa, cuanto más gobernador de una ínsula.)

—Sancho Panza to the barber, *Don Quixote*

It is a commonplace in Spanish Golden Age studies that Cervantes is the most modern and Quevedo one of the least modern of seventeenth-century writers. From our vantage point some four hundred years later and from within a culture that is the product of advanced capitalist organization and liberal ideologies, this would still seem to be the case. But such a judgment obscures the fundamental contradictions present within each writer, some of which I only began to outline in the preceding chapters. Quevedo's powerful attempt to construct an autonomous speaking subject in his poetic text, once translated into philosophic discourse, was not unrelated to the Cartesian formulation of the *res cogitans*.[1] Situated within this other kind of narrative, Quevedo's text would seem to prefigure not only the

---

[1] I have clearly framed my readings of Quevedo and Cervantes within historical rather than philosophical discourse. For a recent analysis of *Don Quixote* which is more heavily indebted to philosophy, see Anthony J. Cascardi, *The Bounds of Reason: Cervantes, Dostoevsky, Flaubert* (New York: Columbia University Press, 1986).

200

most modern but also the most influential tradition in the West since the desire for the autonomous subject has consistently informed all discussion of subjectivity since the end of the seventeenth century. Indeed, it is the intervention into Cervantes studies of the romantic version of this self-contained entity that has produced overly subjectivist readings of *Don Quixote* and has forced into the background the 1615 novel's interest in the social construction of the subject. The emphasis on the individual's apparent self-generation in the first *Don Quixote*, unlike the sociocultural processes of subjectification so central to the second text and to *Persiles y Sigismunda*, coincided with the ascendancy of a bourgeoisie founded on the solitary monad who made his way in a hostile world. Because of this modern emphasis on individualism even readers as perceptive as Erich Auerbach have virtually ignored Cervantes's 1615 sequel and thus have seriously misread the entire Cervantine project.[2] In some cases, critics such as Lukács, who also privileged the 1605 text, used it to construct a typology of the novel of "abstract idealism" in which a problematic hero with an "unquestioning, concentrated interiority" and incapable of self-doubt blindly attacks the objective world.[3] On the basis of such appropriations, Cervantes was quickly transformed into one of the principal fathers of both modern narrative and liberal humanism. Given the hegemony in literary studies of the bourgeois subject, it is no surprise that Cervantes has been rewritten most recently as having somehow anticipated fundamental concepts of both Freudian and Lacanian analysis. As for Quevedo, he continues to be consigned to the realm of the linguistically brilliant but historically bound and hopelessly reactionary.

I am convinced that contemporary accounts of both writers tell us more about the social context in which those accounts are

---

[2] See Erich Auerbach's chapter "The Enchanted Dulcinea," in *Mimesis: The Representation of Reality in Western Literature*, trans. W. R. Trask (Princeton: Princeton University Press, 1953).

[3] Lukács's formulation is in *The Theory of the Novel*, trans. Anna Bostock (Cambridge: MIT Press, 1975).

being drafted than they do about early modern Spain. It is my contention that the texts of Cervantes and Quevedo are at the same time both "forward" *and* "backward" looking in terms of the historical shifts in subjectivity in the West. Such an apparent contradiction can only be understood if we bracket all teleological models of history and mediate the traditional subject/object division with a concept of "objective potentiality," or "habitus."[4] This is to say that the idea of the individual was already inscribed within the collective possibilities of early modern Spain; in Chapter 2 I sketched its vague outline in a variety of discursive practices but noted its inability to displace dominant and residual subject forms based on blood and status. The "new" subject of class discourse, the gendered body, emergent concepts of the family and the nation, therefore, could be hinted at but not fully realized until material and discursive formations were significantly rearranged. Given that early modern Spanish culture was this intricate field of possibilities, it would be a mistake to claim that Quevedo's writings were strictly "reactionary" (although Quevedo himself probably was so) or that Cervantes was a progressive who somehow foresaw the historical, philosophical, and literary future. When Pierre Vilar asserted in his 1956 essay "The Age of Don Quixote" that the two novels are above all books about seventeenth-century Spain, he stated a truism that should govern our understanding of the writings of all Cervantes's contemporaries. The great achievement of the creator of Sancho and Don Quixote, however, was to have experimented with traditional concepts of the subject and in so doing to have pushed farther than anyone else the literary representation of emergent subject positions. That this textual experiment both angered and unsettled the dominant social groups of the day is made explicit by Avellaneda's response; that Cervantes himself rethought and to some extent retreated from what he had found in 1605 is shown by the shifts in emphasis in the 1615 text. This

---

[4]The concept of "habitus" is central to the work of Pierre Bourdieu and is developed at length in his *Outline of a Theory of Practice*, trans. Richard Nice (Cambridge: Cambridge University Press, 1977).

is not to say that Cervantes's second *Don Quixote* is a conventional book that merely represents the traditional values of Spanish and Catholic culture. On the contrary, its emphasis on the discursive construction of subjectivity and its appeal to ethics implicitly critiques essentialist "selfhood" as well as contemporary social conditions. At the same time, Cervantes demonstrates the impracticality and final undesirability of a solitary monad disconnected from all forms of collective values.

This last point is nowhere more apparent than in the characterization of Roque Guinart in the 1615 novel. I have argued that Quevedo felt an attraction to the picaresque voices he created in the poetry precisely because they figured forms of subjectivity which appeared to be "freer" within the aristocratic context. The first Don Quixote, while by no means reducible to the discourse of the picaresque, nonetheless also challenged the limits of what the subject could be. Not until the introduction of the minor characters of the second novel is Don Quixote's individuality deflected and dispersed. I am suggesting that with these supplemental figures, especially Ginés de Pasamonte and the bandit Roque, Cervantes underscores the dangers of setting oneself too far apart from the community. Roque is of special interest because he is based on a historical figure known as Roca Guinarda, who operated in the area around Barcelona in the early decades of the seventeenth century. The powerful charismatic authority of Cervantes's representation of him is grounded in cultural legend and historical fact and thus situates the character in an ontological space different from that of Don Quixote. In a sense Roque, in his extralegal life-style, combines the desire for singularity and self-determination with a kind of social power Don Quixote had failed to achieve. It is probably true that an earlier Don Quixote (that of the 1605 text) would have been less judgmental of the bandit's profession. But by the time he encounters Roque late in the second novel, the bandit's admission that his identity originates in the sickness of personal revenge: "undefinable desires for vengeance" ("no sé qué deseos de venganza") reinforces the knight's ethical stance. He therefore urges Roque to seek conversion:

"Sir Roque," he replied, "the beginning of health lies in the knowledge of the disease, and in the sick man's willingness to take the medicines the doctor prescribes. You are sick; you know your complaint, and Heaven, or rather God, who is our doctor, will apply medicines to cure you, medicines which generally cure slowly, not suddenly and by a miracle. What is more, wise sinners are nearer to a cure than foolish ones, and since you have shown your good sense in your speech, you have only to keep up your courage, and hope for an improvement in the sickness of your conscience."

(Señor Roque, el principio de la salud está en conocer la enfermedad y en querer tomar el enfermo las medicinas que el médico le ordena: vuestra merced está enfermo, conoce su dolencia, y el cielo, o Dios, por mejor decir, que es nuestro médico, le aplicará medicinas que le sanen, las cuales suelen sanar poco a poco y no de repente y por milagro; y más, que los pecadores discretos están más cerca de enmendarse que los simples; y pues vuestra merced ha mostrado en sus razones su prudencia, no hay sino tener buen ánimo y esperar mejoría de la enfermedad de su conciencia.) (2:60)

The consequences of Don Quixote's advice for his own project are poignantly obvious: the gradual transformation of the chivalric enterprise from unbridled subjectivism to an identity founded on social (that is, communal) interests and the eventual investment in religious, although not necessarily orthodox, categories. Don Quixote's palinode at the end of his career and his "return" to the church mean only that in early modern Spain secular social structures could not provide a space for an ethical individualism; religion, then, in what are otherwise virtually "nonreligious" texts (Cervantes's two *Don Quixotes*), becomes the only practice through which such a subject might be constructed.

In the chapter on Quevedo, I made a case for reading specific textual elements in terms of the survival of traditional forms in dissimilar, even antithetical historical contexts. My assertion that the lyric subject of Quevedo's love poetry is in part the product of the poet's being compelled to use ideologically empty models (the sonnet) must be refined, however, for it seems clear that even though the original scene of the "Petrarchan revolution" and its construction of an emergent individual had passed by the time Quevedo was writing, the sonnet still "worked" in one way or another within seventeenth-century Castilian culture. Put another way, the sonnet was not merely an anachronistic curiosity but continued to have real use value in Quevedo's Spain.

As Fredric Jameson has theorized this complex issue, every literary form transmits an ideological content that is able to outlive its original sociohistorical ground: "The ideology of form itself, thus sedimented, persists into the later, more complex structure as a generic message which coexists—either as a contradiction or, on the other hand, as a mediatory or harmonizing mechanism—with elements from later stages."[5] In terms of its basic component parts, of course, the sonnet remains the same for both Petrarch and Quevedo. In seventeenth-century Spain, however, the original "message" of the sonnet is delivered in the ideologically hostile territory of a culture that seeks to block even the idea of an autonomous individual. I have already discussed the extreme contradictions that arose from this situation, as well as the effects produced within specific texts. What we must ask ourselves now is how the sonnet functioned positively in its new context? The issues of patronage and the political economy of courtly society will be the necessary supplement to any future reading of seventeenth-century Spanish poetry.

In my chapter on Cervantes, I discussed "wonder" or "awe" as a sensation with much more cultural power in the seventeenth century than it possesses today. The hegemony of the unified and self-determining subject has in essence radically transformed the potential social uses of wonder, driving it more and more into the realm of private experience and away from the communal activities of storytelling, public ceremonies, and shared aesthetic responses—all of which still characterized early modern society. In saying this I am not positing a radical disjunction between an

[5] Jameson, *The Political Unconscious*, p. 141.

imaginary world of wholeness and immanence and a later world of fragmentation and loss of meaning, although in the past theorists such as Benjamin and Lukács have found this to be a useful heuristic device for understanding literary forms. Rather, my point is that in seventeenth-century Spain two forms of wonder coexisted—one rooted in the experience of the community and manifested through the human body, the other the emerging product of the increased privatization of the subject, now apprehended primarily through the effects of language on the intellect. The first of these forms of wonder shapes the bulk of Cervantes's text; the second characterizes Quevedo's—hence the traditional critical preoccupation with the latter's stylistic and linguistic abilities. If my hypothesis is correct, Quevedo hopes to shock the reader with his language precisely in order to magnify (through the poetic voice of the narrator) the sense of distance between text and public. In this way, he clears further space for a voice that speaks as an individual, that is, an entity not only other to his general audience but alienated from his implicit interlocutor and even from the material of the poem itself. Cervantes, on the other hand, chooses to represent the communal uses of wonder in both *Don Quixotes* and in *Persiles y Sigismunda* in order to show how that sensation can be either an effective ethical device or a tool of the governing elites for the subjection and manipulation of human beings.

It is not surprising, given his preference for exploring subjectivity within social configurations, that early in his career Cervantes sought success in the theater. His move to narrative forms can be attributed not only to individual talent or lack of success with other genres but also to the realization that the reading strategies implied by the early modern novel combined a sense of the reader as private subject in isolation with the more traditional and widespread practice of public readings within a communal space. It has often been pointed out that the "Tale of Foolish Curiosity" ("El curioso impertinente") is only one of several oral performances in the first novel, and a chapter heading late in the second novel suggests how, in this transitional moment, the mode of communication and the production of subjectivity were shifting ground: "Which treats of what the reader shall see or the listener hear" ("Que trata de lo que verá el que lo leyere, o lo oirá el que lo escuchare leer"). While the problematic of reading is not as fully developed in *Persiles y Sigismunda*, the very structure of the text, built on the idea of the pilgrimage, once again privileges the group over the individual. The sense of community produced by activities such as public readings and pilgrimages stands in sharp contrast to Quevedo's representation of the desire for isolation and silent reading, through which a different, more intimate form of the subject takes shape.[6] Although this posture has something to do with an earlier ascetic tradition, the remnants of which are much more explicit in prose works such as the *Sueños* or *El Buscón*, where the narrative voice maintains a rigid distance from the implied reader, it also figures forth the more modern attraction to privacy for the sake of pleasure.

A central purpose of my argument has been to show that within the same ideological context a variety of dissimilar positions for the subject can exist. In contrast to some overly deterministic variants of the Marxian paradigm which posit one mode of production marching inexorably toward the next (and hence the passage from so-called feudal forms of subjectivity to early modern, bourgeois ones), we must be able to imagine the simultaneous coexistence of contradictory concepts in contest on the discursive terrain. Let us return to our example from Cervantes: according to one teleological model, the defeat of Don Quixote by Sansón Carrasco is the novelistic version of the triumph of the absolutist state bureaucracy over the great landholding knights. This view of Don Quixote as the representative of an anachronistic, seemingly useless ideology represses what is "new" or potentially radical about Don Quixote's project in its new context (its capacity for "magnifying the given tasks in the imagination" as Marx says in the *Eighteenth Brumaire*).[7] While it is true that Don

---

[6] For a discussion of related issues based on a phenomenological method and drawing on classical authorities, see B. W. Ife, *Reading and Fiction in Golden-Age Spain: A Platonist Critique and Some Picaresque Replies* (Cambridge: Cambridge University Press, 1985).

[7] Marx, *Eighteenth Brumaire*, p. 596.

Quixote attempts to revive defunct literary and social forms, placed into seventeenth-century Spanish society his behavior figures forth future discursive constructs (the autonomous individual, complex privatization, and so on) that in fact work against absolutism's attempted containment and management of subjects. At the same time, a strictly dualistic reading obscures the fact that Carrasco himself is somehow "attracted to" Don Quixote's differentness, even though he is the primary agent of its recuperation. Don Quixote and Carrasco, then, are not the allegorical emblems of two monolithic modes of production, one being replaced by another; instead, each is the locus for contradictory and complementary tendencies inherent in the same ideological conjuncture.

The idea of the social field as an open and nonsutured space has been theorized in a number of recent studies.[8] What such a deessentializing strategy offers us in terms of rethinking subjectivity as a social construct is an approach to the issue of agency, that is, the ways in which subjects are able to improvise actions within a particular discursive formation. If the subject is the provisional site of intersecting and contradictory discourses and institutional practices, unable to fix itself for any but the most fleeting of moments, the potential for contestation and change would seem to be permanently foreclosed. I find myself deeply dissatisfied with this notion. I have no doubt that my locating of a "contestatory unconscious" in the texts of Quevedo and Cervantes is at least in part the product of my own desire to read acts of resistance into them. The cultural and historical effects of that resistance in the seventeenth century was most assuredly limited. Still, even in the *Don Quixote* of 1615, the idea of the subject as agent and the difficulties with which agency is achieved are insistent preoccupations of the early modern writer.

[8] See, for example, the collection *Rethinking Ideology: A Marxist Debate*, ed. Sakari Hanninen and Leena Paldán (New York: International General, 1983), especially Michel Pecheux's "Ideology: Fortress or Paradoxical Space," pp. 31–35. See also the work of Ernesto Laclau and Chantal Mouffe, in particular *Hegemony and Socialist Strategy: Towards a Radical Democratic Politics*, trans. Winston Moore and Paul Cammack (London: Verso, 1985).

I will conclude with one final textual example—the battle between Don Quixote and Tosilos (2:56). This complex episode in reality begins several chapters earlier (2:48) when Don Quixote is first approached by Doña Rodriguez and asked to vindicate the name of her daughter, who has been wronged by the son of a wealthy farmer. In chapter 52 Don Quixote is barely recovered from the attack by cats perpetrated by the duchess and is considering his departure when Doña Rodriguez broaches the topic again and begs Don Quixote to come to her aid. In a comment important for what I have said about the duke as a failed governor, she adds: "For to expect justice from the Duke, my master, is to ask for pears off an elm tree" ("Porque pensar que el duque mi señor me ha de hacer justicia es pedir peras al olmo"). Doña Rodriguez's request, it seems, is not one of the duke's calculated entertainments but a spontaneous event that leaves the ducal pair as shocked as anyone: "Even the Duke and Duchess, though they suspected that this was some new trick which their servants had prepared for Don Quixote, were puzzled at the earnestness of the lady's demonstrations of grief" ("Y aunque los duques pensaron que sería alguna burla que sus criados querían hacer a don Quijote, todavía, viendo con el ahínco que la mujer suspiraba, gemía y lloraba, los tuvo dudosos y suspensos"). The knight accepts responsibility and challenges the laborer in absentia; actually, since the youth is in Flanders, the duke orders his lackey Tosilos to impersonate the daughter's lover, "first priming him thoroughly in his part" ("industriándole primero muy bien de todo lo que había de hacer"). What had begun as an unexpected slippage in the duke's otherwise carefully laid out program, however, gets further out of hand when Tosilos, already on the field of battle, looks into the crowd, unexpectedly falls in love with the daughter, and then turns to the man in charge:

> "Sir, isn't this a battle to decide whether or not I'm to marry that lady?"
> "That is so," was the reply.
> "Then," said the lackey, "My conscience pricks me, and it

would be a sin if I went on with this battle. So I declare myself beaten, and I'm willing to marry the lady at once." The marshal of the lists was amazed at Tosilos' speech, and being in the secret of the plot did not know how to reply to him with so much as a word. Don Quixote drew up in mid-career, seeing that his adversary was not attacking. The Duke could not conceive why there were not going on with the battle, but the marshal of the lists went to tell him what the lackey had said, which left him astonished and extremely angry.

(—Señor, ¿esta batalla no se hace porque yo me case, o no me case, con aquella señora?

—Así es—le fue respondido.

—Pues yo—dijo el lacayo—soy temeroso de mi conciencia, y pondríala en gran cargo si pasase adelante en esta batalla; y así, digo que yo me doy por vencido y que quiero casarme luego con aquella señora.

Quedó admirado el maese de campo de las razones de Tosilos; y como era uno de los sabidores de la máquina de aquel caso, no le supo responder palabra. Detúvose don Quijote en la mitad de su carrera, viendo que su enemigo no le acometía. El duque no sabía la ocasión por que no se pasaba adelante en la batalla; pero el maese de campo le fue a declarar lo que Tosilos decía, de lo que quedó suspenso y colérico en estremo.)

I close with this passage because it is one of the most striking examples in early modern Spanish literature of the relative unpredictability of any system that seeks to circumscribe the subject's actions. Even in the most carefully scripted situation, the agent's ability to improvise and devise oppositional strategies remains powerful; the intended interpellation of Tosilos is renegotiated and ultimately acted out in unforeseen ways. Although any cultural text will prescribe preferred subject positions, because the subject is constituted by a multiplicity of discourses and practices, it can refuse any single interpellation that would necessarily exclude all others.

Anthony Giddens has described this process of negotiation as a consequence of the "duality of structure." That is to say, the various discourses that constitute the subject, besides constraining or limiting what the subject can be, may also produce the potential for the subject's agency: "Structure thus is not to be conceptualised as a barrier to action, but as essentially involved in its production."[9] Or as Joan Cocks puts it: "For even in a highly structured social life, rules cannot anticipate every possible variation in how an appropriate action may be performed, or every kind of action participants might conceive of taking, to say nothing of every abstract possibility of action inconceivable only because no one has taken it yet."[10] The unintended results of action, then, are the moments of the subject's freedom from the control of the so-called dominant, the moments when the prison houses of ideology and social organization give way to irony and being "in" on the game, the moments of already knowing that one is being manipulated and therefore of manipulating the manipulator. The reinterpellation of Tosilos, whom the duke had inserted into the discourses of aristocratic eroticism and courtly masquerade ("first priming him thoroughly in his part"), empowers him sufficiently to cease to be the lackey, refuse participation in the spectacle, and assert his decision to marry Doña Rodriguez's daughter.

The Tosilos episode illustrates Giddens's point that "power relations . . . are always two-way, even if the power of one actor or party in a social relation is minimal compared to another."[11] Clearly, the agency of most subjects in seventeenth-century Spain was limited to the kind of microresistances figured in the picaresque poetry of Quevedo and certain episodes in Cervantes's two *Don Quixotes*. It has been one of my claims throughout this book, however, that it would be an error to think that the dominant ideology (or the often misunderstood "power") always

[9]Anthony Giddens, *Central Problems in Social Theory*, p. 70.
[10]Joan Cocks, *The Oppositional Imagination: Feminism, Critique, and Political Theory* (London: Routledge, 1989), p. 122.
[11]Giddens, *Central Problems in Social Theory*, p. 93. For an elaboration of Giddens's ideas from a more conventional Marxist position, see Callinicos, *Making History*.

already blocked or co-opted the potential for action. Power may indeed be everywhere, but it is not homogeneous, and relations of power are not articulated in a single way once and for all. Thus we find that the kind of "surreptitious creativities" Michel de Certeau attributes to the colonized peoples of the New World are represented throughout the literature of seventeenth-century Spain.[12] The relatively intricate observational organization of the Habsburg monarchy (a prelude to Foucault's paranoid myth of the panoptic society) finds its literary analogue in the kingdom of the duke and duchess, a space that despite its strong sense of control from above, reveals the fissures and unintended consequences exemplified by the lackey Tosilos. It is there, I would argue, in the localized and seemingly banal microresistances figured in the cultural products of the period, that we must investigate the limits of subjectivity and agency in early modern culture. It is not that the tentative constitution in literature of the subject as individual marked a real threat to aristocratic power. Nevertheless, its discursive presence signaled that aristocratic ideologies were being rearticulated. More important, it is at the level of local struggles that we must locate the problem of agency in our own time in order to connect otherwise dispersed sites of contestation and emergent subjectivities, working all the while to construct ever more inclusive projects aimed at the transformation of society.

[12] See Michel de Certeau, *The Practice of Everyday Life*, trans. Steven Rendall (Berkeley: University of California Press, 1984), p. 32. Not unlike both Tosilos and Governor Sancho, the indigenous peoples in de Certeau's account were able to "metaphorize the dominant order: they made it function in another register."

Bibliography

Almansa y Mendoza, Andrés. *Cartas de Andrés de Almansa y Mendoza: Novedades de esta corte y avisos recibidos de otras partes, 1621–1626*. Madrid: M. Ginesta, 1886.

Alonso, Dámaso. *Ensayos sobre poesía española*. Madrid: Revista de Occidente, 1944.

———. *Poesía española*. 4th ed. Madrid: Gredos, 1962.

Alonso Hernández, José Luis. *Léxico del marginalismo del siglo de oro*. Salamanca: Universidad de Salamanca, 1977.

Amador de los Ríos, José. "Sobre el libro llamado de los pensamientos variables." In *Historia crítica de la literatura española*. Vol. 7, app. 4. Madrid: Joaquin Muñoz, 1865.

Anderson, Benedict. *Imagined Communities: Reflections on the Origin and Spread of Nationalism*. London: Verso, 1983.

Arco, Ricardo del. "La vida privada en la obra de Cervantes." *Revista de archivos, bibliotecas y museos* 56 (1950): 577–616.

Arenal, Electa, and Stacey Schlau. *Untold Sisters: Hispanic Nuns in Their Own Works*. Albuquerque: University of New Mexico Press, 1989.

Ariès, Philippe. *Centuries of Childhood: A Social History of Family Life*. Trans. Robert Baldrick. New York: Random House, 1962.

Atienza Hernández, Ignacio. *Aristocracia, poder y riqueza en la España moderna: La casa de Osuna, siglos XV–XIX*. Mexico City: Siglo XXI, 1987.

Auerbach, Erich. "The Enchanted Dulcinea." In *Mimesis: The Representation of Reality in Western Literature*. Trans. W. R. Trask. Princeton: Princeton University Press, 1953.

Avellaneda, Alonso Fernández de. *Don Quixote de La Mancha (Part II): Being the Spurious Continuation of Miguel de Cervantes' Part I*. Trans. A. W. Server and J. E. Keller. Newark, Del.: Juan de la Cuesta, 1980.

213

——. *El ingenioso hidalgo Don Quijote de La Mancha que contiene su tercera salida y es la quinta parte de sus aventuras* (1614). Ed. Fernando García Salinero. Madrid: Castalia, 1971.

Barker, Francis. *The Tremulous Private Body: Essays on Subjection.* London: Methuen, 1984.

Barthes, Roland. *The Pleasure of the Text.* Trans. Richard Miller. New York: Hill and Wang, 1975.

——. *Sade/Fourier/Loyola.* Trans. Richard Miller. New York: Hill and Wang, 1976.

Bataillon, Marcel. *Pícaros y picaresca: La pícara Justina.* Madrid: Taurus, 1969.

Beinart, Haim, ed. *Records of the Trials of the Spanish Inquisition in Ciudad Real.* Jerusalem: Israel National Academy of Science and Humanities, 1974.

Beverley, John. *Aspects of Góngora's "Soledades."* Amsterdam: John Benjamins, 1980.

——. "Class or Caste: A Critique of the Castro Thesis." In *Papers of the Américo Castro Centennial Symposium.* Syracuse, N.Y.: Syracuse University Press, 1988.

Blanco Aguinaga, Carlos. "Dos sonetos del siglo XVII: Amor-locura en Quevedo y Sor Juana." *Modern Language Notes* 77 (1962): 145–62.

——. "Tradición y originalidad en 'Cerrar podrá . . .'" *Filología* 8 (1962): 57–78.

——. "Unamuno's 'yoísmo' and Its Relation to Traditional Spanish 'Individualism.'" In *Unamuno Centennial Studies.* Ed. Ramón Martínez López. Austin: Department of Romance Languages, University of Texas, 1966.

Blanco Aguinaga, Carlos, Julio Rodríguez Puértolas, and Iris Zavala, eds. *Historia social de la literatura española.* Vol. 1. Madrid: Castalia, 1978.

Bossy, John. "The Counter-Reformation and the People of Catholic Europe." *Past and Present* 47 (1970): 51–70.

Bourdieu, Pierre. *Outline of a Theory of Practice.* Trans. Richard Nice. Cambridge: Cambridge University Press, 1977.

Braudel, Fernand. *Civilization and Capitalism, 15th–18th Century.* Vol. 2: *The Wheels of Commerce.* Trans. Sian Reynolds. London: W. Collins, 1982.

——. *The Mediterranean and the Mediterranean World in the Age of Philip II.* Vol. 1. Trans. Sian Reynolds. New York: Harper Colophon, 1972.

——. *On History.* Trans. Sarah Matthews. Chicago: University of Chicago Press, 1980.

Bravo Villasante, Carmen. *La mujer vestida de hombre en el teatro español.* Madrid: Mayo de oro, 1988.

Cabrera, Alonso de. *Sermones.* Vol. 1. Nueva biblioteca de autores españoles, 3. Madrid: Bailly, 1930.

Cabrera de Córdoba, Luis. *Relaciones de las cosas sucedidas en la corte de España desde 1599 hasta 1614*. Madrid: J. Martín Alegría, 1857.

Callinicos, Alex. *Making History: Agency, Structure, and Change in Social Theory*. Cambridge: Polity Press, 1978.

Caro Baroja, Julio. *Las formas complejas de la vida religiosa: Religión, sociedad, y carácter en la España de los siglos XVI y XVII*. Madrid: Akal, 1978.

———. "Honour and Shame: A Historical Account of Several Conflicts." In *Honour and Shame: The Values of Mediterranean Society*. Ed. J. G. Peristiany. Chicago: University of Chicago Press, 1966.

Casado Lobato, María Concepción. "Autores franceses en la biblioteca de un escritor del siglo XVII: Bernardino de Rebolledo (1597–1676)." In *Livre et lecture en Espagne et en France sous l'ancien régime: Colloque de la Casa de Velázquez*. Paris: AOPF, 1981.

Casalduero, Joaquin. *Sentido y forma del Quijote (1605–1615)*. Madrid: Insula, 1966.

Cascardi, Anthony J. *The Bounds of Reason: Cervantes, Dostoevsky, Flaubert*. New York: Columbia University Press, 1986.

Casey, James, ed. *La familia en la España mediterránea, siglos XV–XIX*. Barcelona: Crítica, 1987.

Casey, James, and Bernard Vincent. "Casa y familia en la Granada del antiguo régimen." In *La familia en la España mediterránea, siglos XV–XIX*. Ed. James Casey. Barcelona: Crítica, 1987.

Castro, Américo. *De la edad conflictiva: Crisis de la cultura española en el siglo XVII*. 4th ed. Madrid: Taurus, 1976.

———. "En el umbral de la historia." *Nueva Revista de Filología Hispánica* 7 (1953): 242–45.

——— "An Introduction to the *Quijote*." In *An Idea of History: Selected Essays of Americo Castro*. Trans. S. Gilman and E. L. King. Columbus: Ohio State University Press, 1977.

———. *El pensamiento de Cervantes*. Barcelona: Noguer, 1972.

———. Prólogo to *El ingenioso hidalgo Don Quijote de la Mancha*. 19th ed. Ed. Américo Castro. Mexico City: Porrua, 1979.

Cervantes, Miguel de. *The Adventures of Don Quixote*. Trans. J. M. Cohen. London: Penguin, 1982.

———. *Don Quijote de la Mancha*. Ed. Martín de Riquer. Barcelona: Juventud, 1971.

Chartier, Roger. "Les pratiques de l'écrit." In *Histoire de la vie privée*. Vol. 3: *De la Renaissance aux Lumières*. Paris: Seuil, 1986.

Chevalier, Maxime. *Cuentecillos tradicionales en la España del Siglo de Oro*. Madrid: Gredos, 1975.

———. "*Don Quichotte* et son public." In *Livre et lecture en Espagne et en France sous l'ancien régime: Colloque de la Casa de Velázquez*. Paris: AOPF, 1981.

———. *Lectura y lectores en la España de los siglos XVI y XVII*. Madrid: Turner, 1976.

Clavero, Bartolomé. *Mayorazgo: Propriedad feudal en Castilla, 1639–1836*. Madrid: Siglo XXI, 1974.

Close, Anthony. *The Romantic Approach to "Don Quixote": A Critical History of the Romantic Tradition in "Quixote" Criticism*. Cambridge: Cambridge University Press, 1978.

Cocks, Joan. *The Oppositional Imagination: Feminism, Critique, and Political Theory*. London: Routledge, 1989.

Cohen, Walter. *Drama of a Nation: Public Theater in Renaissance England and Spain*. Ithaca: Cornell University Press, 1985.

Colie, Rosalie. *The Resources of Kind: Genre Theory in the Renaissance*. Berkeley: University of California Press, 1973.

Cortés Echánove, Luis. *Nacimiento y crianza de personas reales en la corte de España, 1566–1886*. Madrid: CSIC, 1958.

Coto, Sebastián. *Discurso médico y moral de las enfermedades por que seguramente pueden las religiosas dejar la clausura* (1639).

Covarrubias, Sebastián de. *Tesoro de la lengua castellana o española* (1611). Madrid: Turner, 1977.

de Certeau, Michel. "Mystic Speech." In *Heterologies: Discourse on the Other*. Trans. Brian Massumi. Minneapolis: University of Minnesota Press, 1986.

———. *The Practice of Everyday Life*. Trans. Steven Rendall. Berkeley: University of California Press, 1984.

Domínguez Ortiz, Antonio. *El antiguo régimen: Los Reyes Católicos y los Austrias*. Madrid: Alianza, 1973.

———. *Las clases privilegiadas en el antiguo régimen*. 3d ed. Madrid: Istmo, 1985.

Durling, Robert M. *The Figure of the Poet in Renaissance Epic*. Cambridge: Harvard University Press, 1965.

Eagleton, Terry. *Against the Grain: Essays, 1975–1985*. London: Verso, 1986.

Efron, Arthur. *Don Quixote and the Dulcineated World*. Austin: University of Texas Press, 1971.

Elliott, J. H. *Imperial Spain, 1469–1716*. New York: New American Library, 1963.

Eslava, Antonio de. *Noches de invierno* (1609). Madrid: Saeta, 1942.

Ettinghausen, Henry. "Quevedo, ¿un caso de doble personalidad?" In *Homenaje a Quevedo (Actas de la II Academia literaria Renacentista)*. Ed. Victor García de la Concha. Salamanca: Universidad de Salamanca, 1982: pp. 27–44.

Fernández Alvarez, Manuel. *Economía, sociedad, y corona: Ensayos históricos sobre el siglo XVI*. Madrid: Cultura Hispánica, 1963.

Foucault, Michel. *The Archaeology of Knowledge.* Trans. A. M. Sheridan Smith. New York: Harper and Row, 1972.

———. "The Ethic of Care for the Self as a Practice of Freedom." In *The Final Foucault.* Ed. James Bernauer and David Rasmussen. Trans. J. D. Gauthier, S.J. Cambridge: MIT Press, 1988.

———. "The Subject and Power." *Critical Inquiry* 8 (1982): 777–95.

García de la Concha, Victor, ed. *Homenaje a Quevedo (Actas de la II Academia literaria renacentista).* Salamanca: Universidad de Salamanca, 1982.

Giddens, Anthony. *Central Problems in Social Theory: Action, Structure, and Contradiction in Social Analysis.* Berkeley: University of California Press, 1979.

Gilman, Stephen. *Cervantes y Avellaneda: Estudio de una imitación.* Trans. Margit Frenk Alatorre. Mexico City: Fondo de Cultura Económica, 1951.

———. *The Spain of Fernando de Rojas: The Intellectual and Social Landscape of "La Celestina."* Princeton: Princeton University Press, 1972.

Girard, René. *Deceit, Desire, and the Novel: Self and Other in Literary Structure.* Baltimore: Johns Hopkins University Press, 1965.

Gnósofo, Cristóforo [pseud.]. *El Crótalon.* Ed. Augusto Cortina. Buenos Aires: Espasa-Calpe, 1942.

Godzich, Wlad, and Nicholas Spadaccini, eds. *Literature among the Discourses: The Spanish Golden Age.* Minneapolis: University of Minnesota Press, 1986.

Gramsci, Antonio. *Selections from the Prison Notebooks of Antonio Gramsci.* Ed. and trans. Quintin Hoare and G. N. Smith. New York: International, 1978.

Granjel, Luis S. *La medicina española del siglo XVII.* Salamanca: Universidad de Salamanca, 1978.

Gumbrecht, H. U. "The Body versus the Printing Press: Media in the Early Modern Period, Mentalities in the Reign of Castile, and Another History of Literary Forms." *Poetics* 14 (1985): 209–27.

Hanninen, Sakari, and Leena Paldán, eds. *Rethinking Ideology: A Marxist Debate.* New York: International General, 1983.

Herrera, Fernando de. *Anotaciones* (1580). In *Garcilaso de la Vega y sus comentaristas.* Ed. Antonio Gallego Morell. Granada: Universidad de Granada, 1966.

———. *Poesía castellana original completa.* Ed. Cristóbol Cuevas. Madrid: Cátedra, 1985.

Herrero, Javier. "Arcadia's Inferno: Cervantes' Attack on the Pastoral." *Bulletin of Hispanic Studies* 55 (1978): 289–99.

Herrero Garcia, M., ed. *Cuentos de los siglos XVI y XVII.* Biblioteca literaria del estudiante, 23. Madrid: Instituto-Escuela, 1926.

Huarte de San Juan, Juan. *Examen de ingenios* (1575). Biblioteca de autores españoles, 65. Madrid: Atlas, 1953.

Ife, B. W. *Reading and Fiction in Golden-Age Spain: A Platonist Critique and Some Picaresque Replies.* Cambridge: Cambridge University Press, 1985.

Jameson, Fredric. *The Political Unconscious: Narrative as a Socially Symbolic Act.* Ithaca: Cornell University Press, 1981.

———. "Religion and Ideology." In *1642: Literature and Power in the Seventeenth Century.* Ed. Francis Barker. Essex: University of Essex, 1981.

Jauralde Pou, Pablo. "La poesía de Quevedo." In *Homenaje a Emilio Orozco.* Granada: Universidad de Granada, 1980.

———. "La transmisión de la obra de Quevedo." In *Homenaje a Quevedo (Actas de la II Academia literaria renacentista).* Ed. Victor García de la Concha. Salamanca: Universidad de Salamanca, 1982.

Juderías, Julián. *Don Francisco de Quevedo y Villegas: La época, el hombre, las doctrinas.* Madrid: Jaime Ratés, 1922.

Kagan, Richard L. *Students and Society in Early Modern Spain.* Baltimore: Johns Hopkins University Press, 1974.

Kamen, Henry. "Una crisis de conciencia en la Edad de Oro en España: Inquisición contra 'limpieza de sangre.'" *Bulletin Hispanique* 88 (1986): 321–56.

———. *Inquisition and Society in Spain in the Sixteenth and Seventeenth Centuries.* Bloomington: Indiana University Press, 1985.

Laclau, Ernesto, and Chantal Mouffe. *Hegemony and Socialist Strategy: Towards a Radical Democratic Politics.* Trans. Winston Moore and Paul Cammack. London: Verso, 1985.

La Roche, Josette Riandière. "Du discours d'exclusion des Juifs: Antijudaïsme ou antisémitisme?" in *Les problèmes de l'exclusion en Espagne (XVIe–XVIIe siècles),* ed. Augustín Redondo. Paris: Publications de la Sorbonne, 1983.

Lázaro Carreter, F. *Estilo barroco y personalidad creadora: Góngora, Quevedo, Lope de Vega.* 3d ed. Madrid: Cátedra, 1977.

León, Luis de. *La perfecta casada.* Madrid: J. Pérez del Hoyo, 1972.

Lida, Raimundo. *Letras hispánicas.* Mexico: Fondo de Cultura Económica, 1958.

Lida de Malkiel, María Rosa. *Juan de Mena: Poeta del prerrenacimiento español.* México: Nueva Revista de Filología Hispánica, 1950.

Lukács, Georg. *History and Class Consciousness: Studies in Marxist Dialectics.* 3d ed. Trans. Rodney Livingstone. Cambridge: MIT Press, 1973.

———. *The Theory of the Novel.* Trans. Anna Bostock. Cambridge: MIT Press, 1975.

Macrí, Oreste. *Fernando de Herrera.* 2d ed. Madrid: Gredos, 1972.

Mandel, Oscar. "The Function of the Norm in *Don Quixote*." *Modern Philology* 55 (1958): 154–63.

Marañón, Gregorio. *El conde-duque de Olivares: La pasión de mandar*. Madrid: Espasa-Calpe, 1959.

Maravall, José Antonio. *La cultura del Barroco: Análisis de una estructura histórica*. Barcelona: Ariel, 1975. English translation: *The Culture of the Baroque*. Trans. Terry Cochran. Minneapolis: University of Minnesota Press, 1986.

———. *Estado moderno y mentalidad social (siglos XV a XVII)*. Vol. 1. Madrid: Revista de Occidente, 1972.

———. "Interés personal por la casa propia en el Renacimento." *Revue de littérature comparée* 52 (1978): 255–66.

———. "Moral de acomodación y caracter conflictivo de la libertad (notas sobre Saavedra Fajardo)." *Cuadernos Hispanoamericanos* 257 (1971): 663–93.

———. *El mundo social de "La Celestina."* Madrid: Gredos, 1964.

———. *La oposición política bajo los Austrias*. Barcelona: Ariel, 1972.

———. "Sobre el pensamiento social y político de Quevedo (una revisión)." In *Homenaje a Quevedo (II Academia literaria renacentista)*. Ed. Victor García de la Concha. Salamanca: Universidad de Salamanca, 1982.

———. *Teatro y literatura en la sociedad barroca*. Madrid: Seminarios y Ediciones, 1972.

———. *Utopía y contrautopía en el Quijote*. Santiago de Compostela: Pico Sacro, 1976.

———. *Utopia y reformismo en la España de los Austrias*. Madrid: Siglo XXI, 1982.

Marcus, Leah S. *Childhood and Cultural Despair: A Theme and Variations in Seventeenth-Century Literature*. Pittsburgh: University of Pittsburgh Press, 1978.

Martínez Ruiz, José [Azorín]. "La casa de Miranda." In *Con permiso de los cervantistas*. Madrid: Biblioteca Nueva, 1948.

Marx, Karl. *Eighteenth Brumaire of Louis Bonaparte* (1852). In *The Marx-Engels Reader*. 2d ed. Ed. Robert C. Tucker. New York: W. W. Norton, 1978.

Mas, Amédée. *La caricature de la femme, du mariage, et de l'amour dans l'oeuvre de Quevedo*. Paris: Hispanoamericanas, 1957.

Medvedev, P. N., and M. M. Bakhtin. *The Formal Method in Literary Scholarship*. Trans. Albert J. Wehrle. Baltimore: Johns Hopkins University Press, 1978.

Merleau-Ponty, Maurice. *Adventures of the Dialectic*. Trans. Joseph Bien. Evanston, Ill.: Northwestern University Press, 1973.

Molho, Maurice. *Cervantes: Raíces folklóricas*. Madrid: Gredos, 1976.

———. "Cinco lecciones sobre *El Buscón*." In *Semántica y poética*. Barcelona: Crítica, 1977.

———. *Introducción al pensamiento picaresco*. Salamanca: Anaya, 1972.

Moore, Roger. Review of D. Gareth Walters, *Francisco de Quevedo: Love Poet*. In *Revista canadiense de estudios hispánicos* 12 (1988): 520–24.

Morales, J. L. *El niño en la cultura española*. Vol. 1. Madrid: n.p., 1960.

Murillo, Luis. *The Golden Dial*. Oxford: Dolphin, 1975.

———. "Narrative Structures in the *Novelas Ejemplares*: An Outline." *Cervantes* 8 (1988): 231–50.

Olivares, Julián. *The Love Poetry of Francisco de Quevedo: An Aesthetic and Existential Study*. Cambridge: Cambridge University Press, 1983.

Ortega y Gasset, José. *Papeles sobre Velázquez y Goya*. Madrid: Revista de Occidente, 1950.

Pagden, Anthony. "Identity Formation in Spanish America." In *Colonial Identity in the Atlantic World, 1500–1800*. Ed. Nicholas Canny and Anthony Pagden. Princeton: Princeton University Press, 1987.

Parker, Alexander A. *The Approach to the Spanish Drama of the Golden Age*. Diamante 6. London: Hispanic and Luso-Brazilian Councils, 1957.

Pecheux, Michel. "Ideology: Fortress or Paradoxical Space." In *Rethinking Ideology: A Marxist Debate*. Ed. Sakari Hanninen and Leena Paldán. New York: International General, 1983.

Percas de Ponsetti, Helen. "Authorial Strings: A Recurrent Metaphor in *Don Quijote*." *Cervantes* 1 (1981): 51–62.

Pérez de Ayala, Martín. *Discurso de la vida*. Buenos Aires: Espasa-Calpe, 1947.

Petrarca, Francesco. *Petrarch's Lyric Poems: The "Rime Sparse" and Other Lyrics*. Ed. and trans. Robert M. Durling. Cambridge: Harvard University Press, 1976.

Pfandl, Ludwig. *Historia de la literatura nacional española en la Edad de Oro* (1929). Trans. Jorge Rubio Balaguer. 2d ed. Barcelona: G. Gili, 1952.

Pike, Ruth. *Aristocrats and Traders: Sevillian Society in the Sixteenth Century*. Ithaca: Cornell University Press, 1972.

Pineda, Juan de. *Diálogos familiares de la agricultura cristiana* (1589). Biblioteca de autores españoles, 163. Madrid: Atlas, 1963.

Pinelo, Antonio de León. *Anales de Madrid (desde el año 447 al de 1658)*. Ed. Pedro Fernández Martín. Madrid: Instituto de estudios madrileños, 1971.

Pinheiro da Veiga, Tomé. *Fastiginia o fastos geniales* (1605). Valladolid: Colegio de Santiago, 1916.

Porreño, Baltasar. *Dichos y hechos del rey D. Felipe II* (1628). Ed. A. González Palencia. Madrid: Saeta, 1942.

Pozuelo, José María. *La lírica amorosa de Quevedo.* Murcia: Universidad de Murcia, 1977.

Price, R. M. "A Note on Three Satirical Sonnets of Quevedo." *Bulletin of Hispanic Studies* 40 (1963): 79–88.

Quevedo, Francisco de. *La hora de todos y la fortuna con seso* (written ca. 1635; published 1650). Ed. Luisa López Grigera. Madrid: Castalia, 1975.

——. *Obra poética.* Ed. José Manuel Blecua. 4 vols. Madrid: Castalia, 1969–81.

——. *Obras completas.* Ed. Felicidad Buendía. Vol. 1. 6th ed. Madrid: Aguilar, 1966.

——. *Poemas escogidos.* Intro. José Manuel Blecua. Madrid: Castalia, 1972.

Quiñones, Juan de. *Memorial de Juan de Quiñones dirigido a F. Antonio de Sotomayor, inquisidor general, sobre el caso de Francisco de Andrada, sospechoso de pertenecer a la raza judía, discutiendo sobre los medios de conocer y perseguir a ella* (17th century). Biblioteca Nacional, Madrid. Varios especiales, box 8, no. 16.

Ramírez-Araujo, Alejandro. "El moro Ricote y la libertad de conciencia." *Hispanic Review* 24 (1956): 278–89.

Redondo, Augustín, ed. *Autour des parentes en Espagne aux XVIe et XVIIe siècles: Histoire, mythe, et littérature.* Paris: Sorbonne, 1987.

Regan, Mariann S. "The Evolution of the Poet in Petrarch's *Canzoniere.*" *Philological Quarterly* 57 (1978): 23–45.

Rico, Francisco, ed. *La novela picaresca española.* Vol. 1. Barcelona: Planeta, 1967.

Riley, E. C. *Cervantes's Theory of the Novel.* Oxford: Clarendon Press, 1962.

Rivadeneira, P. Pedro de. *Historia eclesiástica del scisma del reino de Inglaterra* (1588). In *Obras escogidas*, Biblioteca de autores españoles, 60. Madrid: Atlas, 1952.

Rivers, Elias. "Language and Reality in Quevedo's Sonnets." In *Quevedo in Perspective: Eleven Essays for the Quadricentennial.* Ed. James Iffland. Newark, Del.: Juan de la Cuesta, 1982.

——. *Renaissance and Baroque Poetry of Spain.* Prospect Heights, Ill.: Waveland Press, 1988.

——. "Some Ideas about Language and Poetry in Sixteenth-Century Spain." *Bulletin of Hispanic Studies* 61 (1984): 379–83.

Robles, Juan de. *El culto sevillano* (1631).

Rodríguez, Juan Carlos. *Teoría e historia de la producción ideológica: Las primeras literaturas burguesas (siglo XVI).* Madrid: Akal, 1974.

Rodríguez-Moñino, Antonio. *Construcción crítica y realidad histórica en la poesía española de los siglos XVI y XVII.* Madrid: Castalia, 1965.

Rojas, Fernando de. *La Celestina.* Madrid: Alianza, 1988.

——. *The Celestina*, trans. Lesley Byrd Simpson. Berkeley: University of California Press, 1966.

Rosales, Luis. *Cervantes y la libertad*. Vol. 2. Madrid: Sociedad de Estudios y Publicaciones, 1960.

Salillas, Rafael. "Poesía rufianesca." *Revue hispanique* 13 (1905): 18–75.

Salomon, Noël. *La vida rural castellana en tiempos de Felipe II*. Trans. Francesc Espinet Burunat. Barcelona: Ariel, 1982.

Sartre, Jean-Paul. *Critique of Dialectical Reason*. Trans. Alan Sheridan-Smith. London: Verso, 1982.

Shils, Edward. *Center and Periphery: Essays in Macrosociology*. Chicago: University of Chicago Press, 1975.

Smith, Paul. *Discerning the Subject*. Minneapolis: University of Minnesota Press, 1988.

Snell, Ana María. *Hacia el verbo: Signos y transignificación en la poesía de Quevedo*. London: Tamesis, 1982.

Stallybrass, Peter, and Allon White. *The Politics and Poetics of Transgression*. Ithaca: Cornell University Press, 1986.

Stevenson, Laura. *Praise and Paradox: Merchants and Craftsmen in Elizabethan Popular Literature*. Cambridge: Cambridge University Press, 1984.

Tennenhouse, Leonard. *Power on Display: The Politics of Shakespeare's Genres*. New York: Methuen, 1986.

Teresa de Avila. *Libro de las fundaciones* (written 1573, published 1610). Biblioteca de autores españoles, 53. Madrid: Atlas, 1952.

Thirsk, Joan. "The European Debate on Customs of Inheritance, 1500–1700." In *Family and Inheritance: Rural Society in Western Europe, 1200–1800*. Ed. Jack Goody, Joan Thirsk, E. P. Thompson. Cambridge: Cambridge University Press, 1976.

Tierno Galván, Enrique. "Humanismo y sociedad" (1964). In *La novela picaresca y otros escritos*. Madrid: Tecnos, 1974.

——. "Notas sobre el Barroco." In *Desde el espectáculo a la trivialización*. Madrid: Taurus, 1961.

Unamuno, Miguel de. *Ensayos*. Vol. 1. Ed. Bernardo G. de Candamo. Madrid: Aguilar, 1970.

——. "El individuo, producto social" (1897). In *Obras completas*. Vol. 9: *Discursos y artículos*. Madrid: Escelcier, 1971.

Vassberg, David E. *Land and Society in Golden Age Castile*. Cambridge: Cambridge University Press, 1984.

Vega, Joseph de la. *Confusión de confusiones* (1688). Reprint by Sociedad de Estudios y Publicaciones (n.p.: n.d.).

Vicens Vives, Jaime. *An Economic History of Spain*. Vol. 1. Trans. Frances M. López-Morillas. Princeton: Princeton University Press, 1969.

Vilar, Pierre. "The Age of Don Quixote." *New Left Review* 68 (1971): 1–13.

Vossler, Karl. *La soledad en la poesía española*. Madrid: Revista de Occidente, 1941.

Walters, D. Gareth. *Francisco de Quevedo: Love Poet*. Cardiff: University of Wales and Washington, D.C.: Catholic University of America, 1985.

Weber, Alison. *Teresa of Avila and the Rhetoric of Femininity*. Princeton: Princeton University Press, 1990.

Weiger, John. *The Individuated Self: Cervantes and the Emergence of the Individual*. Athens: Ohio University Press, 1979.

———. *The Substance of Cervantes*. Cambridge: Cambridge University Press, 1985.

Williams, Raymond. *Marxism and Literature*. Oxford: Oxford University Press, 1977.

Wright, L. P. "The Military Orders in Sixteenth- and Seventeenth-Century Spanish Society." *Past and Present* 43 (1969): 34–70.

Zabaleta, Juan de. *Día de fiesta por la mañana* (1654). In *Costumbristas españoles*. Vol. 2. Ed. Evaristo Correa Calderón. Madrid: Aguilar, 1964.

Zahareas, Anthony N., and Thomas R. McCallum. "Toward a Social History of the Love Sonnet: The Case of Quevedo's Sonnet 331," *Ideologies and Literature* 2 (1978): 90–99.

Zayas, María de. "Noche décima." In *Desengaños amorosos: Parte segunda del Sarao y entretenimiento honesto* (1647). Madrid: Aldus, 1950.

Index

agency, 208–12
Alonso, Dámaso, 105 n. 6, 112, 131
Anderson, Benedict, 94
Ariès, Philippe, 62
Avellaneda, Alonso Fernández de,
    50, 155–60
    Cervantes's *Don Quixote* and, 161–
    79

Barthes, Roland, 188
Blanco Aguinaga, Carlos, 16 n. 16,
    133
blood:
    Cervantes and, 50, 159
    circulation of, 45
    discourse of, 39–53
    discourse of virtue and, 41, 159
    n. 4
    Quevedo and, 151–52
    vengeance and, 167–68
body, discourse of the, 53–61
    the State and, 53–54
Braudel, Fernand, 8–14, 37 n. 4
Burckhardt, Jakob, 38

Cabrera, Alonso de, 64, 92
Cabrera de Córdoba, Luis, 53
capitalism, 82–89, 151–52

Carrasco, Sansón (*Don Quixote*),
    179–91, 207
Casalduero, Joaquin, 180
Castro, Américo, 11, 14, 17–18,
    180
La Celestina, 10, 75
Cervantes, Miguel de:
    difference between 1605 and 1615
        Don Quixote, 176–79
    Novelas ejemplares, 159
    Persiles y Sigismunda, 194–96, 201,
        206–7
    Quevedo and, 7–9, 153–54, 201–
        2
    social positions of, 154–55
Cervantes criticism, 176 n. 16
charismatic authority, 182–89
children, early modern, 62–67
class, 74–89
    appropriateness of term, 46 n. 11,
        74–77
    social force and, 77
Cohen, Walter, 26 n. 29
comedia (early modern Spanish the-
    ater), 19–21, 26, 138
contract and construction of indi-
    vidual, 80–81
conversos (Jewish converts to Catholi-
    cism), 40–41, 88

Counter Reformation, 6 n. 5, 95
Covarrubias, Sebastián, 63, 92, 182
Crótalon, 10–11

de Certeau, Michel, 27, 31, 212
deeds, discourse of, 49, 52
Descartes, René, 23, 192
determination, 30
discursive formations, 36, 40
    contradiction and, 34–35, 151–52, 201–3
Domínguez Ortiz, Antonio, 35, 39 n. 5, 51 n. 17
Duke and Duchess (*Don Quixote*), 190–97

Efron, Arthur, 181
Eiximenis, Francesc, 56
Eslava, Antonio de, 50–52

family, discourse of the, 61–74
    children within, 62–67
    household vs., 62–63
    "femaleness," 55, 58
    blood and, 60
    gender and, 26–27
Foucault, Michel, 5 n. 4, 6 n. 5, 36, 160, 170–71
Furió Ceriol, Fadrique, 41

Garcilaso de la Vega, 117–22
Giddens, Anthony, 79, 210–11
Gilman, Stephen, 65 n. 36
Girard, René, 189
"Golden Age" Spain (*Siglo de Oro*), 11–13
Gramsci, Antonio, 6 n. 6, 131 n. 31
Guillén de Castro, 89
Guinart, Roque (*Don Quixote*), 203–4

Harvey, William, 45
Herrera, Fernando de, 112, 122–25
hidalgo (minor Spanish nobleman), 48

Hippocrates, 57–58
Huarte de San Juan, Juan, 48–49, 57

individual: 5, 32, 38, 52, 71, 87
    freedom (*libertad*) and, 93
individualism, 91
    Cervantes criticism and, 200–201
    early modern English culture and, 90–91
    early modern Spanish culture and, 15, 19, 94

Jameson, Fredric, 114, 205
Juan de Dios, 33–35

Kamen, Henry, 41 n. 7

labor and class consciousness, 82–84
Lazarillo de Tormes, 10, 141, 157, 196 n. 32
Lida, Raimundo, 105, 130
Lukács, Georg, 22, 74

Maravall, José Antonio, 13 n. 12, 19, 81, 187–88
Marx, Karl, 22, 31, 62, 76, 83, 93, 207
Mas, Amédée, 134–35, 146–47
menstruation, 42–44
Merleau-Ponty, Maurice, 74
mode of communication, 68
Murillo, Luis, 73 n. 48, 184 n. 23

nationalism, discourse of, 89–94

otherness, construction of, 44, 95–96

Panza, Sancho (*Don Quixote*), 79–81, 86–87, 183
Parker, A. A., 26
Perry, Mary Elizabeth, 27 n. 31
Petrarca, Francesco, 110–17
    Garcilaso de la Vega and, 117–22

Petrarchan lyric, 108
  ideological "homelessness" of,
    114–17, 126–31
  Spanish tradition and, 111–32
Pfandl, Ludwig, 105
pícaros and the picaresque, 134–51,
    157
  "freedom" and, 147–48
  language (*germanía*), 141, 144–48
Pineda, Juan de, 56
Pinelo, Antonio de León, 65
poetry and poetic speakers in
    Quevedo, 35–36
  function of courtly, 99–100, 106–
    8
  picaresque, 134–51
  sonnet form and, 109–13
  subjectivity and, 131–34
Porreño, Baltasar, 34 n. 1
primogeniture (*mayorazgo*), 66–67
privacy and reading practices, 67–
    70
psychoanalysis, 61, 70–72
purity of blood (*limpieza de sangre*),
    41–44, 155

Quevedo, Francisco de:
  El Buscón, 28, 101
  canonical status of, 101–2, 106
  Cervantes and, 7–9, 153–55,
    201–2
  Garcilaso de la Vega and, 118–22
  "modern" qualities of, 100–103
  Petrarch and, 115 n. 18, 128–29,
    204–5
  politics and, 103–5, 108
Quiñones, Juan de, 42–44

Rebolledo, Bernardino de, 70

religious discourse, 34–35, 37, 87–
    88
Rivers, Elias, 100
Rojas, Fernando de, 10, 75

Salucio, Agustín, 41
Sartre, Jean-Paul, 24–25, 100
Shils, Edward, 185–86
subjectivity:
  agency and, 208–12
  aristocratic, 32–34, 132
  bourgeois individual and, 5
  emergent forms of, 168–71, 202
  literary rivalry and, 157–60
  Karl Marx on, 22, 31
  "self" vs., 29 n. 32
  theory of, 2–7, 22
  wonder and, 192–95
  writing and, 32–33, 98, 131–34

Teresa de Avila, 47, 56, 109
Tierno Galván, Enrique, 18–19, 23,
    128, 149
Timoneda, Juan de, 59
Torquemada, Antonio de, 77
Tosilos (*Don Quixote*), 209–11

Unamuno, Miguel de, 15–16

Vega Carpio, Lope de, 171–72
virtue, discourse of, 41, 47–53

Weiger, John, 29 n. 32
wet-nurses (*nodrizas*), 64
Williams, Raymond, 1, 36–37
wonder (*admiratio*), 192–95, 205

Zabaleta, Juan de, 51
Zayas, María de, 61

Library of Congress Cataloging-in-Publication Data
Mariscal, George.
  Contradictory subjects : Quevedo, Cervantes, and seventeenth century
Spanish culture / George Mariscal.
    p.   cm.
  Includes bibliographical references and index.
  ISBN 0-8014-2604-9 (alk. paper)
    1. Quevedo, Francisco de, 1580–1645—Criticism and interpretation.
  2. Cervantes Saavedra, Miguel de, 1547–1616—Criticism and
  interpretation.   3. Subjectivity in literature.   4. Individualism in
  literature.   5. Spain—Civilization—1516–1700.   I. Title.
  PQ6424.Z5M28   1991
  860.9'003—dc20   91-13369